ELEMENTS

OF

ENGLISH GRAMMAR.

T0382452

THE ELEMENTS

OF

ENGLISH GRAMMAR

WITH A CHAPTER ON ESSAY-WRITING

BY

ALFRED S. WEST, M.A.

TRINITY COLLEGE, CAMBRIDGE,
FELLOW OF UNIVERSITY COLLEGE, LONDON.

CAMBRIDGE:
AT THE UNIVERSITY PRESS.

1907

Key to the Questions contained in West's Elements of English Grammar and English Grammar for Beginners, by ALFRED S. WEST, M.A. Cambridge University Press. Second Impression. Price 3s. 6d. net.

CAMBRIDGE
UNIVERSITY PRESS

University Printing House, Cambridge CB2 8BS, United Kingdom

Cambridge University Press is part of the University of Cambridge.

It furthers the University's mission by disseminating knowledge in the pursuit of education, learning and research at the highest international levels of excellence.

www.cambridge.org
Information on this title: www.cambridge.org/9781316633441

© Cambridge University Press 1907

First edition 1893
Reprinted 1894, 1895, 1897
New edition 1898
Reprinted 1899, 1901, 1902, 1903, 1905
Revised edition (101,000 to 115,000), 1907
First paperback edition 2016

A catalogue record for this publication is available from the British Library

ISBN 978-1-316-63344-1 Paperback

PREFACE.

THIS book contains the Elements of English Grammar, but it does not profess to be a complete manual of the English Language. Boys and girls from thirteen to seventeen years of age are the readers whose wants it has been written to supply. For a treatise intended to meet the requirements of older students, a different choice of materials would often have been made, and the materials chosen would have been treated in a different fashion. Hence it will be found that in the following pages no mention is made of some of the questions which are discussed in larger works ; that other questions are touched upon, but not probed to the bottom ; that here and there a definition lacks completeness, logical accuracy being sacrificed to intelligibility ; and that the details of early English accidence have been inserted only when modern forms would be inexplicable without them. There are elementary books which furnish information so copious that young readers cannot see the wood for the trees. One who undertakes to instruct boys and girls needs constantly to bear in mind ὅσῳ πλέον ἥμισυ παντός—how much the half is greater than the whole, in order that he may avoid 'the human too much.' The things which have been deliberately left out of this small volume would have made a big book.

When we reflect that of every hundred boys and girls now learning English Grammar probably not more than one will ever read a page of any English author who wrote before the age of Elizabeth, it seems needlessly cruel to the remaining ninety-and-nine to inflict upon them the exhaustive study of historical English accidence. The average pupil, for whom the English Grammar lesson means mastering lists of strong verbs in half-a-dozen conjugations,—or learning that the comparative of *near* has assumed such diverse forms as *nyra, nearra, nerre, nere, nerrer*, or that the word *which* has at different times been written *hwilc, whulc, whulch, wuch, wich,* and *whilk,*— deserves our sympathy when he complains that English Grammar is rather dull. Tell him that " English Grammar without a reference to the older forms must appear altogether anomalous, inconsistent, and unintelligible," and he will say that, if it is necessary to encounter grim battalions of these older forms on every page, the subject had better be left severely alone, since it is hardly worth while going through so much to get so little.

Dull, no doubt, some parts of English Grammar, and of any other grammar, inevitably are, but the subject as a whole is far from being so dull as teachers and treatises frequently succeed in making it. A good teacher, who takes an interest in the matter himself, will secure the interest of a class of quite small boys,—not merely of the good boys at the top, but of the rank and file, of all, indeed, save the hopeless residuum who 'have taken the whole of science' for their aversion,—while he sketches for them the gradual growth of our language, or talks over with them the difference between Common and Proper nouns, or tells them the derivation of curious words like *liquorice*, or *treacle*, or *rhubarb*, or supplies them with faulty sentences which are to be pulled to pieces and put right. Yet even these topics may be so handled as to produce depressing results.

An hour a week is the time usually allotted to the study of English Grammar at those schools in which the conflict of studies allows it a place in the educational routine. A class reading every week seven pages of this book will work its way to the end in the course of the school year. No attempt has been made to divide the contents into 'Lessons,' since the number of pages suitable for senior students would be too many for juniors. As each chapter usually completes the treatment of some important and distinct branch of the subject, the chapters vary greatly in length, and the amount to be prepared for each lesson must be determined at the discretion of the master.

Of the Questions at the end of the Chapters, most have been chosen from the Cambridge Local Examination Papers of the last twenty years; the Oxford Local Examination Papers and the Papers of the Royal College of Preceptors have furnished others, and a few have been made for their present purpose. They are of very different degrees of difficulty. Occasionally they raise points which are interesting, but not important enough to deserve discussion in the text of the chapter to which they are attached. In such cases solutions or helps towards solution have been added. At the close of a protracted exposition of an abstract principle, the practical teacher often has cause to feel that he has been beating the air, when the use of a concrete example enables him to drive his point home at once. To meet his needs, a good supply of sentences for correction has been added to the concluding chapters on Syntax. There is reason to hope that the boys and girls who attack these problems will find the benefit, not merely in the confidence with which they will face the Examiner, whom most young seekers after Truth nowadays expect to meet round the other side of the Tree of Knowledge, but also in the formation of the habit of thinking for themselves. In this case the English Grammar lesson will prove to be a means of education and not simply an opportunity for instruction.

Private students can obtain from the *Key* whatever assistance they require to enable them to answer correctly every Question in the book. Much of the information furnished in the *Key*, though unsuitable for junior pupils, may be of some interest and service to their teachers.

The matter contained in these pages has but slight claims to originality. The writer of an elementary textbook, traversing ground well-trodden by many predecessors, would probably go astray, if he endeavoured at any cost to be original. Many of the following chapters owe something, and occasionally they owe much, to Mr Mason's *English Grammar* and to Prof. Bain's *Higher English Grammar*. Use has been made also of Dr Gow's suggestive *Method of English*, of Dr Angus's *Handbook of the English Tongue*, of Mr Low's *English Language*, of Dr Abbott's *How to Parse*, of Dr Morris's *Historical Outlines of English Accidence*, and of Professor Skeat's *Principles of English Etymology* and *Etymological Dictionary*. Acknowledgment of indebtedness to these and to other writers has in some places been made, but much of the well-worn material, of which an elementary work on English Grammar must be composed, is the common property of all who choose to write upon the subject.

My cordial thanks are due to several friends for suggestions which have enabled me to improve in many respects the original draft of this book. To Dr Keynes, late Fellow of Pembroke College, Mr R. T. Wright, late Fellow and Tutor of Christ's College, and Mr J. H. Flather, of Emmanuel College, my obligations are great for help in the work of revision. With his customary kindness Professor Skeat has sent me many valuable criticisms. At the same time it must be clearly understood that, for the shortcomings of the following pages, the responsibility rests entirely with me.

ALFRED S. WEST.

CONTENTS.

THE ELEMENTS OF ENGLISH GRAMMAR.

CHAPTER I.

HISTORICAL SURVEY.

1. Britons and Englishmen. The people who lived in our island fifteen hundred years ago were not Englishmen, nor did they speak the English language. When, in our flights of rhetoric or poetry, we declare that we glory in the name of Britons, or sing that Britons never shall be slaves, our intentions are patriotic, but our language is apt to be misleading. Britons we may indeed call ourselves, if in doing so we mean nothing more than this, that we are inhabitants of Britain. But when we speak of ourselves as Britons, or as a British race, let us bear in mind such facts as these :—that we are in the main of English origin; that our English forefathers conquered the Britons, deprived them of their lands, and made many of them slaves; that the English settled in the country belonging to the Britons, and that their descendants have remained here ever since. Firmly grasping these truths, we may, if we like, apply the name of Britons to our fellow-countrymen, just as we apply the name of Great Britain to our country. No danger of misconception lurks in the use of the word

'Britain' as the geographical name of our island, for our island remains the same: it is the population which has changed.

2. **The Roman Conquest.** As the result of his invasions in B.C. 55 and the following year, Julius Caesar exacted from the British tribes the payment of an annual tribute to Rome. His advance into the country reached only as far as St Albans, and nearly a century passed before the Romans returned. In the year A.D. 43, the Roman legions were sent to Britain again, and in the course of the next forty years the country was reduced to subjection as far as the Tyne. Half a century later, the limit of Roman conquest was pushed further north to the Clyde. The Romans held the country as we hold India to-day. They did not intermarry with the Britons as they intermarried with the natives of Gaul or of Spain. Their occupation of Britain was a military occupation, and the Britons preserved their own language, though it was not until A.D. 410 that the Romans, after a tenure of nearly four hundred years, finally left the island.

3. **The Britons were a Keltic race,** and in some parts of our islands a Keltic language is still spoken. Welsh is a Keltic dialect; so is Manx; so is the native Irish, or Erse; so is the dialect of the Highlands of Scotland[1]. If we wish to have a notion of the sort of language which an ancient Briton spoke, we must remember that it was like the Welsh of to-day and therefore very different from English. The people of South Britain called themselves *Cymry*, as the Welsh call themselves now. *Cambria* and *Cumbria* preserve for us this name 'Cymry' in a Latin form.

4. **The English Conquest.** In the year A.D. 449, a generation after the departure of the Romans, Hengist

---

[1] Lowland Scotch is an English dialect.

the Jute settled in Kent, and in the course of a century the conquest of the country was for a second time fairly complete. The account of the successive invasions,—first of Jutes, then of Saxons, and then of Angles, all closely allied tribes,—must be looked for in a history of the English people, not in a book on the English speech. But to these two questions an answer ought to be given here :

(1) **Who were these settlers ?**
(2) **Where did they come from ?**

(1) They were **Teutonic** tribes. The people, whom we call Germans, call themselves *Deutsch*. The word is familiar to us in the form *Dutch*. The Romans, getting as near as they could to the name by which these German tribes called themselves, made the word *Teutoni* and gave it a Latin declension. From this we derive the convenient term *Teutonic*. If we pronounce the stems of *Teut-oni* and of *Deut-scher* with their proper vowel sounds, the resemblance is close. We disguise this resemblance by giving to the vowel of the word *Teutonic* the sound of the *eu* in *feud*. We use the word *Teutonic* to signify 'belonging to the German race,' but if we said that English, or Dutch, or Flemish, was a 'German' language, the term might be misleading, as we commonly employ the word *German* in a narrower sense, to signify the language spoken to-day in Berlin and taught at school to English boys and girls who are said to be 'learning German.' This German which is spoken at the present day in Germany is itself one of the Teutonic dialects.

Thus the Jutes and Saxons and Angles were very different people from the Britons. The Jutes, Saxons, and Angles,—or to call them by a collective name, the *English*, —were Teutonic tribes. Their speech was akin to Dutch, and it was the parent of our own. The Britons were a Keltic race, and their language was as different from the language of their Saxon conquerors as the Welsh language of to-day is different from our modern English.

(2) To find the **district from which these tribes came,** we must turn to the map of North Germany and Denmark.

The Angles are believed to have come from the duchy of Schleswig.

Crossing its northern border we pass into Jutland, which is part of Denmark. The south of Jut-land was probably the home of the Jutes.

If we move southwards again into Holstein, we find on the west coast two rivers forming respectively its northern and southern boundaries, the Eider and the Elbe. From this neighbourhood it is supposed that the Saxons came.

Neglecting these details, we may remember that **the English people came from Schleswig-Holstein,** or that the English people came from the country to the north of the mouth of the Elbe; that they came between the years A.D. 450 and 550; and that having come they stayed.

As the district from which these invaders came is a low-lying, flat part of the continent, we call them **Low Germans,** to distinguish them from their Teutonic kinsmen living in the interior of the country, where the ground is higher. What we call to-day the 'German' language is *High German.* Dutch, Flemish, spoken in parts of Belgium, and Frisian, still spoken in the districts from which our ancestors came, are Low German dialects. Thus the terms *High* and *Low,* as applied to German, have a geographical origin. No stigma of inferiority is attached to us when we are described as a 'Low German' race.

5. What became of the Keltic race, the Britons?

They were driven into the west and the north of the island,—into Devon and Cornwall, into Wales, into Westmoreland and Cumberland. Those who remained in the parts which were under English rule were made slaves. Their Keltic language was spoken only amongst themselves. Henceforth the language of the country was English.

6. Anglo-Saxon. The term *Anglo-Saxon* has a twofold application, (1) to people, (2) to language.

(1) Whether the name 'Anglo-Saxons' meant originally Angles *and* Saxons or Saxons *of* England (as distinguished from Saxons of North Germany) is a point which we need not now discuss. At an early age the term was used to denote the Teutonic tribes generally in England and at the present day by 'Anglo-Saxons' we signify people of English race.

(2) Applied to language *Anglo-Saxon* is a misleading term, suggesting as it does that the English settlers all spoke one dialect. Now there were at least three dialects in use, viz. Anglian in Northumbria (north of the Humber), Frisian in Mercia (the Midlands), and Saxon in Wessex (south of the Thames). Most of the literature which has come down to us from that early period is written in the Wessex dialect and to this dialect scholars in the 17th century gave the name Anglo-Saxon. Our standard Modern English traces its descent from the Mercian dialect, not from the so-called 'Anglo-Saxon' of Wessex.

7. Roman missionaries. Our English forefathers were heathen. We preserve relics of their worship in the names of the days of the week. Roman missionaries were sent to this country in the year A.D. 597 to teach them Christianity. Latin became again one of the tongues of Britain, the language of its worship and of its literature. Trade brought in other words from a Latin source.

8. The Northmen. During two and a half centuries, from about A.D. 800 to 1050, England was exposed to frequent inroads of the Danes, or Northmen, inhabitants of Scandinavia and not merely of Denmark. These Northmen, from Denmark, Norway, and Sweden, were a Teutonic race, so they were akin to the English whom they harassed; but we place them in a group apart from High or Low Germans and call this group the *Scandinavian*.

9. The Norman Conquest. The Normans, who established themselves in our country in A.D. 1066, were originally, like the Danes, Northmen or Scandinavians.

But they had been settled on French soil for about 150 years and had acquired a French dialect, the French of northern France, called the *langue d'oïl.* The word *oïl,* the same word as *oui,* signifies *yes.* The *langue d'oïl* was the dialect in which people said *oïl* for *yes,* as distinguished from the *langue d'oc* in which they said *oc.* This French language was in the main a form of Latin, containing, however, a certain amount of Keltic, for the Gauls were a Keltic race, though they adopted the speech of their Roman conquerors. So the French influence upon our English tongue is really a Latin influence in disguise.

10. **The Revival of Learning.** The sixteenth century is the time of the Revival of Classical Learning, or of the Renaissance as it is sometimes called. The capture of Constantinople by the Turks in A.D. 1453 had caused the flight of the cultured Greeks who lived there, and they sought refuge in the cities of Italy. To Florence flocked eager students out of many lands to acquire from these learned exiles a knowledge of ancient literature. Curiosity respecting Greek and Roman antiquities spread widely, and Greek and Latin writers were zealously read. The consequence was that an enormous number of new words, borrowed directly from the Latin, passed into our English vocabulary. Hundreds of words were introduced and dropped, as there was no need of them : hundreds more remained. Very different was the way in which words of Latin origin came in at this time from the way in which they came in under the influence of the Norman Conquest. At the Revival of Learning the words were borrowed by scholars from books. Under the Norman kings they were introduced by the daily speech of foreigners who had taken our England and made it their own.

11. Other incidents in our history deserve mention in an account of the influence of political events on the formation of our speech. Thus, in the reign of Mary, Spanish

influence was strong; in the reign of Elizabeth, English volunteers helped the Dutch against the Duke of Parma; in the reign of Charles II., French was the fashion at Court. But the Spanish and Dutch and French words which thus secured a footing in our language are few.

12. We will close this chapter with a short **summary of the chief historical events** which have affected the formation of our English speech as it exists to-day, and in the next chapter we shall say something about the character of the words which we owe to these events.

1. The original inhabitants of this country were Britons, a Keltic race, speaking a language like Welsh. They were subjugated by the Romans, who remained here from A.D. 43 to 410. They were then subjugated by the Jutes, Saxons, and Angles, tribes belonging to the Low German branch of the Teutonic stock. These English people came from the district north of the mouth of the Elbe at different times between A.D. 450 and 550, and their descendants have stayed in this country ever since.

2. A.D. 600 to 1000. The Christian missions introduced some words of Latin origin, and the growth of trade brought in others.

3. A.D. 800 to 1050. The Danes made frequent incursions, and from 1017 to 1042 Danish kings ruled in England. By 'Danes' are meant not only people of Denmark, but people of Norway and Sweden also. Like the English they were a Teutonic race, but we call theirs the Scandinavian branch.

4. A.D. 1066 to 1400. The Normans were also originally Scandinavians, but they had adopted the language of France during their occupation of that country for 150 years before they conquered England; and for 150 years after their conquest of England,—until the death of John and the final severance of England from Normandy,—great efforts

were made to extend the use of the French language in
this country. The blending of the Norman-French and
English languages did not take place till long after the
Conquest. The Normans in England continued to speak
French: the English continued to speak English, and books
were written in English. Nearly two centuries elapsed
before there was a real amalgamation. About the year
1250 French words began to pass freely into the native
vocabulary, and by the year 1400 French had ceased to be
the speech of the nobility in England. The French language is in the main a form of Latin, though the Gauls were
a Keltic race.

5. The Revival of Letters, or of Classical Learning,
or the Renaissance, affected our language from the time of
Henry VII. to the end of Charles I.'s reign, *i.e.* during the
16th and the first half of the 17th century.

CHAPTER II.

CONSTITUENTS OF THE ENGLISH VOCABULARY.

13. IN the previous chapter we mentioned the leading events in the history of our country which have exercised an influence upon the formation of our language as it exists to-day. In this chapter we shall answer the question,—**What sorts of words do we owe to these events** in our history?

14. I. Keltic words in English. The Keltic words in our ordinary English speech are few. When we bear in mind that in some parts of our island the British inhabitants were nearly exterminated by their English conquerors and that British civilization was practically destroyed, we are not surprised to find that the influence upon our English speech of the intercourse between Britons and Englishmen was very slight. Keltic names of places indeed are numerous. *Avon* is a Keltic word for 'river,' and there are many Avons in England. *Aber*, as in *Aberdeen, Aberystwith, Berwick* (*i.e. Aberwick*), meaning 'the mouth of a river'; *Pen* or *Ben*, 'a mountain,' as in *Penzance, Ben Nevis*; *Llan*, 'a sacred enclosure,' as in *Llandaff, Lampeter*; *Caer* or *Car*, 'a castle,' as in *Caermarthen, Carlisle*,—all of these are of Keltic origin, and there are others besides, but geographical names have no claim to be reckoned as a part of our ordinary vocabulary. Several words which were formerly supposed to have passed from Keltic into English are now known to have passed in a contrary direction from English into Keltic. A few Keltic words may have come to us through the Norman French. At a later date we borrowed a few more from Welsh, from Irish, and from Gaelic, the language spoken in the Highlands of Scotland, all of which belong to the Keltic group. But our indebtedness to Keltic is small. We may sum it up thus:

1. Geographical names, which are no part of our ordinary vocabulary:

2. A few words handed down from the original Britons, or introduced through the Norman French:

3. A few borrowed from Welsh (*e.g. cromlech, flannel, flummery*), from Irish (*e.g. fun, shamrock, shillelagh*), and from Gaelic (*e.g. clan, gillie, whiskey*).

15. II. **The Latin Element in English.** Though the Romans held this country for nearly four hundred years, they left us no Latin words in our vocabulary as a legacy from their occupation. But it must be remembered that the Romans never came in contact with the English after the English had established themselves here. The Romans took their final departure in A.D. 410, and it was not until A.D. 449 that the first English settlement was made. The Romans probably introduced many Latin words into the language of the Britons, but the Britons contributed very few words to our English speech, and of those which they did contribute none happened to be of Latin origin. We can trace **the effect of Roman occupation** however in several **names of places.** When we meet with a word like *Don-caster*, or *Circen-cester*, or *Chester*, we recognise the Latin *castra* and know that these places were once Roman military stations. So in *Lin-coln* we have *colonia:* in *Wall's End* and in *Walton, vallum* appears in disguise. When the English arrived and found a place called 'Chester,' they would continue to call it

' Chester,' just as when we occupied New South Wales and found a place called ' Wagga-Wagga,' we continued to call it ' Wagga-Wagga,' and in this way we may say that the Romans have left their mark upon our language. But their influence is seen only in a few geographical names. This Latin element is sometimes called the *Latin of the First Period.*

16. In A.D. 597, St Augustine was sent by Pope Gregory to teach Christianity to the English, and in the course of the next four centuries several Latin words, connected with the Christian faith and ritual, were introduced into the language. Translations from Latin originals brought in others. Commerce was extending also between England and other European nations, from whom were borrowed terms of Latin origin, new names for new things. Let us picture to ourselves the influence which a missionary settlement would have to-day upon the language of a tribe of African savages. From the Christian teachers they would borrow such words as *bible, hymn-book, chapel,* and add this English element to their African speech. Then after a while the trader would follow, and the language of the natives would be enriched with such words as *rifle, gunpowder, gin.* In like manner, between the years A.D. 600 and 1000, Roman ecclesiastics introduced words of which *altar, creed, font, candle,* are examples, while, in consequence of enlarged knowledge owing to extended trade, such words as *cheese, cook, linen, poppy, pear,* found their way into our language. This Latin is called the *Latin of the Second Period.*

17. We saw that **Norman-French** was in the main a **language of Latin origin.** Hence we may say that the words which we owe to our Norman conquerors are Latin words which have come into the language indirectly, Latin words ' once removed.' This Latin element is called the *Latin of the Third Period.*

Now, if we consider how complete the Norman Conquest was and how rapidly it was effected, we may feel some surprise that it is an English language and not a French language which we speak to-day.   Norman lords occupied the lands from which English owners had been ejected. Normans held the higher offices in church and state.   Deliberate efforts were made to extend the use of the French language.   Boys at grammar schools had to turn Latin into French.   Cases in the law-courts were carried on in French.   Yet in spite of all, English survived and prevailed. One important event which contributed largely to this result was the loss of the French possessions in John's reign (1206).   Norman barons had to make their choice between life in France and life in England, and those who settled in England at length threw in their lot with the English and ceased to be French.   Then again the war with France in Edward III.'s reign made everything French unpopular. In this reign boys were no longer required to construe their Latin into French, and English was used instead of French in the law-courts.

To the Normans we owe many words which relate to (1) feudalism, chivalry and war; *e.g. homage, fealty, banner, lance, battle, captain:* (2) law, government and office; *e.g. attorney, assize, reign, council, baron, duke:* (3) the church; *e.g. cloister, penance:* (4) hunting; *e.g. chase, leveret:* and also (5) many abstract terms, *e.g. nature, art, science, glory*[1].

The Normans gave us many more words which do not come under these heads.   An interesting example of the way in which the language of a country illustrates its

[1] Words of French origin introduced between 1250 and 1400 have been called Anglo-French, to mark the fact that they belong to a separate French dialect, developed in England and different from any of the forms of French spoken on the Continent.   They constitute a valuable element of our vocabulary, many of them being as much required for daily use as the words of native origin.

history is supplied by the names of certain animals and
of the meats which they furnish. When the beast is alive, we
call it an *ox,* or a *sheep,* a *calf,* or a *pig.* These are English
words. When it is cooked for the table, we call it *beef,*
mutton, veal, pork. These are French words. From these
facts we might draw the inference that the English peasant
looked after the stock on the farm, and his Norman master
ate the joints in the hall. Sir Walter Scott puts this point
forcibly in *Ivanhoe.*

18. *The Latin of the Fourth Period* comprises those
words of Latin origin which were introduced in swarms
during the time of the **Revival of Classical Learning,**
or have passed into our language since that date. The
age of the Tudors was one in which men's minds expanded
rapidly, and new ideas required new words for their expression. The Reformation in religion; the diffusion of literature owing to the recent invention of printing; geographical
discovery; progress in science,—all these things rendered
the old vocabulary inadequate, and the fashionable study of
classical authors showed where fresh words were to be found.
For one who has learnt a little Latin, it is an easy matter to
identify a Fourth-Period word on the page of a modern
book. From the same Latin original we may have another
word, which has come to us through the Norman-French,
disguised beyond easy recognition in the course of centuries
of oral transmission. Compare the following:

Original Latin.	Borrowed directly.	Through Norman-French.
captivus	captive	caitiff
factionem	faction	fashion
factum	fact	feat
fidelitatem	fidelity	fealty
persequor	persecute	pursue
senior	senior	sir
quietus	quiet	coy
traditionem	tradition	treason.

In the classical form assumed by several words of

Norman-French origin, we see another consequence of the New Learning.   Thus *dette* was changed to *debt*, *vitaille* to *victual*, *aventure* to *adventure*.

19.   Summary of borrowings from Latin.   The Latin element in modern English is connected with one or another of the following four leading events :

1.   **Roman occupation of Britain,** A.D. 43 to 410. Latin words found in names of places ; *e.g. Dorchester.*

2.   **Introduction of Christianity** among the English, A.D. 597.   During this period, extending from A.D. 600 to 1000, about 150 Latin words were brought in, many of them through the influence of the church and others through commercial intercourse.

3.   **Norman Influence,** A.D. 1066—1400.   Latin introduced indirectly through the Norman-French and also directly, Latin being at that time the language of the learned professions, law, medicine and divinity.

4.   **Revival of Letters,** the 16th century and first half of the 17th, or the period extending from the Tudors to the Commonwealth.   Words of all kinds.

20.   Before leaving this subject we must touch on a few other points of interest connected with the Latin element in our language.

Though our language is the English language, it contains more words of Latin than of native origin.   In saying this we mean that, if we take a dictionary and count up the total number of words, we shall find that Latin has furnished us with more than we obtained from our English forefathers.   But then we do not *use* more Latin words than English words, although we have more of them.   This last sentence contains eighteen words.   Of these eighteen, only two are of Latin origin, the words *use* and *Latin*.   All the rest are native English.   Two in eighteen is a trifle over 11 per cent.   By way of contrast let us examine a sentence taken at random from an essay of Matthew Arnold's :

"All our good secondary schools have at present some examination proceeding from the universities; and if this kind of examination, customary and admitted already, were generalised and regularised, it would be sufficient for the purpose."

Here we have thirty-five words, and thirteen of them come from the Latin source. This gives 37 per cent. of foreign origin as compared with eleven per cent. in the former passage.

One more sample, this time a verse of Wordsworth's:

> "Six feet in earth my Emma lay,
> And yet I loved her more—
> For so it seemed,—than till that day
> I e'er had loved before."

From these four lines, containing six-and-twenty words, the Latin element is altogether absent.

Now, how is it that the dictionary proportion of Latin words in English and the proportion in use are so different?

Because (1) in the dictionary every word counts once and only once. *That, and, if,* count as one English word each, and *regularise, generalise, secondary,* count as one word each. But we can hardly make a sentence without bringing in such words as *that, and, if,* whilst we may pass months or years or a life-time without bringing into our sentences such words as *regularise, generalise, secondary.* We should find it a trouble-some business to make a sentence ten words long without using a single native English word, for the English words are the mortar, so to speak, by which the sentence is bound together. Take these words away, and the sentence tumbles to pieces. Take away the classical words, and we can in most cases substitute for them words of English origin.

Again, (2) by far the greater number of the words in the dictionary are words which we never use at all,—words which we should never meet with, unless we chanced to see them when we were looking in the dictionary. How many words there are in the English language, it is not an easy matter to say. Some persons would give 100,000 as the number, others 200,000, others 400,000. These startling discrepancies do not imply any incapacity to count correctly on the part of the people who furnish the estimates; they arise from a difference of opinion as to what is to be reckoned as a word. Suppose we accept the lowest of the three totals mentioned above, and say that there are 100,000 words now current in our language; we might then roughly distribute them thus without any great error in the proportion: Latin 60,000, English 30,000, Greek and other sources 10,000.

But how many of these words are in ordinary use? To this question it is impossible to give a definite answer. Shakespeare employed twice as many words to express his thoughts as anybody else, and he said all that he had to say with about 15,000 words. Milton needed only half that number. An educated man of to-day has a vocabulary of some five or six thousand words. Two thousand suffice for an average mechanic; one thousand for a schoolboy; half that number for an illiterate labourer. We give these numbers by conjecture, but probably they are not very wide of the mark. At any rate we may safely say this, that for every word which the best educated man makes use of, there are at least ten, perhaps twenty, in the dictionary, which he never uses at all. And most of these are words of foreign extraction. The question may be asked,—What are these words for, if we never use them? Vast numbers of them are words of what we call a technical character; they belong to different arts and crafts and sciences, and are used by the men who follow those arts and crafts and sciences and by nobody else. Thus the doctor employs hundreds of technical words not used by the rest of us; then there are the words peculiar to botany and chemistry; the words of mining, of building, of seamanship, and so on. Every occupation furnishes its contribution of terms which are as completely unknown to people generally as so many words of Winchester slang.

But (3) even when we are dealing with words in ordinary use, words of which everybody knows the meaning, the more simple and familiar the subject in hand, the more does the English element predominate. The words which denote the things nearest and dearest to us, the things which we have known from our childhood, are of English origin. *Father* and *mother, house* and *home, rain, wind, day, night, sun, moon,*—these are English words. And hence it is that Wordsworth, describing an old man's feeling about his daughter's death, naturally uses an unmixed English diction as best suited to his purpose. How feeble a Latinized paraphrase would sound by the side of the simple English words which go home to our hearts!

> "And yet I loved her more—
> For so it seemed,—than till that day
> I e'er had loved before."

"It appeared to me that I entertained an intenser affection for her than I had previously experienced." The force of the passage has gone, and the sentence reads as if it were taken from the pages of a third-rate novelist. On the other hand, the extract from Matthew Arnold abounds in Latin words, because he is dealing with a scientific subject and resorts to scientific language. Our English forefathers knew nothing of 'regularising' and 'generalising,' of 'secondary schools' and 'universities.' We should be puzzled to express the passage in words of English origin. Thus the Latin element in a man's style will vary according to his subject. If he is writing on a philosophical subject, the proportion of Latin words must necessarily be high, because English will not provide him with the vocabulary which he requires. If he is writing a story or a poem about love or family life, the proportion of Latin words will be low, because English words will be more effective for his purpose. But however high the proportion may be, we shall never come across a passage five lines long in which there are as many

Latin words as there are words of native origin. When we say of a man that he writes a Latinised or classical style, we mean that he often prefers to use a Latin noun, verb, or adjective, when an English noun, verb, or adjective would express his meaning. The other words in his sentences are for the most part English and must be English, since about these no choice is possible.

It is sometimes said that we ought always to use an English word instead of a Latin word if we can. But a hard and fast rule of this sort is not to be laid down for universal application as a maxim of style. The Latin word may sometimes be the more effective or exact, though an English word might also serve the purpose. A good writer will select the best word regardless of its derivation. Still, half-educated persons have such a hankering after Latin words in preference to English words, for the expression of common-place notions about things of every-day life, that there is safety in laying down the rule, at any rate for them, that the English word should always be taken, and the Latin word should be left. The habit of saying 'Allow me to assist you to potatoes,' instead of 'Let me help you to potatoes,' or 'Let me give you some potatoes'; of using 'period' or 'epoch' instead of 'time'; 'individual' instead of 'man'; 'commence' instead of ' begin,' and so on, is detestable[1].

21. III. **Greek words in English.** The Greek element in English is important, and its amount is rapidly increasing. In date of introduction it corresponds with the Latin of the Fourth Period. There are indeed a few ecclesiastical terms of Greek origin, which reached us through a Latin channel before the Norman Conquest, *e.g. deacon, monk, apostle, bishop, psalm.* But with the exception of a score of words like these, belonging to the vocabulary of the Christian church, the Greek which we have in modern English has been adopted since the Revival of Learning for purposes of scientific nomenclature. Greek is a language which lends itself readily to the formation of compounds. So was old English, but this power of making new words by the combination of other words seems to have perished through the influence of the Norman French. At any rate, our language possesses it no longer. If we consider the ease with which long compound words can be formed in

---

[1] See Abbott and Seeley's *English Lessons,* p. 105.

modern German, it seems curious that our own Teutonic language should lack the same facility. But such is the case. And as compound terms are increasingly necessary to express the complex ideas of science, we fall back on Greek to supply our needs. *Telephone, microscope, thermometer, photograph,* are examples of Greek compounds, and, if we translate these words into their English equivalents, the advantage which we gain from the use of Greek is apparent.

22. **IV. Scandinavian words in English.** It is not always an easy matter to determine what words we owe to the Norsemen, as the Norsemen belonged to the Teutonic race, and their vocabulary resembled that of our own Low-German dialect. Still, there are some words which we can identify as Scandinavian in their origin. We may trace the Danes on the map of England by the ending *-by*, which means 'town,' as in *Derby, Whitby:* the same word is preserved in *bye-law.* This ending occurs for the most part in the district once occupied by the Danes, called the Danelagh, in the north and east of England. *Fell,* as in 'Scawfell,' *force,* 'a water-fall,' as in 'Stockgill-force,' are other examples of Danish geographical names. To the Danes we owe also the word *are,* which took the place of the English form of the 3rd person plural of the verb *am.* Other additions which they made to our vocabulary are seen in the words *fellow, sky, scant, ugly.* The common termination *-son* in names of persons, *e.g.* 'Johnson,' 'Anderson,' is Danish. Words meaning 'son of,' Patronymics as they are called in grammar, were formed in Old English by the addition of the ending *-ing, e.g.* 'Atheling.'

23. **V. Words from various sources.** We have now completed our account of the chief sources from which the vocabulary of modern English has been enriched.

Words have been borrowed from a large number of other languages, but no great advantage will be gained by burdening the memory with lists of terms for which various foreign countries have been placed under contribution. The student who is asked to mention a word which we have taken from an Indian or Chinese source should think of something peculiar to India or China, and examples will suggest themselves. Thus *punkah* or *rupee* may occur to him as Hindustani words, *nankeen* or *tea* as Chinese. A few illustrations are added of common words borrowed from miscellaneous sources :

Modern French—*bouquet, etiquette, programme.*
Italian—*bandit, grotto, regatta.*
Spanish—*armada, cigar, don.*
Portuguese—*caste, molasses, verandah.*
Modern German—*meerschaum, plunder, waltz.*
Dutch—*sloop, skipper, yacht.*
Russian—*drosky, rouble, steppe.*
Hebrew—*cherub, seraph, shibboleth.*
Arabic—*alkali, sheik, sherbet.*
Persian—*bazaar, ghoul, shawl.*
Malay—*amuck* ('to run amuck'), *gong, sago.*
North-American—*skunk, squaw, tomahawk.*

QUESTIONS.

1. These six Latin words occur in names of places and are marks of the Roman occupation of Britain :—*castra*, 'a camp'; *colonia*, 'a colony'; *fossa*, 'a ditch'; *portus*, 'a harbour'; *strata*, 'a paved road'; *vallum*, 'a rampart.' Mention names in which these Latin words survive.

2. The following Latin words furnish us with pairs of derivatives which came into our language (1) indirectly through the Norman-French, (2) directly at the Revival of Learning. Give the pairs of derivatives :—*fragilis, pœnitentia, securus, pauper, redemptionem.*

3. What other forms have we of the words *privy, royal, story, blame*? Which of the forms came into the language first? Why do you think so?

4. Pick out the words of Latin origin in the 19th Psalm.

5. Mention the periods at which words of Latin origin were largely introduced into English. Give instances of words introduced at each period.

6. Give the words of English origin in common use which most nearly answer to the following :—*expansion, construction, ridiculous, fortitude, depression, depart, transgression, elevation, probability, virtuous.*

7. Of the elements composing the English vocabulary, which is (1) the largest, and (2) the oldest?
To what European dialects is English most nearly akin?

8. Assign to its proper language the italicised part of each of the following words :—*Car*lisle, Don*caster*, Der*by*, Lin*coln*.

9. How is it that so many rivers in England bear the name of *Avon*? In what forms does *Ex* appear in names of places?

[*Avon* is a Keltic word for 'river' and *Ex* for 'water.' The name *Avon* or *Ex*, given by the British inhabitant to the river in his neighbourhood, would be preserved by the English settler. Hence we have upwards of a dozen rivers called 'Avon' in England, and 'Ex' in various disguises is even more common : *e.g. Ex*-eter, *Ax*-minster, *Ux*-bridge, *Usk, Ouse*. In Scotland alone there are more than half-a-dozen rivers called *Esk*.]

10. Rewrite the following passage, substituting, where possible, words of English origin for those derived from Latin :—
' The old man trusts wholly to slow contrivance and gradual progression. The youth expects to force his way by genius, vigour, and precipitance. The old man deifies prudence. The youth commits himself to magnanimity and chance. Age looks with anger on the temerity of youth, and youth with contempt on the scrupulosity of age.'
Johnson.

11. From what causes and in what ways have foreign words obtained a footing in the English language?
[Mention as the chief agencies (1) conquest, (2) commercial intercourse, (3) literary influence.]

12. Give illustrations of the way in which a study of the sources of the English language corroborates what we learn from English history.

13. What languages had been spoken in this island, or were being spoken in it, when the English Conquest took place?
Were they in any way akin to the speech of the Angles and the Saxons?

14. What do you know of the origin of each of the following words? Comment on their connexion with facts of English history :—
Avon, Chester, Grimsby, cloister, cherry, beef, potion, poison.

15. Describe with illustrations the influence of the Celtic and of the Scandinavian languages upon our English vocabulary.

16. Mention eight English words which have come to us from different foreign languages and state the source of each.

17. What is the source of each word in the following sentence?—
'Meanwhile the great rhetorical fabric gradually arose. He revised, erased, strengthened, emphasized, with indefatigable industry.'

18. What is the origin of the words *priest, bard, fealty, punkah*? What kind of intercourse led to the adoption of each of these words into our vocabulary?

19. Write any four consecutive lines of English poetry and underline the words of non-Teutonic origin.

20. Illustrate the influence of the social and political institutions of the Normans upon the English vocabulary.

21. What is meant by speaking of a word of foreign origin as 'acclimatized' or 'naturalized'?

[See § 92, 1. We may also describe as 'imperfectly naturalized' a foreign word which retains in English its foreign pronunciation, *e.g. ennui.* Think of some more examples.]

22. How do we obtain names for new ideas and new inventions? Give instances.

[Bear in mind that in some cases these novelties are named after the men by whom they were introduced.]

23. 'English has borrowed largely from other languages.'

Does this seem to you an advantage or a drawback?

Give a few examples of words thus borrowed.

[A language should have a vocabulary large enough to express the ideas of the people who use it. In what respects would English be deficient without its Latin or Greek element? On the other hand, there is a risk that the synonyms of a mixed vocabulary may land a speaker or writer in tautology or fallacious argument. Thus an orator advocated 'freedom of speech' on the ground that every man ought to have 'unrestricted liberty of expressing his sentiments.']

CHAPTER III.

THE INDO-EUROPEAN OR ARYAN FAMILY OF LANGUAGES.

24. WHEN we are learning Greek or Latin, French or German, we come across some words that are the same in form as their English equivalents and many more words that are very like them. Take the English words *one, three, me, is.* Everybody can see the resemblance of these words to the French *un, trois, me, est*; to the Latin *unus, tres, me, est*; to the German *ein, drei, mich, ist*; to the Greek ἕν, τρεῖς, με, ἐστί. A knowledge of other languages of Europe would enable us to carry the comparison further with the certainty of finding in them corresponding resemblances. From the fact that these similarities exist we are not to draw the inference that our English ancestors **derived** the word *me* from the Latin, or that the Romans **derived** their word *me* from the Greek. We did not wait for the Romans to supply us with a necessary word like *me*, nor were the Romans without it until they took it from the Greeks. With regard to the French words *un, trois, me, est*, the case is different; they do 'come from' the Latin *unus, tres, me, est*, for the Romans conquered Gaul, and the Gauls adopted in the main the language of their conquerors. But *me* was good English before the Normans came to England. Such words as *secure, convict, hospital, detect*, have really 'come from' the Latin: we borrowed them directly. But it would be a great mistake to suppose that wherever we find a likeness between words in two languages, there has been any borrowing at all, direct or indirect.

Now resemblances such as we see between words like *one, three, me, is,* in a number of different languages, are too many for them to be the result of chance. If then the similar words in one language have not been taken from those in another, **how are we to account for the similarity ?**

25. The explanation is this, that **the various languages have proceeded from a common source.** Suppose that many of the nations of Europe and Asia are descended from a tribe which existed some thousands of years ago. Suppose that, as this tribe increased in numbers, it became a difficult matter to supply the growing population with food. We know what happens in our own time and country when men find a difficulty about getting a livelihood in the place of their birth. They go somewhere else. Sometimes they move from the country districts and settle in the large towns. Sometimes they leave the old country and seek their fortunes in a new one. The men who cut themselves adrift from their old moorings are, as a rule, the younger, more vigorous, and more enterprising members of the community. The old folk stay on at home. In much the same fashion we may imagine that this primitive nation witnessed long ago the exodus of many of the more hardy and energetic of its members. With their tents and their cattle, these younger men would wander away from the family settlement, until they found a district which seemed attractive as a permanent resting-place, a district with a river at hand and pasture for the herds. And here the descendants of these emigrants would remain until in their case was repeated the history of what had happened to their fore-fathers. The pressure of an increasing population would make a fresh migration necessary, and a part of the tribe would again set out to found a new settlement. Suppose

that, three or four thousand years later, a traveller came upon the descendants of the original tribe, scattered abroad through Europe and Persia and India, he would find that, in spite of the changes which removals and the lapse of many centuries had brought about in their languages, these languages contained beneath the surface many points of resemblance.

Now this supposition that from an early race of men there started forth, at different times, parties of emigrants from whom have sprung a posterity which occupies a portion of Asia and almost the whole of Europe, is a supposition only. Historical records on the subject we have none. We cannot therefore speak of these migrations with the same certainty which we feel when we speak of the English coming from Schleswig-Holstein, or of the Normans coming from France. In proof of these invasions of Saxons and Normans we can produce written testimony. The migrations of our supposed primitive tribe are matters of inference, but the inference is one which we feel justified in drawing, because it enables us to **explain the existence of these similarities** between many of the languages of Europe and Asia.

A comparison of most of the languages of Europe with many of the languages of India discloses to us the fact that, instead of being totally different, they present many points of resemblance,—so many indeed that we are driven to the conclusion that these languages have **proceeded from a common source.** This collection of languages we call the **Indo-European** or **Aryan Family** of Languages.

26.   It is believed that three or four thousand years ago there lived, somewhere between the Hindu-Kush mountains and the Caspian Sea, a tribe, or tribes of the same race, called **Aryans.** Though we have no written memorials of these Aryans, the habits and character of the people are

known to us as inferences from facts revealed by philological research. Experts in the Science of Language tell us that these Aryans lived in towns, kept cattle, ploughed the ground, used metals, made boats, could count up to a hundred, recognised family relations, and had various names for God. And the line of argument by which they establish these conclusions is of this kind:—If, say they, we find existing in various disguises, in a number of different languages, the same word to express 'horse,' 'sheep,' 'plough,' 'spear,' then the tribe from which these modern races have sprung must have had a word for horse, sheep, plough, spear, and if they had the word, they must have been acquainted with the thing. Thus we see once more how language throws a light upon history, or even reveals to us history which is otherwise hidden.

27. Of these Aryan languages some are more closely allied than others. The more closely allied languages we arrange in classes which we call **Stocks**. Then again we subdivide a stock into classes of still more closely allied languages, and these subdivisions we call **Branches**. Let us treat our own language in this fashion. In the first place, it belongs to the **Teutonic** stock. But many other languages belong to this stock, some of which resemble English more closely than others. Dutch, Flemish, German, Icelandic, Norwegian, Swedish, Danish, are all of them Teutonic languages, but they fall into different groups. English we said was a **Low-German** language : so is Dutch ; so is Flemish. Modern German is the only representative of the High-German branch. Although on the Continent High-German is of greater importance than the Low-German languages, Low-German is of greater antiquity. Indeed High-German is a development from Low-German and began its separate existence about the seventh century Then again the languages of Iceland, Norway, Sweden, and Denmark, form a third group, which we call Scandinavian.

The Teutonic stock is thus subdivided into three branches, viz. Low-German, High-German, and Scandinavian, and it is a full designation of the **English language** to say that it is a member of the **Low-German branch** of the **Teutonic stock** of the **Indo-European or Aryan family** of languages.   We might describe Dutch and Flemish as sister languages of English, and German and Norwegian as its first-cousins[1].

Another stock of considerable interest to us is the **Romanic, or Italic**, since to this stock belong the Latin, from which we have borrowed largely, and the modern representatives of the Latin,—Italian, French, Spanish,— Romance languages as they are called, *Romance* because they come from a Roman source.   Then again there is the **Hellenic or Grecian** stock, which is represented by the Modern Greek.

The **Keltic** stock also has peculiar interest for us, because the inhabitants of our island before the arrival of our English forefathers were Kelts, and Keltic dialects are spoken at the present day in parts of Great Britain and Ireland.   The Keltic stock falls into two branches, the Cymric and the Gadhelic.   Under the former head are placed the Welsh language and the Armorican, a dialect spoken in Brittany.   The old Cornish, which died out two centuries ago, belonged to the same branch.   In the Gadhelic group are included the native Irish or Erse, the Gaelic of the Highlands, and the Manx of the Isle of Man.

---

[1] The oldest of the Teutonic languages of which written records are extant is Gothic, sometimes called Mœso-Gothic.   This was the language spoken by the Western Goths, or Visigoths, who settled in Mœsia, a district corresponding to the present Servia and Bulgaria.   About the year A.D. 350 Bishop Wulfila (or Ulphilas) translated the Bible into Gothic, and of this translation portions have come down to us.   These literary remains are of great linguistic value, as they are earlier by some centuries than any other Teutonic records: the next earliest are Anglo-Saxon and Old High-German.

28. The language brought to this island in the fifth and sixth centuries by our English forefathers was a pure or unmixed Teutonic speech. An unmixed language in the main it long continued to be. Contributions of words from foreign sources came in slowly at first. On the other hand, although **Modern English** is in its essentials a **Teutonic** language, it contains a large **Italic** element, has received considerable additions to its vocabulary from the **Hellenic** source, and possesses a slight **Keltic** ingredient. Thus four different stocks have contributed to its formation: it is a **mixed** or **composite** language: its words have been borrowed from many different sources.

29. Two groups of European languages remain to complete the list of stocks into which the European members of the Aryan family are divided: these are the **Slavonic,** of which Russian is an important example, and **Lettish,** which is represented at the present time by dialects in Eastern Prussia.

As the name *Indo-European* implies, some of the languages of Asia belong to this family. These languages fall into two groups. One group is the **Indian,** which includes Sanskrit, a dead language with an important literature ; the modern dialects of India which are sprung from Sanskrit, such as Hindustani, Bengali, and others ; and Cingalese, the dialect of Ceylon. The other group is the **Iranian** or Persian.

There are thus eight stocks into which the Aryan or Indo-European family is subdivided, two of them Indian and six European. It must not be supposed from the use of the word 'Indo-European' that *all* the languages of India and *all* the languages of Europe belong to the same family. The languages of India we will not discuss in further detail, but it must be borne in mind that **the following European languages are not members of this great family :**—Turkish, Hungarian, the language of the Laps in Lapland, the language of the Fins in Finland, and the Basque, spoken in the Pyrenees.

30. Of the other families of languages, the **Semitic** is the most important. To it belongs Hebrew, in which the greater part of the Old Testament is written, and it contains also Arabic. Besides the Aryan and the Semitic Family, other distinct groups of languages spoken in various parts of the world have been recognised, *e.g.* the languages of China, of Farther India, of Japan, of South America. Many languages have not yet been studied with the view of tracing their relationships.

31. The Table on the next page shows the relationship of some of the principal members of the Indo-European or Aryan Family of Languages. The names of dead languages and dead dialects are printed in italics.

TABLE SHOWING SOME OF THE LANGUAGES BELONGING TO THE ARYAN OR INDO-EUROPEAN FAMILY.

Celtic stock	Romanic or Italic stock	Hellenic stock	Teutonic stock	Lettic stock	Slavonic stock	Indian stock	Iranian or Persian stock
Cymric branch — Gadhelic branch	*Latin*	*Greek*	Low German branch — High German branch — Scandinavian branch		Russian	*Sanskrit*	Persian
British — Irish	Romance Languages, viz.	Mod. Greek				Hindustani	
Cornish — Gaelic	Italian		English — German — *Gothic*			Bengali	
Welsh — Manx	French		Dutch — Icelandic				
Breton	Spanish		Flemish — Norwegian				
	Portuguese		Swedish				
			Danish				

CHAPTER IV.

THE DIVISIONS OF GRAMMAR.

32. In the preceding chapters we have sketched the gradual process by which was formed the English language as we have it now; we have marked those events in the history of our island which produced important effects upon our language; and we have shown the relationship of English to other members of the same family of languages. We have ascertained what the English language is, where it came from, when it arrived. We now pass on to treat of the grammar of the English language; and first let us inquire **what we mean by Grammar.**

33. We can speak a language, or we can write a language, or we can both speak and write a language. All languages were spoken before they were written. Some languages spoken by uncivilized tribes in Africa are not written yet. At the present day Latin and ancient Greek are written but not spoken. For this reason we call them dead languages. English, French, and German are spoken and written. Now it is clear that there must be a right way and a wrong way of writing and speaking these languages. **To deal with the correct way of writing and speaking them is part of the business of Grammar.** An African savage knows nothing of grammar, but he knows that the missionary does not speak his language properly. In time the missionary may come to know the language as thoroughly as the natives know it, and may state a number of rules and principles concerning the use of the language,—rules and principles to which the natives conform in their daily speech, without having ever heard of the existence of such rules and principles. These rules and principles constitute an important part of the grammar of the language. But we need not travel so far away as Africa for an illustration. Take the case of an English child, brought up in an educated family. At an early age such a child would speak good English though he had never learnt grammar, perhaps had never even heard of the subject. On the other hand, a child brought up in an ignorant household would speak bad English, would make mistakes in pronunciation or use wrong forms of expression. Without any grammatical training in either case, these children would speak correctly or incorrectly, would pick up good English or bad English, through the influence of the people with whom they came in contact. So it is hardly a true account of the matter, at any rate so far as one's own language is concerned, to say, as is sometimes said, that grammar *teaches* us to speak and write correctly. We learn to speak and write correctly by mixing with educated persons and reading well-written books. What grammar does is this: it **treats of the language** generally, its sounds, letters and words; it supplies us with a number of **rules for the correct way of using the language**, and it examines **why** certain ways of using the language are right, and certain others are wrong, not merely stating **rules**, but adding **reasons**. Thus, suppose a person says 'Ask him to let you and I go out'; we see that the grammar is bad, and if we alter the sentence to 'Ask him to let you and me go out,' we make the necessary grammatical correction. But if we go on to add that *let* is a transitive verb and requires an objective case after it, we give a reason for altering *I* to *me*. We state not merely that one form of expression is wrong and the other right, but *why* one is wrong and the other right. We give a principle as well as a rule.

34. Some writers on grammar have described it as an Art and others as a Science. An Art consists of a collection of rules, with more or less practical skill to carry them out. A Science consists of the principles on which the Art is based. Now a man may be a successful artist in many subjects without understanding the principles which underlie his Art. He may have the knack of playing a tune on the piano after he has heard it whistled in the street, though he may be unable to read music from the printed page. Or he may be able to paint a landscape, though he knows nothing of the principles of perspective. And in like manner he may speak and write excellent English, though he has never been taught a line of grammar. But he would certainly be more likely to avoid mistakes as a musician, if he had learnt the principles of harmony, or as a painter, if he had learnt the principles of perspective, or as a writer and speaker, if he had learnt the principles of grammar. So even from the point of view of practical utility, we may fairly say that grammar deserves to be studied. A knowledge of grammar will not indeed make a man a *good* writer, in the sense of furnishing him with a pleasant or striking style, but it will help to make him a *correct* writer, and many of our masters of English style would have written better, if they had paid more attention to grammatical rules. If therefore anybody is disposed to say that learning grammar is a waste of time, because it is quite possible to speak and write correctly without a knowledge of it, we may fairly reply that a knowledge of grammar is of some use even as a safeguard against speaking and writing wrongly, things which we are all of us apt to do. But this is not the chief reason after all for studying grammar. We study many subjects of which it would be difficult to say precisely what is the 'good,' unless we were satisfied that the knowledge of the subject is a *good in itself*. It is a knowledge of such subjects which constitutes a liberal as distinct from a commercial education. We may study chemistry simply because it is interesting to know something of the constituents of the world around us, not because we intend to become chemical manufacturers. We may study animal physiology simply because it is interesting to know something of the structure of our own bodies and of the bodies of other animals. We have been breathing and digesting all our lives, and we shall breathe no better for knowing the composition of the atmosphere, and digest no better when we have learnt the nature of the gastric juice, than we breathed and digested before we acquired this information. But we do not feel that the time given to chemistry or physiology has therefore been wasted. An intelligent man likes to understand the things which he sees around him. These things are too numerous for us to understand much of many of them. We must pick and choose according to our tastes. But a man who knows nothing but what is of 'use' to him, in the sense of its providing him with the means of getting his living, is likely to be a dull fellow, uninteresting to himself and to his neighbours. Now to English-speaking people the English language ought to be an attractive subject of study. When we think of the series of great writers who have used this language,—of Chaucer, Shakespeare, Milton, Wordsworth, Tennyson,—when we reflect how this language is spoken to-day by many millions of people besides the inhabitants of our own little island,—by the people of the United States and Canada, of Australia and South Africa,—so that it bids fair to become the universal medium of intercourse among the chief commercial nations of the world, we can hardly fail to realise that our English tongue well deserves our attention, and that we ought not to rest satisfied with merely using it correctly, but that we should give some time and trouble to gaining information about its history and character. And some of this information a book on English grammar will give.

35. **Grammar**, then, has to do with **language, and language is made up of words**. A language, as we saw, may be spoken, or written, or both. Spoken words are sounds which may be pronounced rightly or wrongly, as a short experience shows us when we are learning French or German. One part of Grammar deals with the **correct pronunciation of words**, and is called **Orthoëpy**. But under this head we shall treat of a good deal besides the right pronunciation of words. We shall inquire what is the total number of elementary sounds which our English vocabulary with its 100,000 words contains. We shall classify these sounds. We shall touch upon some of the tendencies to substitute one sound for another and look for an explanation of these tendencies. That branch of the subject which has to do with topics of this sort is sometimes called **Phonology,** or the **theory of spoken sounds.**

36. Then again, words may be **written** as well as **spoken**, and they may be **written rightly or wrongly**. The branch of grammar which deals with the **correct writing or spelling of words** is called **Orthography**. We write, or spell, with letters, so orthography deals with the alphabet.

37. If we are asked,—Are Orthography and Orthoëpy **essential or necessary parts of Grammar?** we may answer in this way: If a language is spoken but not written, as is the case with the languages of savage tribes, its grammar will contain Orthoëpy but not Orthography. If a language is a dead language,—if it is written but no longer spoken,—its grammar will contain Orthography, but its Orthoëpy will be uncertain or impossible. But either Orthography or Orthoëpy a grammar must contain, for a language must be either written or spoken, if we know it at all.

38. After examining the sounds and signs, or letters, of which spoken or written words are composed, we shall pass on **to consider words themselves.** We shall show that the words contained in the vocabulary of our language may be arranged in classes according to their meaning, as nouns, verbs, prepositions, etc. Then we shall inquire what changes of form, or inflexions, any of these words undergo, and what is the effect of these changes on the meaning of the words. We might also push our investigation further, and discuss the relation of English words to words in other languages, and determine the channel through which they passed into our own. As an example of these different operations, take the word *mother.* Of this word as it stands by itself, we can say that it is a noun, in the singular number ; that it makes a possessive case singular *mother's,* and a plural number *mothers* ; that compounds can be formed from it such as *mother-country,* and derivatives such as *motherly* ; that it is connected with, though not borrowed from, the Latin *mater,* Greek μήτηρ, German *mutter,* and so forth. Now that part of grammar in which we **treat of words taken separately, classifying** them and considering their **origin and form,** is called **Etymology,** and a very important part of the subject it is.

39. But when we speak or write, it is rarely the case that words stand alone in this fashion. It is true that sometimes they occur thus: for example, we may say 'Mother!' as an exclamation, or if we are asked 'Who gave you that book?' we may answer, 'Mother,' which is a short way of saying 'Mother gave it me,' or 'Mother did.' But usually words occur in sentences, and then we can describe what is the relation in which each word in the sentence stands to the rest. The part of grammar which **treats of words** when they are regarded **in their relation to other words,**— of words when they form parts of groups of other words,—is called **Syntax.** So far as Grammar is studied as an Art,— as a subject of practical usefulness to prevent us from making mistakes in speaking or writing,—Syntax is the more important department. But in so far as we study grammar in the spirit of scientific curiosity, for the sake of learning something about our English tongue, Syntax is of no more importance than Etymology. In the following pages however no attempt has been made to keep the treatment of Etymology rigorously distinct from that of Syntax. For in discussing the forms of words it is often an advantage to deal with their uses when they are related to other words.

40. When we have dealt with the sounds of our speech, the signs or letters which represent them, the words taken separately, and words arranged in sentences, our treatment of the subject will be finished. Recognition is indeed frequently given to another department of Grammar, called Prosody. The aspect of this word must not mislead the reader into thinking that Prosody has to do with prose, for prose is just what Prosody does not deal with. Prosody has to do with Verse, with compositions in metre. Now it is clear that Prosody is not an essential department of grammar, for there might well be a language in which there were no compositions in verse, no metre, and therefore no Prosody. As a fact there is probably no language without metrical compositions of some sort, such as hymns to the gods or chants before going into battle, and if there is metre, then there are principles which regulate the employment of the metre, and these principles constitute Prosody. But there is no necessity for the existence of metrical compositions in every language. Most of us pass our lives and express ourselves only in prose. We may conceive that an entire nation expressed itself only in prose, and had never expressed itself in anything else.

But as soon as a language presents us with compositions in metre, Prosody becomes possible. And most languages do contain compositions in metre amongst their oldest literary possessions. This is naturally the case, since verse is easier to recollect than prose, and is often better worth recollecting. Consequently, in an early age verse is handed down, while prose perishes.

The common blunder must be avoided of supposing that rhyme is the same thing as verse, or that poetry is the same thing as either. Verse is the name applied to the arrangement of words in metre. In modern English verse, this arrangement is such as to allow the accent, or stress of the voice, to fall at regular intervals, like the beats in music. This regular recurrence of accented and unaccented syllables is called rhythm.

A study of metres helps us to appreciate and enjoy the skill which our poets have shown in devising varied and appropriate measures for their verse. But the adequate discussion of this subject would occupy too much space in our book. Moreover, as grammarians we are concerned not with the effective use of language but with its correct use. Questions of style are appropriate to treatises on Composition or Rhetoric rather than to a treatise on Grammar, and the metrical arrangement of words is a matter of style.

41. It will be convenient if we bring together the chief results which we have reached in this chapter.

Grammar has sometimes been described as the Art of speaking and writing correctly. But people may possess the Art of correctly using their own language without having any knowledge of grammar. We define it therefore as **the Science which treats of words and their correct use.**

It contains the following departments,—Orthoëpy, Orthography, Etymology, and Syntax.

Orthoëpy deals with the correct pronunciation of words.

Orthography deals with the correct spelling or writing of words.

Etymology deals with the classification of words, their derivation and inflexion.

Syntax deals with the combination of words in sentences, their government, agreement, and order.

CHAPTER V.

ELEMENTARY SOUNDS IN ENGLISH.

42. WE have assumed that the English dictionary contains 100,000 different significant sounds or words, five or six thousand of which are in use as the vocabulary of the average well-educated man. These different sounds are composed of a very limited number of **simple** or **elementary** sounds. Just as chemistry teaches us that out of some seventy elements are formed the boundless varieties of substances which nature and man's art present to us, so an examination of the sounds which we utter in pronouncing English words shows us that they are made by combining about forty sounds which are simple or elementary. Take, for example, the words *bat* and *but*. Each word contains three simple sounds in combination, but two of the simple sounds, *b* and *t*, are the same in each.

43. Vowels and Consonants. Our first business will be to ascertain the **different sorts of sounds** which we make in speaking. The division of letters, which serve as the signs or symbols of sounds, into **vowels and consonants**, is known to everybody. Let us carefully inquire into the nature of the distinction between these sounds.

Open your mouth and let the breath pass out unchecked while you utter the sound of *a* in *path*, or of *e* in *feed*, or of *o* in *note.* The sound can be **continued** until you are out of breath. Now pronounce the letter *b* in *bad*, not calling it *bee*,—' *bee*' is merely its name as a letter of the alphabet. Pronounce it as if you intended to say *bad*, but changed your mind and stopped as soon as the first letter had escaped. The sound is an **instantaneous** one. There is a sudden explosion of the *b'*, and to prolong it is impossible. Why? Because the sound is made by closing the lips and tearing them rapidly apart. Observe how a man who stammers pronounces the word *bad.* He does not prolong the sound of *b*,—he could not prolong it,—but he repeats it, closing and separating his lips until at length he gets the word out. Again, take the sounds *d* and *t*, pronouncing them as we should do, if we started saying words of which they form the first letter and stopped as soon as we had got the first letter out. Begin to say *dog*, or *ten*, and check yourself at the end of the *d'* or *t'*. No amount of effort will enable you to continue the sound uninterruptedly.

Shall we say then that vowels are sounds which we can prolong indefinitely, in other words, which we can keep on making without a break, and consonants are sounds which come to an end instantaneously? Further experiments will show that this ground of distinction fails. Take the sounds represented by *f, v, s, sh, l, m, n, r.* Like the vowel sounds, these sounds can be prolonged while the breath holds out. The distinction between vowels and consonants consists rather in this. A vowel is a sound by the aid of which we can pronounce any other sound at the ordinary pitch of the voice. A consonant is a sound by the aid of which we cannot pronounce any other sound at the ordinary pitch of the voice. Pronounce once more the sounds *p'*, *b'*, *t'*, *d'*, without any accompanying vowel. The parting of the lips in *p'* and *b'* is just audible: so is the click of the tongue against the teeth in *t'* and *d'*. We cannot say that absolutely no sound is produced. If we practised these experiments in a company of silent people, we should make noise enough to attract attention. But the sounds would not be uttered at the ordinary pitch of the voice. Conversation across the table in these tones would be inaudible, and a speech in so low a key to a public meeting would be no better than dumb-show. Add a vowel to these silent letters however; say *pay, be, toe, daw,* and you can make yourself heard a hundred yards away. But let us try the combination of *p, b, t, d,* with those other consonants which we saw could be uttered by themselves, *f, v, s, sh, l, m, n, r.* If we place together *pr, bn, tl, dz,* we shall not find that we have obtained a combination which can be pronounced at the natural pitch of the voice. Instead of saying, therefore, that vowels are sounds which can be uttered alone, and consonants are sounds which can be uttered only by the aid of a vowel, let us put the matter thus:

Vowels are sounds by the aid of which any consonantal sound can be audibly produced.

Consonants are sounds which will not enable us to produce audibly sounds which are by themselves almost inaudible.

44. This account of the difference between vowels and consonants does not agree with the account which is usually given. It is commonly said that vowels are sounds which can be produced alone, and that consonants are sounds which can be produced only by the aid of a vowel. But though this statement of the matter suits the derivation of the words, —for *vowel* comes from *vocalis,* which means 'capable of being sounded,' and *consonant* comes from *cum,* 'together,' and *sonans,* 'sounding,' *i.e.* 'what is sounded along with something else,'—it does not seem to suit the facts of the case. If a public speaker incurs the hostility of his audience, the *ssss...*of their disapproval can be heard very well without the addition of any vowel to aid its pronunciation. The *sh...!* with which ill-mannered people are rebuked for chattering at a concert; the *mmm?* with which we express our hesitation when an acquaintance makes a statement or a proposal which does not commend itself to our favour, are consonantal sounds which are audible enough when they stand alone.

Then again it is sometimes said that vowels are open sounds and consonants closer and less musical sounds, but this distinction does not seem to throw much light on the subject. Or we are told that vowels are formed without the stoppage of the breath, and that consonants are formed by stopping or by squeezing the breath. All this is interesting, no doubt, to us as physiologists, but it is no concern of ours as grammarians whether we stop our breath or only squeeze it, whether we vibrate our vocal chords or do something with our larynx or pharynx. This is physiology, not grammar. Our business is to distinguish the sounds when produced, not to determine the mode of their production.

45. Classification of Consonantal Sounds. Let us now take the consonantal sounds and consider some broad distinctions between them. Compare the four sounds of *d'*, *t'*, *dh'*, *th'*, as represented in the words *din, tin, thine, thin*, remembering, as before, to make these sounds by beginning to utter the words and stopping short before the vowel is reached. Now in these four sounds, there are two important distinctions to be noticed :

46. Sonants and Surds. (1) In the first place, if we compare *d'* with *t'* and *dh'* with *th'*, we shall observe that although the *d'* and *dh'* are not audible at the ordinary pitch of the voice, still they can be just heard, if an effort is made, while the *t'* and *th'* are scarcely to be heard at all. The same contrast may be noticed in other pairs of sounds : *g'*, if pronounced when isolated from its vowel, is audible, *k'* is less so. The sound of *j'* in *jest* is audible when it stands alone ; *ch'* in *chest* is less so. The sound of *b'* is just audible ; *p'* is almost silent. Various names have been used to express this distinction. Some writers call one set of sounds **Hard** and the other **Soft** ; others call one set **Sharp** and the other **Flat**. Let us compare once more *b'* and *p'* and ask ourselves which is hard and which is soft, which is sharp and which is flat. If it strikes us that the application of these metaphors is obvious,—if these terms at once convey their appropriate meaning to our minds,—by all means let us continue to make use of them. Possibly however we may not be struck by the suitability of the

epithets, and in that case the old words **Sonant and Surd**
will express the difference more plainly for us. **Sonant**
means **sounding, surd** means **noiseless.** Supposing
that we fail to see the fitness of calling *p* hard or sharp
and *b* soft or flat, we can see the fitness of calling *p* surd and
b sonant, for we have only to pronounce both letters and
observe which of the two we can hear most of. By continuing the experiment, we can distribute all the sonants and
surds in their right classes, and this is a much better plan
than learning the lists by heart and then putting the wrong
names at the top. If we pronounce *b, g, d, j, dh, z, zh, v, w,*
without an accompanying vowel, we can hear them. These
we call **sonants.** If we pronounce their correlatives *p, k,
t, ch, th, s, sh, f, wh,* without a vowel, they are almost inaudible. These we call **surds.**

To make this distinction clear, we will give these pairs
of sounds in two columns with a word to illustrate each.
They are variously distinguished as—

Sonant, Flat, Soft, Voiced.		Surd, Sharp, Hard, Breathed.	
b,	bin	*p,*	pin
g,	gat, gate	*k,*	cat, Kate
d,	do	*t,*	to
j,	jest	*ch,*	chest
dh,	thine	*th,*	thin
z,	maze	*s,*	mace
zh,	azure, pleasure	*sh,*	shine, sure
v,	vat	*f,*	fat
w,	wear	*wh,*	where
y,	yet		—
		h,	hat

The sound represented by **wh** is pronounced by Scotchmen and
Irishmen, but is vulgarly neglected in southern England. Many people
make no difference in sound between *what* and *wot, when* and *wen,
where* and *were, while* and *wile.*

The surd corresponding to the sonant **y** resembles the German *ich*
sound. It may be heard occasionally in such English words as *hue,
human.*

The letters **w** and **y** are used sometimes with the force of consonants, and sometimes with the force of vowels. In *wit* and *yes* they are consonants: in *few* and *they*, vowels. Hence they are called **semivowels**. In the sound given to *w* at the beginning of a word you may detect a close resemblance to the vowel-sound in *cool* or *rude*. Pronounce slowly *oo-it, oo-et*: then increase the speed as you repeat the word, and you will find that you are saying *wit, wet*. Again, take a word beginning with a *y*, such as *yes*, pronounce it slowly, and you will recognise in the sound of its first letter the long vowel sound in *feed*. A person who gives a hesitating ' yes ' in reply to a question says *ee-es*.

By some writers **h** is not admitted to a place among the consonants, but is regarded as merely an audible emission of breath before vowels or semi-vowels, and called the 'aspiration.' Thus in Greek the original *h* ceased to be a letter and became simply a 'rough breathing.'

Now let us return to our four sounds *d, t, dh, th*, and observe what other distinction can be drawn between them, besides the distinction of sonant and surd.

47. Stops and Continuants. (2) The sounds *d* and *t* are sudden, abrupt, instantaneous, explosive: it is impossible to prolong them. The sounds *dh, th* (as in *thine* and *thin*, for we often make the sound of *dh*, though we never use this sign for it) are continuous: they can be prolonged if we keep on breathing. Hence they are called **Continuants** or **Spirants** (from the Latin *spiro*, ' I breathe '). The letters *p, b, k, g, t, d*, are called **Stops** or **Mutes**, because the sounds are silenced with a sudden halt. From the same circumstance they are also called **Checks,** or **Explosives.** Grammarians have exercised much ingenuity in finding a variety of terms to express the same distinction, thereby rendering the matter more difficult than it naturally is.

We will now make a second list of consonantal sounds, classified according as they are Stops or Continuants :

Stops, Mutes, Checks, Explosives : *p, b, k, g, t, d.*
Continuants, Spirants : *ch, j, th, dh, s, z, sh, zh, f, v, wh, w, y, h.*

With the exception of *ch* and *j* all these sounds are simple or elementary : *ch*, pronounced as in *church*, $= t + sh$, *tshurtsh*, and *j*, as in *jest*, $= d + zh$, *dzhest*. These two composite sounds have been called *consonantal diphthongs*.

48. To complete the number of our elementary consonantal sounds we must add the **Liquids**, viz. *l, m, n, r*, and *ng* (pronounced as in *sing*). These are all sonants in English. Owing to the fact that the sounds of *l, m, n, r* flowed smoothly on and readily combined with other consonants, the Greek grammarians two thousand years ago called them 'fluid' or 'pliant' letters, and this epithet the Latin grammarians translated as 'liquid.'

49. The following list[1] contains all the **simple** or **elementary consonantal sounds** in English:

Stops			Continuants		
	p,	pin		*th,*	thin
	b,	bin		*dh,*	thine
	k,	Kate		*s,*	mace
	g,	gate		*z,*	maze
	t,	to		*sh,*	shine
	d,	do		*zh,*	azure
Liquids				*f,*	fat
	l,	lay		*v,*	vat
	m,	may		*wh,*	where
	n,	nay		*w,*	wear
	r,	ray		*y,*	yet
	ng,	sing		*h,*	hat

The reader must keep clearly in mind the fact that we are dealing with elementary **sounds,** not with our way of writing them. Owing to the deficiencies of our alphabet we are obliged to use combinations of two letters,—*digraphs*, as grammarians call them,—to represent six of these con-

---

[1] Adopted, as is also the table of Vowel-sounds on p. 45, from Miss Soames's *Introduction to the Study of Phonetics*. In these sections much use has been made of Miss Soames's book, and also of Mr Nesfield's *English Grammar Past and Present*, pp. 277—282, to which the student is referred for a more detailed treatment of the subject. At the end of Mr Nesfield's book a note by Professor Skeat on Vocalic Sounds in Modern English has been reprinted.

sonants. But the sounds are simple and indivisible. The sound of *z* in *azure* is different from the sound of *z* in *zebra*. To mark that difference we have written it *zh*, but it is not a compound of *z + h*: it is really an elementary sound. The sounds of *dh* in *thine* and of *th* in *thin* are different, but they are both of them elementary: they are not compounds of *d + h* and of *t + h*. We need a separate letter for each, but we do not possess such a letter for either. And the same thing is true of the other digraphs, *sh*, *wh*, and *ng*.

The letter *r* is called a **Trill**, because of the vibration in the sound, or in some part of the vocal apparatus by which it is produced. Roll out an *r* as a Frenchman does, *rrrr*, and this will be recognised at once. There is very little of a trill about our English pronunciation of the letter. With us the sound of *r* is heard only when the *r* is followed immediately by a vowel in another syllable or another word. Thus we can hear it in *fairest, starry, stir up*, but not in *fair play, star gazing, stir the fire*. Literary critics are often severe upon such rhymes as *morn* and *dawn*, *ought* and *fort*, which they describe as execrable. On the contrary, in the ears of educated people south of the Humber such rhymes are perfect, as the *r* in *morn* and *fort* is silent.

Sibilants are hissing sounds. They can be picked out easily from among the spirants : they are *s, z, sh, zh*.

50. *Classification of Consonantal Sounds according to Vocal Organs.*

These consonantal sounds may be classified on quite a different principle. Hitherto we have dealt with them according to their characteristic differences as sounds. But we can also arrange them according to the part of the vocal apparatus chiefly concerned in their production. Thus we have :—

Lip-sounds, Labials	. *p, b, f, v, wh, w.*
Teeth-sounds, Dentals . . .	. *t, d, th, dh, s, z.*
Roof-of-mouth sounds, Palatals	. *sh, zh, y.*
Throat-sounds, Gutturals . . .	. *k, g.*
Mouth-of-windpipe sound, Glottal .	. *h.*
Nose-sounds, Nasals	. *m, n, ng.*
Tongue-sounds, Linguals . . .	. *l, r.*

The reader will observe that these classes are not mutually exclusive. Thus, for example, *m* is both labial and nasal, *n* dental and nasal, *f* and *v* dental as well as labial.

51. Enumeration of Vowel-Sounds. Vowel-sounds are either simple or compound in their character.

Compound vowel sounds are called **Diphthongs**. The words in the following columns illustrate the sixteen simple or elementary vowel-sounds employed in our English speech. Of these sixteen vowel-sounds, eight are long and eight are short.

Long vowels	Short vowels
father	a*ttend*
*fu*r	*p*u*tty*
fairy	*p*at
fatal	*p*et
*fee*t	*p*it
*faw*n	*p*ot
*foe*man	*pillo*w
*foo*l	*p*ut

In studying this list, direct your attention to the vowel-*sound* of each word. The ways in which we represent these sounds in *spelling* are various, and, from our present point of view, unimportant. Thus, for example, the vowel-sound of *fur* appears also in *herd, firm, work, learn, myrtle*: the vowel-sound of *pet* appears also in *head, many, bury, says, heifer, friend, guest*.

The Obscure or Natural Vowel a. The vowel-sound exemplified by the **a** in *attend*, at the top of the column of short vowels, frequently occurs in English words, but only in unaccented syllables. It may be heard at the end of *vill*a, *sudd*en, *cupb*oard, in the middle of *mirac*l*e, tend*ency, *harm*ony, at the beginning and end of A*meri*ca, *gra*mmari*a*n, *verand*ah. It is called the Obscure vowel, or the Natural vowel,— natural, because the sound is produced with the minimum of effort. Hence boys who get into difficulties over their construing, and orators who are at a loss to proceed with their speeches, occupy the intervals with this sound. This natural vowel bears a closer resemblance in sound to the vowel-sound of *putty* or *fur* than to that of *pat*, with which it has often been wrongly identified.

Observe that many words written with an *r* at the end are pronounced in the south of England with this Natural vowel in place of the *r*. Say the words *hair, here, poor, our*, by themselves or when followed by words beginning with a consonant, and you will hear no *r*. On the stage and in the comic papers this substitution of the Natural vowel for *r* is caricatured, when the dandy is represented as saying 'De-ah me! What a bo-ah!' If however final *r* is followed by a vowel, it has its consonantal sound. Compare, *e.g.*, *dear aunt* and *dear me, poor Ellen* and *poor Tom*.

52. Diphthongs are blends or combinations of two vowel-sounds which are run together in pronunciation. At this point great care is needed not to be misled by the diphthongs of print, *æ*, *œ*, neither of which, in our English pronunciation, is a true diphthong at all. The *æ* of *Cæsar* is no diphthong in sound; it is the same as the pure vowel-sound of *feet*. So is the *œ* of *fœtid*. The *ea* in *lead*, *ie* in *field*, *ei* in *receive*, are none of them true diphthongs: they are only more or less clumsy ways of showing the length of an elementary vowel-sound.

The true diphthongs in English,—those in which two vowel-sounds are run into one,—are five in number : viz.

i in *fine*: this is a blend of the *a* in German *mann*,— a sound of *a* which is extinct in modern English except provincially,—and of the *i* in *pit*. The blend of the *a* in *father* with the *i* in *pit* gives us the broader diphthongal sound heard in *aye*, when we say 'The Ayes have it.'

oi in *noise*: this is a blend of the vowel-sounds in *fawn* and *pit*.

ou in *house*: this is a blend of the vowel-sounds in *father* and *put*.

u in *use*: this is a blend of the vowel-sounds in *pit* and *fool*.

In a drawling pronunciation it is possible to detect the elementary vowel-sounds which form the diphthongal blend. Persons of defective education will talk of 'a bee-ootiful baw-ee,' or 'a na-ice ha-use,' when they mean 'a beautiful boy' or 'a nice house.' It should be specially observed that although the *i* in *fine* is a single letter, it is diphthongal in sound, and the same is true of the *u* in *use*. These diphthongal sounds can be represented in many other ways. Thus *i* is heard in *try*, *die*, *dye*, *sigh*, *guide*, *buy*, *aisle*, *eye*. *Oi* is expressed by *oy* in *boy*, by *uoy* in *buoy*. *Ow* or *ough* often occurs instead of *ou*. Diphthongal *u* is variously written as *ue* (*sue*), *ui* (*suit*), *eu* (*feud*), *you*, *yew*, *ewe*.

Consider next the vowel-sounds of *fate* and *foe*. It is undeniable that these are really diphthongal. In each case the vowel with which we start glides into a different vowel with which we close. Thus we pronounce *fate* as *fay-eet* or *fay-it* and *foe* as *fo-oo*. If you question this statement run up or down the scale singing *fate* or *foe* and note the result. Unless you have been taught singing by a good master, before you have reached half way the vowel-sound which you are producing will be *ee* or *oo*. *Fay-eet* and *fo-oo* are blends as complete as *na-ice* or *ha-use*. And hence some authorities class the vowel-sounds of *fate* and *foe* with the true diphthongs. There is some convenience however in placing them in the list of elementary vowel-sounds while recognising that in the standard speech of southern England they have acquired a diphthongal character. For when they occur at the end of a syllable which is followed by another syllable their sound is almost if not quite pure. Thus in *fa-tal, la-dy, na-vy*, and in *foe-man, no-ble, po-ker*, the secondary vowel-sound, which is prominent in *fate* and *foe*, is scarcely perceptible. Our English tendency to turn long vowels into diphthongs makes it a difficult matter for us to acquire the right pronunciation of such words as *été* and *drôle* in French, or *geh* and *so* in German, for in French and German these vowel-sounds are pure. But the feat, though difficult, is not impossible.

The reader may have felt surprised at finding in the list of short vowel-sounds the *o* of *pillow*. That this *o* differs from the *o* in *pot* is obvious enough, but he may have been inclined to identify it with the *o* of *foe*. As we have just seen, the *o* of *foe* finishes in the sound of *oo* : now the *oo* element is almost inaudible in the *o* of *pillow*. This short *o* occurs only in unaccented syllables, whether at the beginning of a word, as in *omit*, in the middle, as in *proceed*, or at the end, as in *pillow*. To substitute the Natural vowel for this final *o* and say *fella, winda*, instead of *fellow, window*, is a vulgarism.

In dealing with the letter *r* we pointed out that its characteristic trilled sound is heard in English only when the *r* is followed by a vowel in the next syllable or the next word. And in dealing with the Natural vowel we saw that an untrilled *r*,—an *r* followed by a consonant,—is often replaced by this vowel-sound. When we pronounce the word *fair*, what we really say is *fae-a*, the Natural vowel taking the place of *r*. It is only in words such as *fair-y, fair-est, car-ing, bear-er*, words with a trilled *r*, that the *pure* long vowel-sound is heard. A similar substitution takes place when we say *beer, boar, boor*; our actual pronunciation is *bee-a, bo-a, boo-a*. In each case we begin with one vowel-sound and end with another. But the blend is not complete. The component parts remain distinct. You will find many lines in Shakespeare in which such words as *fire* and *dear* form two syllables, but no actor could make more than one syllable of a word containing a true diphthong, such as *fight* and *doubt.* We may therefore call these combinations **Imperfect Diphthongs.**

53. We have now enumerated 23 pure consonants, 16 pure vowels, 5 true diphthongs, and 4 imperfect diphthongs. Of our pure vowels two would be placed by some authorities amongst the diphthongs. Adhering however to the scheme adopted in the preceding pages, we give 39 as the sum-total of elementary sounds in English as spoken to-day.

Now if we run over the **letters of the alphabet,** we shall see that some of them find no place in our classification. The following letters are **absent** from the list :—**c, q, j, x.** Why is this ?

The letter *c* is absent because it **represents no sound** in English not **already represented** by *k, s,* or *sh. Cat* is pronounced precisely as *kat* would be pronounced, *city* as *sity, special* as *speshal.* Thus the letter *c* is superfluous.

The letter *q* occurs only before *u* and, in combination with it, represents the sound of $k+w$, a compound, as in *queen,* or, more rarely, the simple sound of *k,* as in *quay, cheque.*

For a different reason we reject the other two letters. They do not stand for **simple** or **elementary** sounds at all, but **represent compounds.** So—

j is a combination of $d+zh$,
x ,,   ,,   ,, $k+s$ in *excel,* or of $g+z$ in *exert.*

Notice that not only *can* these sounds be represented by a combination of letters, but they *ought* to be represented thus. For it is the business of the alphabet to furnish us with separate signs for **simple** sounds but not for **compound** sounds. If the alphabet contains a shorthand symbol *x,* representing in one letter the sound of $k+s$, why, we may reasonably ask, should it not contain other shorthand symbols, say, a shorthand symbol for $a + n + d$? Such a symbol we do indeed possess in the form &, but we do not regard this symbol as a letter of the alphabet, and nobody but an American humourist would employ it in spelling other words, writing 'h&some' for *handsome* and 'underst&' for *understand.* The like criticism applies to the compound sound represented by *j.* The objection may be raised that, if *x* is rejected because it can be represented by $k + s$, we ought to get rid of *f* because it can be represented by $p + h$, and that we might spell *fife, phiphe,* just as we spell *philosophy* with a *ph.* But the cases are quite different. The sound of *f* is not a compound of $p + h$. It is a simple sound, and it is entitled to a separate letter. It is the use of the *ph* for *f* which is open to censure from the alphabetical stand-point. We use the *ph* because the words containing it come from the Greek, but if we spelt according to sound, the *ph* would disappear, and we should write *filosofy* instead of *philosophy.*

54. The following points connected with the subject of sounds in English deserve attention :

(1) Two mutes of unequal degrees of sharpness and flatness cannot be easily sounded together in the same syllable ; or, if we employ the terms which we saw reason to prefer, a sonant and a surd in juxtaposition cannot be easily pronounced in the same syllable. We may write them together, but to sound them both as they are written is impracticable. It is important to notice this, because sonants and surds often are thus written together, when we form the plurals of nouns or the past tenses of verbs. The ordinary way of making plurals is to add *-s* to the singular. Now *s* is a surd mute. Add *s* to a noun ending in a surd sound, *e.g. pat,* and the result can be readily pronounced as it is written, *pats.* But add *s* to a noun ending in a sonant sound, *e.g. pad,* and the result cannot be readily pronounced as it is written, *pads.* What we do pronounce is *padz,* two sonants. We naturally make the ending *s* give way and turn it into *z,* instead of preserving the *s* and changing the last letter of the word into *t,* as this latter course would alter the meaning of the noun. If we try the experiment with other nouns ending in sonant letters, *e.g. hog, slab,* we shall find the same tendency at work to assimilate the sound of the surd *s* to the sound of the sonant *g* or *b,* causing us to pronounce the words *hogz, slabz.* The same principle is seen

at work in the past tense of verbs when an *ed* is added to the present. Take the word *walk* and add *ed* : *k* is a surd sound, *d* is a sonant. One or other of the sounds must give way, if we pronounce them in the same syllable. The *d* gives way, otherwise the root itself would be changed, and we pronounce the past tense as if it were written with a surd *t*, *walkt*. The same thing happens with such words as *slap, hiss, cuff,* in which we write *slapped, hissed, cuffed,* but give these forms the sound of *slapt, hisst, cufft*.

(2) Our natural laziness induces us to save trouble in the pronunciation of sounds. Accordingly we find—

i. That sounds which involve a good deal of effort in their utterance tend to disappear from words. Thus *if* was formerly *gif, day* was *daeg, godly* was *godlic.* We no longer sound the *gh* in *light* and similar words, though we continue to write it. Many words which now begin with a *y* began in old English with a *g*.

Again, words have in many instances lost a syllable, sometimes at the beginning, sometimes in the middle, sometimes at the end. If we compare *bishop* with *episcopal*, we see that the word has been shorn of its initial *e* : so *diamond* is *adamant* without the initial *a*: *bus* is *omnibus* after a double decapitation. *Palsy* is the same as *paralysis* with the -*ra*- dropped out : *proxy* is *procuracy* in reduced circumstances. Examples of the tendency to cut words down at the end occur in *cab*, which used to be *cabriolet*, in *miss*, which is a curtailed form of *mistress*, and in *consols*, which represents *consolidated stocks*. School slang supplies illustrations of the same process of abridgment in the words *exam* for *examination*, *trans* and *con* for *translation* and *construe*.

ii. But, curiously, letters have in some cases crept into words, apparently to render the pronunciation easier. If we compare with the Latin *numerus, tener, camera,* the English *number, tender, chamber,* we notice the insertion of a *b* or a *d*. It is supposed that to pronounce these words with the *b* or *d* was found less trouble than to pronounce them without these strengthening letters. An omnibus-conductor calls out *Westmin-i-ster,* as the word thus lengthened is more easily repeated than *Westminster.* Uneducated people often insert a syllable in *umbrella* and speak of an *umb-e-rella.* All such changes are called euphonic, or are said to be made for the sake of euphony, *i.e.* owing to our desire to save ourselves effort in speech when we can.

(3) *Umlaut.* We sometimes find that, when a syllable containing a short vowel is added to a word, there is a tendency to shorten the vowel of the original word into something more nearly approaching conformity with the vowel of the ending. This process is called Umlaut. Thus the addition of the suffix turns *corn* into *kernel, old* into *elder, thumb* into *thimble, fox* into *vixen.*

(4) *Metathesis.* Sometimes the order of the letters in a word is transposed: this change is called metathesis. To say *waps* for *wasp* is a vulgarism now, but it was good Old English. A countryman says *aks* for *ask*, *haps* for *hasp*. The *Ridings* of Yorkshire are *thridings, i.e. third-ings* or 'third parts.' *Nostrils* are *nose-thirles, i.e.* 'nose-holes.'

(5) *Accent* is the stress of the voice laid upon a syllable in a word. *Emphasis* is the stress laid upon a word or words in a sentence. Accent has exercised an influence in producing some of the changes mentioned above. The word *episcopus* was cut down to *bishop*, and *procuracy* to *proxy*, as we said, to economise labour, but it was owing to the fact that the suppressed syllables were unaccented that people felt themselves at liberty to drop them out of these words. We may often observe the tendency to clip words improperly when the neglected syllable carries no accent; thus boys say *ex'cise* for *exercise*, *lib'ty* for *liberty*.

In modern English the tendency is to throw the accent near the beginning of the word, but this tendency is counteracted, sometimes by our desire to lay the stress on the root of the word rather than on a mere prefix, and sometimes by foreign influence, many French and Latin words preserving their own accentuation. The accent rarely goes further back than the third syllable from the end of the word; when it goes further back than this there is a secondary accent, an echo of the first, as in *témporáry, héterodóx, héterogéneous;* but usually its place is on the third syllable from the end, as in *geólogy, extrávagant, miscelláneous, incomprehénsible.* We do not throw the accent as far back as we might in *disórder, interférence, divérsion*, and many similar words, perhaps because we wish to lay stress on the important part of the word and not on its prefix; but no general principle can be stated respecting our usage in this matter. There is no consistency in our practice, for the accent is carried back to the prefix in these words,—*ínnocent, cóntroversy, déference.* In the following words the accentuation is due to foreign influence;—*crusáde, cavalíer, ballóon, routíne, antíque*, are French; *robúst, moróse, benígn, humáne*, are Latin. The words *sénator* and *órator* have become thoroughly naturalized, and we lay the stress on the first syllable, in conformity with the general tendency of accentuation in English. The less familiar *curátor* and *testátor* preserve the accent which they had in Latin.

Many words in English differ in meaning according to their accent. There are upwards of fifty pairs of nouns and verbs like *áccent* and *accént, éscort* and *escórt, rébel* and *rebél*, in which the noun has the accent on the first syllable, and the verb has it on the last. Almost all these words are of Latin origin. In the words *absent* and *frequent* we have verb and adjective distinguished by the accent: in *compact* and *expert* noun and adjective are thus distinguished. Other examples are given in the Questions at the end of this chapter.

QUESTIONS.

1. Say whether the sounds corresponding to the following letters are (1) sonant or surd, (2) mute or spirant, (3) labial, dental, guttural, or palatal;—*k, d, z, f, th, m.*

2. Which of the following combinations cannot be pronounced as they are written? Why not?—*tacks, tags; dogs, docks; staffs, staves; sods, sots; slaps, slabs; jumped, crazed, crashed, robbed, stopped, flocked, flogged.*

3. Explain the nature of the changes which the following words exhibit when they are compared with the corresponding forms supplied by other languages, or by our own language at an earlier stage:— 'enough,' Ger. *genug*: 'I,' Ger. *ich*: 'lord,' O. E. *hlaford*: 'rain,' Ger. *regen*: 'way,' Ger. *weg*: 'morrow, Ger. *morgen*: 'warden' and 'guardian': 'warrant' and 'guarantee': 'story' and 'history': 'spite' and 'despite': 'uncle,' Lat. *avunculus*: 'dropsy,' Gk. *hydrops*: 'miss' and 'mistress': 'petty,' Fr. *petit*: 'peril,' Lat. *periculum*: 'sexton' and 'sacristan': 'citizen,' Fr. *citoyen*: 'firth' and 'frith': 'long' and 'linger': 'old' and 'elder': 'vain' and 'vanity': 'cook' and 'kitchen': 'thunder,' Ger. *donner*: 'city,' Lat. *civitas*: 'priest' and 'presbyter': 'tremble' and 'tremor': 'gender,' Lat. *genere*: 'Birmingham' and 'Brummagem.'

4. How does the accent of the following words affect their meaning?—*affix, contest, frequent, august, torment, refuse, compact, desert, conjure, collect, minute, invalid.*

5. These words were formerly accented in the following way:— *bondáge, advertísement, balcóny, mischíevous, acadèmy, contráry.* Mark the syllable on which the accent falls now. What tendency does the change indicate? What means have we of knowing that a word once bore a different accent from the accent which it bears now?

6. Some letters are said to be superfluous. Exemplify this with respect to some of the letters in the following sentence:—'The fox ran quickly near the city walls.'

7. Give words illustrating the various sounds represented by the letter *a* in English.

Classify the mute consonants into labials, dentals, and gutturals; and also into thin, middle, and aspirate.

[The following table contains the classification required :

	Surds Thin Sharp Hard	Sonants Middle Flat Soft	Aspirate
Labials	p	b	ph, bh
Dentals	t	d	th, dh
Gutturals	k	g	kh, gh

The student must observe that none of these aspirated mutes occur in English. The aspirated mute *ph* is not the *f* sound of *photograph* : it is the *ph* of *uphold*. The *th* is not the sound which we have in *thin* : it is the sound which we have in *at home*. The *kh* is the Greek χ, not the sound of *ch* in *church* or *loch*. The sounds of *ph, th, ch*, as we pronounce them are not Mutes at all : they are Spirants or Breaths. See Abbott and Seeley's *English Lessons*, p. 283.]

8. Distinguish the true from the false Diphthongs in the following words :—*pain, noise, new, people, yeoman, build, now, found, eye, clean, rough.*

9. Distinguish the meanings of *canon* and *cannon* ; *tránspórt* and *transpórt*; *áccent* and *accént*; *dissent* and *descent* ; *ingenious* and *ingenuous*; *désert, desért* and *dessert*; *virtue* and *vertu*; *éxpert* and *expért*; *súpine* and *supíne*.

10. What are Doublets ? How have they arisen ?
[Words which proceed from the same original but have assumed different forms are called ' doublets.' See § 18. The shortening of words owing to the loss of an unaccented syllable also produces doublets : see § 54, (2) i.]

11. From the list of words illustrating the sixteen elementary vowel-sounds in English (given in § 51, p. 45) select the word which has a vowel-sound corresponding to the italicised letter or letters in each of the following words :— h*au*l, y*ea*st, ob*ey*, g*ua*rd, marg*a*rine, t*ou*gh, g*ui*ld, s*ai*d, st*ai*d, f*ea*st, *ea*rth, p*ou*r, t*ou*r, b*u*sy, h*ei*fer, s*ew*, f*er*n, h*oo*d, fl*oo*d, pr*e*tty, wh*a*t, l*eo*pard, g*ao*l, h*ei*r, d*o*ve, w*oo*l, b*ou*quet, *a*ny, p*eo*ple, gamb*o*ge, c*a*nvas, mart*y*r, s*y*rup, f*u*rlough, d*e*ter, br*ew*er, w*i*dow, r*ea*lity, *au*nt, s*au*ce, *a*bate, *o*ppress, mach*i*nery, m*i*schievous, *a*ttack, for*ei*gn, procl*a*mation, prof*e*ssor, comp*a*ny, *i*nfluenza.

CHAPTER VI.

Signs or Letters.

55. How may our 100,000 words or significant sounds be represented best in writing?

One way would be to have a different symbol or picture for every word, after the fashion of the Chinese. But consider how awkward and troublesome such a method of representing our words would be. Think of the burden on the memory of associating even five hundred words with as many distinct pictures. To learn the meaning of five thousand such pictures would require years of study. Try to realise our difficulties if, instead of representing numbers by a combination of the digits o to 9 and by using the device of place, we employed a different symbol for every different number. Our means of numeration would in this case be of a very imperfect character. Now, although 100,000 distinct sounds may exist in English speech, these distinct sounds are formed by the combination of about forty simple or elementary sounds; and a corresponding number of symbols, or signs, or letters, combined together, will enable us to represent all our existing words and as many additional words as our language may hereafter receive. Suppose that the words *gun, rod,* were represented by pictures, and that a person had never learnt these pictures, or having learnt them had forgotten their meaning, he would be at a loss to understand the sense of a passage in which they occurred.

But when he has once learnt the meaning of the signs *g, u, n, r, o, d,* he can combine them so as to represent these words, or can interpret the words when he sees them in print, as rapidly as he can write down the sign for three-hundred-and-twenty-seven, or recognise the meaning of 327, when he has once mastered the use of figures.

56. We saw in the preceding chapter that in pronouncing English words we make use of 16 distinct simple or elementary vowel-sounds and of 23 simple or elementary consonantal sounds. Thus there is a total of 39 simple sounds for which we require 39 separate signs. Diphthongs would be expressed by writing in juxtaposition the signs of those vowels of which they form blends. If we had a perfect alphabet, it would fulfil these two conditions:

1. **Every simple or elementary sound would have a separate sign:**

2. **No such sound would have more than one sign.**

And then, if we always used our perfect alphabet consistently and employed its proper sign for each of these sounds, it would be as easy a matter to spell a word when we had learnt our alphabet, as it is to write down a number when we have learnt the use of figures. Such a system of spelling would be **phonetic**, that is, **spelling according to the sound.** Our spelling is far from being phonetic. The chief cause of this is the imperfect nature of our alphabet. We saw that of the twenty-six letters which it contains, four are useless, *c, j, q,* and *x,* so our twenty-six letters are reduced to twenty-two, by means of which we have to express thirty-nine simple sounds. The alphabet is open to the twofold criticism that it is (1) **Deficient,** to the extent of nearly half the requisite number of letters, and (2) **Redundant,** in possessing four letters which are of no use.

The deficiency is best seen in the vowels, of which we enumerated sixteen: these are represented by five signs, so eleven signs are lacking under this head. Of the twenty-three elementary consonantal sounds, six are without corresponding separate signs,—*zh, sh, dh, th, wh, ng.* This brings up the deficiency to seventeen. Diphthongs, as we said, we propose to indicate by placing together the letters representing the vowel-sounds of which they are composed. We saw that the available signs in our present alphabet are twenty-two in number. Add to these the seventeen signs which are wanting, and we obtain a perfect alphabet of thirty-nine letters with which to represent the thirty-nine simple sounds in our language.

57. A phonetic system would be of immense advantage in saving the time which we spend during our early life in learning how to spell. To master an alphabet of thirty-nine letters would of course take longer than to master an alphabet of twenty-six letters. But the alphabet once learnt, mistakes in spelling would be almost as rare as mistakes are now in writing down numbers. Spelling-books and dictation would be almost unnecessary. This is what we should gain by adopting the system. The drawback to the introduction of the system would be this, that our printed books would be out of date. To the generation which had learnt the new system, our existing literature would be unintelligible until it was reprinted according to the reformed method. This disadvantage would not however be very serious. All the books which are worth reading by the ordinary man might be printed in the revised version at a small cost, and the student who used our present libraries of English works for purposes of research would soon overcome the difficulties of our present spelling well enough to read existing books.

But the system stands no chance of being adopted because of two obstacles in the way. (i) People who have learnt our present mode of spelling will never consent to begin reading over again with a new ABC at middle-age. And (ii) a uniform pronunciation must be adopted throughout the country before a phonetic system can be introduced. If a Lancashire man reverses the vowel sounds in *put* and *butter* and spells phonetically, the words *put* and *butter* would be written with their vowels reversed in the north and in the south of England. On the other hand, if these words are written in the same way throughout the country while the pronunciation varies in different parts, the spelling is no longer phonetic.

It is sometimes urged as an objection against a phonetic mode of spelling, that the etymology, or derivation, of many words would be obscured by its adoption; that the word *city*, for example, if spelt *siti*, would fail to suggest to our minds the Latin *civitas* and its train of ennobling associations. But this line of objection seems a little insincere and pedantic. To the student of English, reflexion and research would reveal the meaning of the word however it might be spelt, and as for the ordinary man, we may be quite sure that when he goes up to town in his omnibus he is thinking of the City in quite other connexions than its ennobling associations with the Latin *civitas*. It is urged again that a phonetic system would obscure words pronounced alike but written differently, such as *chord, cord*; *pear, pair, pare*; *hair, hare*, and so on. But this seems a somewhat childish objection. *Box* and *post* have various meanings, but the context shows us which is the right one, and if we can understand a man who uses the word *hare* in conversation, without his stopping to explain that he means an animal, no one but a person of painstaking stupidity would find any ambiguity in the word when he met with it in print.

58. As our alphabet is defective to the extent of seventeen out of the thirty-nine letters which it ought to contain, extra duty has to be performed by some of the twenty-two available letters.

Take, for example, our sixteen elementary vowel sounds. For want of separate signs to show whether the vowel in a word is to be pronounced long or short, we have recourse to various clumsy devices called *orthographical expedients*. The commonest expedient to show that a vowel is long is to add *e* mute at the end of the word. Accordingly we write *gate, mete, wife, stone*. To show that a vowel is short, we double the consonant which follows it. Accordingly we write *matter, better, bitter, copper, gutter*.

59. The deficiencies of the alphabet would inevitably make our spelling irregular and unscientific, but inconsistency runs riot in our orthography to an extent which is really impressive. We may illustrate this in two ways by showing

(1) how the same sound is represented by a variety of letters :

(2) how the same letter or combination of letters stands for a variety of sounds.

As examples of (1), let us take the sound given to the letter *a* in *fate*. Other ways of representing this sound readily suggest themselves:—*laid, rein, say, prey, gauge, gaol, break, eh.*

Other ways of representing the sound of *o* in *no*:—*coat, rote, soul, roe, yeoman, owe, though, sew, sow.*

The sound of *e* in *me*:—*beat, beet, mete, relief, deceit, key, quay, machine, people.*

The consonants afford fewer examples of these eccentricities, but they afford some.

The *f* sound in *fill* is expressed also in *philosophy, quaff, laugh.*

The *k* sound in *kit* appears in *cat, back, quay, ache.*

The *s* sound in *sin* is represented in *cinder, scent, schism.*

In illustration of (2), we will take examples of single letters, vowel and consonant, and of combinations of letters, the sounds of which are not uniform.

The letter *a* illustrates the variety of uses to which a single sign may be put. It represents five distinct vowel-sounds in *fat, fare, fate, father, fall,* and is used in many words where it is not pronounced at all; *e.g.* it affects the pronunciation of the preceding vowel in *boat, meat*: it has the sound of *o* in *what,* and of *e* in *many.*

As examples from the consonants, take *s,* which is sonant in *praise,* surd in *sing,* stands for *zh* in *measure,* for *sh* in *mansion,* and is silent in *isle* or *aisle.*

The letter *g* has one sound in *gum,* another in *gem*; followed by *h* its sound is sometimes that of *f,* as in *laugh,* and sometimes it is not sounded at all, as in *though.*

Some combinations of letters are very uncertain in their pronunciation: *ough* is a good instance of this. *Though, through, cough, rough, plough,* by no means exhaust the list of various sounds.

Of the English alphabet we may therefore say that it is (1) **Defective,** (2) **Redundant,** and (3) **Inconsistent.**

60. Why is English spelling so difficult?

1. Because the alphabet is **defective,** and its deficiencies are supplied by different devices in different words.

2. Because our spelling has been pretty well fixed for nearly three hundred years, since the translation of the Bible in James I.'s reign supplied a standard of orthography throughout the country, whilst the **pronunciation has changed** largely in the interval.

3. Because **our words have come to us from**

many sources, and we have kept the spelling which they had in the languages from which we took them but have given the words an English pronunciation.   Thus we spell *city* with a *c*, not with an *s*, because it comes from *civitas*; *philosophy* with a *ph* and not with an *f*, *ch*emistry with a *ch* and not with a *k*, because of their Greek origin ; *vic*tuals has a *c* because of the Latin *victus*, from *vivo*; dou*b*t has a *b* because of the Latin *dubito*: *syntax* from the Greek would be obscured in the guise of *sintaks*, and *phlegm* would be changed from its original beyond recognition if we wrote it *flem*.

61. Where did our English alphabet come from, and how did we get it ?

Our alphabet came from the Latin alphabet, the Latin from the Greek, and the Greek from the Phœnician. During the Roman occupation of Britain, the Britons picked up the Latin alphabet, and the English learnt it from the Britons.   Before their migration to this country the English had an alphabet which was in use among the Teutonic tribes, called *Runic*.   Inscriptions containing these *runes* still exist on stones and crosses in Norway and Sweden, in the north of England and in parts of Scotland. When the English settlers adopted the Roman alphabet they preserved two of their own runes, the letters called *wen* and *thorn*.   *Wen* or *w* was written þ; *thorn* or *th* and *dh* was written þ and afterwards ð.   The letters *w* and *th* took their place after the Norman Conquest.   The word *the* would in Old English characters be written þe. Hence has arisen the notion that in Old English it was written *yᵉ* or *ye* and so pronounced.   People who devise programmes for fancy fairs, in what they conceive to be the Early English style, have the idea that the frequent use of *yᵉ* for *the* and the addition of an *e* at the end of every word which ends in a consonant will convert 19th century English into 9th century English. But this is a mistake. Our forefathers said *the* as we say it, though they wrote it with a single sign for the *th*, and correctly so, for the sound is a simple one.

The letter **j** was originally used merely as a different form of **i**, an **i** with a tail to it. The sounds which we now represent by **i** and **j** were not distinguished by symbol till the 17th century. Rather earlier than this, a distinction was made in the use of the letters **u** and **v** so that they represented respectively vowel and consonant.

The word *alphabet* comes from the names of the first two letters of the Greek alphabet, *alpha, beta*.

62.   This seems to be a suitable point at which to give an answer to the question,—**When are Capital letters to be used ?**

1.   At the beginning of every sentence.

2.   At the beginning of every line in poetry.

3.   At the beginning of quoted passages: *e.g.* He said, " Let us go and see."

4.   For Proper names.

5.   For the various names of God.

6.   For titles of office and officials:—Secretaryship of the Treasury, Lord Chancellor: but capitals are often dispensed with in these cases.

7.   Sometimes at the beginning of nouns and adjectives, to call attention to their importance.

8.   For the pronoun *I* and for the interjection *O*.

Questions.

1.   What is meant by Orthography? Point out any orthographical irregularities in the spelling of *scent; island; proceed, precede; sovereign.*

[Through ignorance of the derivation (French *sentir*) the *c* was introduced into *scent*, and the *s* was inserted in *iland* owing to confusion with *isle* or *insula*. Both *proceed* and *precede* contain the Latin *cedo.* Why should this be differently represented in the two words? *Sovereign* has been spelt thus owing to a mistaken idea that it comes from *reign*. It should be *sovran*. *Therefore* should be *therefor.*]

2. Give examples of the different pronunciation of these letters:— *i, u, ie, ti, ch.*

3. In what other ways do we represent the sounds of *au* in *haul*, *o* in *fond*, *g* in *ginger*, *x* in *Xenophon*, *sc* in *science?*

4. Mention words in which the following letters are written but not sounded:— *p, b, gh, t, l.*

5. Give illustrations from the English language (1) of the softening of the final guttural, (2) of the substitution of *d* for *th*, (3) of the loss of letters, (4) of the insertion of the letters *b* and *d*.

6. Show that the orthography and the pronunciation of several English words are at variance. Can you account for the discrepancy?

[Refer to §§ 59 and 60. Dou*b*t, recei*p*t, hym*n*, *ch*ronicle, *h*our, *p*salm, vi*s*count, *k*now, would be suitable examples for annotation.]

7. Give examples in English spelling of—
(1) single letters representing double sounds:
(2) two or more letters representing an indivisible sound:
(3) different letters representing the same sound:
(4) the same letter representing different sounds:
(5) redundant and silent letters.

8. It is said that the introduction of a system of purely phonetic spelling would obliterate traces of the history of many of our words. Show the force of this remark in the case of the following:—*chronometer*, *phantom, vitiate, honour, rheumatism.*

9. Explain the presence of the italicised letters in the following words:—de*b*t, wet*t*er, pa*i*r, favo*u*r, num*b*er, r*h*yme, black*a*moor.

10. Describe some of the anomalies of our modern spelling, and mention words which are not spelt uniformly by standard writers.

[A few typical examples of uncertain orthography are subjoined: add to the list. *Judg(e)ment, recal(l)s, mov(e)able, benefit(t)ed, monied, dul(l)ness, civilize, favo(u)r, gallop(p)ed.*]

11. In what other ways are the following words spelt in current literature?—*programme, rhyme, inflexion, medieval.* Can you say anything for or against them?

[*Programme* was borrowed from the French, not compounded (like *telegram*) from the Greek. *Rhyme* is thus spelt from a wrongly-supposed connexion with *rhythm*. *Inflexion* is the correct form, as the supine-stem of the Latin *flecto* is *flex-*, not *flect-*.]

12. Mention some of the most important facts in the history of our Alphabet.

CHAPTER VII.

ETYMOLOGY.

63. A language is a **collection of articulate and significant sounds.** If we listen to a baby, we find that his utterances consist of such sounds as *ul-ul-ul, ga-ga, um-um,* sounds which are merely noises, like the barking of a dog or the crowing of a cock. Significance, or meaning, they may indeed have, and the observant mother or nurse may understand that one noise is made when the baby wants his bottle and that another expresses his happiness when he has got it. But to persons outside the family circle these cries convey no more meaning than the cries of the farm-yard. Articulate they certainly are not. When the baby says 'pa,' 'ma,' we remark with truth that he is beginning to talk quite nicely. Talk, speech, words,—these terms point to sounds which are significant and articulate, and such sounds in English form the subject-matter with which we have to deal in English grammar. In our daily lives we commonly use words in connexion with other words to form sentences, but we can consider them by themselves, though we do not use them by themselves. The part of grammar which treats of words **taken separately** is called **Etymology** : the part which treats of words as forming **portions of a sentence** is called **Syntax.** In dealing with Etymology we shall often find it useful to cross the confines of Syntax.

64. Etymology deals with the classification of words, their derivation, and inflexion.

There are **various ways of classifying words.** In the dictionary we arrange them in alphabetical order; in the spelling-book we arrange them according to their number of syllables. Now as language is employed by us for the expression of our thoughts, and our thoughts are usually expressed in sentences, for the purposes of grammar we shall group the words of the language in classes **according to their different functions in the sentences** which we form with them to express our meaning. By 'different functions' we mean the special work accomplished by different kinds of words. The function of a pump is to raise water; of a balance to weigh things; of a noun to serve as a name of things; of a verb to make assertions about things. Small differences of function may be neglected in the classification of words, (just as we classify a machine as a pump, whether it is a force-pump or a common-pump), but we cannot usefully reduce the number of classes of words in grammar below eight, and these eight different classes we call the Parts of Speech.

65. The Parts of Speech are the classes into which the words of a language fall, when they are arranged according to their separate functions in a sentence.

The following sentence contains eight words, and the part played by every one of the eight is different:

"Oh! and was he in good health yesterday?"

Oh is an interjection, a sound expressing sudden feeling. We could omit it from the sentence without disturbing the construction: as the derivation of the name implies, it is something 'thrown in.'

And is a conjunction: it joins on the words which follow it to the previous sentence.

Was is a verb.

He is a pronoun.

In is a preposition showing that the noun *health* stands in a certain relation to the rest of the sentence.

Good is an adjective limiting or restricting the meaning of the word *health.*

Health is a noun.

Yesterday is an adverb limiting the application of the verb as regards time.

66. In parsing a word, our first business is to refer it to its proper class among these parts of speech. The form of the word is seldom of help to us in English when we are thus engaged. It is often necessary to look to the context before we can decide in any particular case to what class the word belongs.

Thus in the sentence 'The *after* growth was considerable,' *after* is an adjective: in '*After* me, the deluge,' it is a preposition: in 'Jill came tumbling *after*,' it is an adverb: in 'He called *after* you left,' it has the force of a conjunction. So again the word *stone* has various functions in different sentences. In '*Stone* him to death,' it is a verb: in 'He threw a *stone*,' it is a noun: in 'This is a *stone* fence,' it is an adjective. Once more, the word *but* serves in many capacities. In 'Many are called, *but* few are chosen,' it is a conjunction: in '*But* few are chosen,' where *but* signifies 'only,' it is an adverb: in 'All *but* John were drowned,' where *but* signifies 'except,' it is a preposition: in 'There is no one *but* thinks you mad,' *but* does the work of a relative pronoun with a negative attached, 'There is no one *who* does *not* think you mad.'

67. Attempts have been made to reduce these eight parts of speech to a smaller number of groups. Thus words have been arranged in the following four divisions :

i. Names of THINGS .	1.	Nouns.
	2.	Personal Pronouns.
	3.	Adjectives.
ii. Expressing ATTRIBUTES	4.	Verbs.
	5.	Adverbs.
iii. Expressing RELATIONS	6.	Conjunctions, between sentences.
	7.	Prepositions, between things.
iv. Expressing SUDDEN FEELINGS,	8.	Interjections.

At our present stage there would be no advantage in discussing this or any similar scheme in detail. From the purely grammatical point of view, it is more important to notice that **some of the parts of speech** are **inflected** and **others are not.**

68. **Inflexion is a variation in the form of a word to mark a modification of its meaning.** Thus *-s* in *fathers* denotes that we are speaking of more than one *father*: it is a sign of the plural. So *-ed* in *walked* denotes that the action occurred formerly: it is a sign of the past tense. Again, *-er* in *taller* denotes the presence of a quality in a greater degree than is implied by *tall*: it is a sign of comparison. Again, *-ess* in *authoress* denotes that the person to whom the name is applied is a female: it is a sign of gender. All these **modifications of form,**—*s, ed, er, ess,*—are **inflexions.** Sometimes we have **inflexion without the addition of anything** to the word at all. *Man* makes its plural *men, goose* makes *geese, drink* makes its past tense *drank, fall* makes *fell,* by inflexion. There is **change of** form though nothing has been added. Now applying the possibility of inflexion as a principle of division to the parts of speech, we shall find that the two groups are composed thus :

Inflexional.		*Non-Inflexional.*	
1.	Nouns	5.	Prepositions
2.	Adjectives	6.	Conjunctions
3.	Pronouns	7.	Interjections.
4.	Verbs		

Of Adverbs, some are inflected to mark comparison and others are not. The same remark is true to a smaller extent of Adjectives, but our classification is in the main correct.

69. **The English language has but few inflexions.** A Roman could say *lapidi, lapide*: we have to use prepositions and say *to a stone, by a stone.* A Roman could say *amavisset, amarentur*: we must employ pronouns

and auxiliary verbs, and say *he would have loved, they would be loved.* In Old English there was a fair supply of inflexions, but these were in great measure destroyed by the fusion of Norman and Englishman. The Norman conqueror had to learn our vocabulary, but use our grammatical forms he would not. We pointed out in an earlier chapter that, though our English vocabulary contains twice as many Latin words as native words, we use four or five of the latter for one of the former in our everyday speech, since the words which necessarily occur in every sentence, such as pronouns, conjunctions, and auxiliary verbs, are exclusively of English origin. And we said that we were justified therefore in describing our language as an English and not as a Romance language. We now see that there is a further justification for so describing it in the fact that nearly all of the surviving inflexions, which constitute an important part of the grammar of our language, are of English origin.

A language like ours which has but few inflexions is sometimes called **analytic.** A language like Latin which has many inflexions is called **synthetic.** The distinction is an important one, but the terms **inflexional** and **non-inflexional** would express it equally well and convey the proper meaning to our minds at once.

70. **The sum-total of the inflexions which the words in a language undergo constitutes its Accidence.** Accidence is thus narrower in its meaning than Etymology. **Accidence,** (from Latin *accidere*, 'to happen'), comprises the **changes of form** which happen to words. **Etymology** deals with these **changes of form** and also with the **classification** and **derivation** of words. English grammar has but little accidence, because its inflexions are few, but there is much to be said on the subject of its etymology.

The sum-total of the inflexions marking number and case of a noun or pronoun is called its **Declension.**

The sum-total of the inflexions of a verb is called its **Conjugation.**

71. Before leaving the subject of inflexion, let us note the principal **consequences of the loss of our inflexions in English.**

(1) We **employ prepositions** in place of case-endings, and **auxiliaries** instead of inflexions in verbs.

(2) The **order of words** in a sentence admits of very little variety in modern English. *Brutus occidit Caesarem* could be arranged in six ways : *Brutus killed Caesar* can be arranged in only one. Why? Because to a Roman the form of the ending would show that *Brutus* was the subject and *Caesarem* the object, whether either word stood first, second, or third, in the sentence. Thus for purposes of emphasis a Roman was able to vary the order of his words. With us the place of subject and object is fixed.

(3) There is **nothing in the form of our words** to show whether they are **one part of speech** rather than **another.** Hence one part of speech is often used for another. We can turn a noun into an adjective and talk of an ' *iron* bar,' or into a verb and say ' *Iron* the clothes.' We can make adjectives into nouns and speak of our *equals*, or *betters*, or *inferiors.* We can manufacture adverbs out of other parts of speech and say ' *Crack* went the whip,' ' I am going *home*,' ' He came *safe*,' ' He is not a *bit* surprised.' We also find such expressions as ' *But* me no *buts*,' ' *Uncle* me no *uncle*,' signifying ' Don't say *but* to me,' ' Don't call me *uncle*.' The sense indeed is plain, but such forms would be impossible in a synthetic or inflexional language like Latin.

QUESTIONS.

1. What is the Part of Speech of each of the italicised words in the following sentences?—' *Count* the money.'—' Keep *count* as you go.'—' Foreign coins will not *count.*'—' *Count* is a foreign title.'—' It is slovenly not to *date* your letters.'—' Bring the statement up to *date.*'—' These distinctions belong to *race.*'—' They are *race* distinctions.'—' They are prepared to *race.*'—' The *tender* has left the ship.'—' Confinement made him *tender* for the winter.'—' Infatuation made him *tender* for the contract.'—' *Tender* memories linger round the *spot.*'—' The *spot* stroke is barred.'—' You will *spot* your dress.'—' Woe *worth* the hour.'—' An hour of his time is *worth* half-a-crown.'—' His time is of little *worth.*'—' Mark his *fell* design.'—' His design *fell* to the ground.' ' Tramp o'er moss and *fell.*'—' He tramped o'er moss and *fell.*'—' Strike a *light.*'—' He has a *light* heart.'—' The bonfires are *alight* here.'—' *Alight* here for the Aquarium.'—' Boots repaired *while* you wait.'—' I have waited a long *while.*'—' How can I *while* away the time?'—' Look at the *above* remarks.'—' Look at the remarks *above.*'—' Look at the remarks *above* the notice.'—' I am an *outside* passenger.'—' I prefer the *outside.*'—' I prefer to ride *outside.*'—' The train came *down* the incline.'—' It was the *down* train.'—' It came *down* at a great pace.'—' Clear the *deck*, get the *deck* cabin ready, and *deck* the walls with flags.'—' I walked *past.*'—' I walked *past* the gate.'—' Forget the *past.*'—' Forget all the *past* follies.'—' The *steam* tram has not got up *steam* enough to *steam* up the hill.'

2. What parts of speech may each of the following words be?—*round, close, equal.* Write one short sentence to illustrate each use of them.

3. What is an inflexional language? What parts of speech may be inflected in English? Illustrate your answer by examples.

4. Write down in a column all the parts of speech. Underline the two which you consider most important, and doubly underline the two which you consider least important, giving reasons in each case for your opinion.

5. Form a sentence containing at least six different parts of speech, and point out in it one example of each.

6. Write short sentences illustrating the use of each of the following words as different parts of speech:—*match, mangle, pile, punch, row.*

7. Write short sentences illustrating the different meanings of each of the following words:—*own, that, quick, judge.*

8. Write four short sentences, each of which contains the word *back.* In the first sentence, use the word *back* as a noun; in the second, as a verb; in the third, as an adverb; and in the fourth, as an adjective.

CHAPTER VIII.

Nouns.

72. A noun is the name of anything.

The word *noun* is derived from the Latin *nomen*, which means 'a name.' No sentence can be formed without a noun, or something equivalent to a noun, expressed or implied, and a verb, also expressed or implied. 'Birds fly,' 'Politicians wrangled,' are examples of the simplest form of sentence. Each contains a noun which indicates the thing about which the statement is made, and a verb by means of which we make the statement. The word *verb* is derived from the Latin *verbum*, 'a word,'—the word without which the sentence would collapse. But to discuss whether noun or verb is the more essential to a sentence seems as useless as it would be to inquire which of the two blades in a pair of scissors does more of the cutting. Sometimes, no doubt, it looks as if we could have a sentence without a noun or without a verb. When I say 'Go,' the sense is clear. But the noun, or rather its substitute the pronoun, is understood, and in giving an analysis of the sentence we should supply it and say that the subject is *You* and the predicate *go*. And in older English it was often so supplied, and people said 'Go thou.' Again, if I ask 'Who told you this?' and you answer 'Jones,' the verb is understood, and the full expression would be 'Jones told me this,' or 'Jones did.' Thus these forms of expression are only apparently exceptions to the statement that **every sentence contains noun and verb.** They are elliptical expressions; a word is omitted which is required to complete the grammatical structure of the sentence, but though omitted it is understood.

73. The definition of a noun suggests a few remarks.

1. Guard against the not uncommon blunder of confusing the noun and the thing. The noun is the name of the thing. The paper on which this book is printed is a thing, not a noun: the word *paper* is a noun.

2. Bear in mind that the word 'thing' is here used to denote all objects of thought, whether these objects of thought be things with life or without it, material or immaterial, real or imaginary. In the language of our definition, every object that we can think about, whether it have an existence or not, is a *thing*, and the *name* of such a thing is a *noun*. *Charles, negro, Rome, city, angel, ghost, dragon, point, zero, infinity, nothing,* are nouns, for they are names of objects of thought, *i.e.* of things about which we can think.

3. The objection may be raised,—Are not some of the pronouns names of things too? If so, why should we place them in a separate class? If Brown says 'I broke the window,' is not *I* the name of the thing about which the assertion is made, just as much as *Brown* or *the boy* is, when we say 'Brown broke the window,' or 'The boy broke the window'? And in this criticism there is some force. But these pronouns differ in so important a characteristic from the words which are commonly called nouns, that they deserve to rank as a separate part of speech, although, as their name implies, they are used instead of nouns. For when we say 'The boy broke the window,' the term *boy* brings up to our minds a certain uniform conception; we know what we mean by a 'boy.' But if Brown says '*I* broke the window,' and Brown's companion Smith says '*I* jogged his elbow,' and the master says '*I* shall make you pay for it between you,' *I* changes its meaning in the mouth of each speaker. When Brown and Smith are talking together, Brown calls himself *I* and Smith *you,* while Smith calls Brown *you* and himself *I.* But Brown and Smith are always *boys,* and the master is always a *master,* no matter who it is that uses the words.

4. This further criticism may be made on the definition, that adjectives are, at any rate sometimes, names of things; that *black* is the name of all black objects,—horses, ink, marble, etc.—*round* the name of all round objects,—the moon, a cricket-ball, a wheel, a watch-glass, etc., so that when I say 'The moon is round,' *round* is a name of the moon.

To this objection the answer may be given that in such cases the adjective qualifies a noun which is understood. When I say 'The moon is round,' I mean 'The moon is a round moon' or 'a round thing.' Moreover it is only when the adjective is used as a part of the predicate that this ellipsis of the noun is possible. As the subject of a sentence the adjective cannot stand alone. I cannot say 'Round rotates on its axis,' but must say 'A round object rotates on its axis.' In any case it is the noun which is the name of the thing: the adjective marks merely a quality of the thing.

74. Different classes of nouns.—Common and Proper.

Compare the words *river* and *Henry*. What important difference is there between them? Not this, as is sometimes said, that *river* can be applied to an indefinite number of objects and *Henry* to only one, for *Henry* can be applied to an indefinite number of objects also : eight Henrys sat on the throne of England. The difference lies in the fact that, when we use the word *river*, it has for us a **certain uniform sense.** The word suggests to our minds the conception of flowing water, banks, source, outfall, and so forth. If we found a piece of water in a park and were inclined at first sight to call it a river, but afterwards discovered that it contained neither inlet nor outlet and that we could walk all round it, we should say 'This is not a river ; this is a lake.' The word *river* has a meaning, and its meaning does not suit a stagnant sheet of water. But a person called 'Henry' might equally well have been called 'John,' for the name 'Henry' has no meaning. We say that the Thames is a 'river,' because it has certain qualities which the word *river* suggests to our minds. But 'Henry' is merely a **mark, arbitrarily set** upon a person to distinguish him from other people. Any other mark would have done just as well. And for one reason or another such marks or names are often changed. Thus, Sir Robert Walpole became Earl of Orford. During the greater part of his life he was known by the mark *Walpole :* for the last few years he was known by the mark *Orford. Walpole* and *Orford* are names without meaning, so if we once know to whom they are to be attached as marks, it makes no difference which name we choose for the purpose. If a football club changes its colours, the team is indicated by a new mark. When Walpole became Orford he was indicated by a new mark. But if we called a river an 'elephant' or a 'bedstead,' we should talk nonsense, because these words are not merely marks but contain meanings, and their meanings in no wise correspond with the qualities presented by a river. Once upon a time, no doubt, people's names had a meaning and were bestowed upon them because people possessed certain qualities. The original Redhead may have got his name from the colour of his hair, the original Tomson from the circumstance that he was the son of Tom. But Redhead's posterity perpetuate the name, though they may be black-haired boys or bald-headed men, and a Tomson of to-day may have taken the name to enable him to receive a legacy, though his name was formerly Robinson. This important distinction is expressed in grammar by the words Common and Proper. A common noun is applied to a number of things because they are alike, or possess some quality in common, whereas a proper noun, though it may be applied to several objects, is not applied to these objects because they are alike or possess any quality in common.

There are some nouns which contain a meaning but are applicable to only one thing. Such nouns we call **Singular.** In the mouth of a Christian or of a Jew, the name *God* is a Singular noun, for Christians and Jews recognise only one God. *Whiteness* is a Singular name, for although the quality which we call 'whiteness' is found in many objects, the quality is one and the same. Several nouns present the peculiarity of being sometimes Singular and sometimes Common. If I say 'Space is infinite,' 'Time flies,' the nouns are Singular: if I say 'This space is larger than that,' 'I have seen him several times,' they are Common.

~The reader will perceive on reflexion that Proper names are really a special class of Singular names. When we make use of a Proper name, we apply it to some particular individual only. But Singular nouns with a meaning are few and hard to find in any language, whilst meaningless Singular nouns are many, and they meet us at every turn. Hence it is that, in a classification of Nouns for the purposes of Grammar, we usually distinguish between Common and Proper nouns, and not between Common and Singular nouns, of which latter kind Proper nouns are a sub-class.

We may define these three classes of nouns thus :

A Common Noun is one which can be applied to an indefinite number of things in the same sense.

A Singular Noun is one which cannot be applied to more than one thing in the same sense.

A Proper Noun is a singular name assigned to an individual as a mere distinguishing mark.

75. We may notice that (1) **Proper Nouns** are sometimes **used as Common Nouns**, and (2) **Common nouns** are sometimes **used as Singular nouns**, that is, as names possessing a meaning, but applicable to **only one** individual.

(1) **Proper nouns become common in two** ways:

(*a*) When they indicate a **class resembling the individual** denoted by the proper name. 'A village Hampden' means a village patriot: of an ill-tempered woman we may say 'She is a regular Xanthippe :' we may speak of promising young cricketers as 'youthful Graces.' When parsing words thus employed, describe them as proper nouns used as if common. Note however that when we speak of 'the Browns' or 'the Smiths,' meaning all the people called 'Brown' or 'Smith,' without implying that they have any common quality besides the possession of the same name, these words, though plural, are still proper. But if we mean by 'the Marlboroughs and Wellingtons' not the people called Marlborough and Wellington, but great soldiers like Marlborough and Wellington, the proper nouns have passed into common nouns.

(*b*) **Proper nouns become common** also when **things are named after** the persons or places which bear these names. *Atlas, boycott, macadam, phaeton, brougham,* come from names of persons; *cypress, guinea, worsted, landau,* from names of places[1].

(2) On the other hand a **Common noun** may be used with such qualifying epithets as **to become Singular.** 'The last of the Tudors,' 'the present Lord Chancellor,' 'the highest mountain of Europe,' are compound names which can be used correctly of only one object. And even without the qualifying words we sometimes interpret the meaning of common nouns in a restricted sense. A child who says, 'Father told me to do this,' narrows the meaning of 'father' and uses the noun as if it were a singular noun. Similarly, by 'the Queen' we signify Alexandra, by 'the Prince,' the Prince of Wales. These words are like Proper nouns in this respect, that they can be applied to only one individual in the same sense: they are unlike them in this respect, that they have a meaning, while *Alexandra* and *George* have none.

76. Names of Materials. Nouns denoting certain materials, *e.g.* mud, zinc, gold, rice, arsenic, are never found

[1] The original form of the personal name or place name is some-times disguised, as in *camellia* (Kamel), *filbert* (St Philibert), *petrel* (St Peter), *volcano* (Vulcan), *cambric* (Cambrai), *currant* (Corinth), *sherry* (Xeres), *gypsy* (Egypt).

in the plural: others of precisely similar character occur in the plural, but always in some special sense. *Men* means more than one man, but *tins* does not mean more than a certain quantity of tin, nor *sugars* more than a certain quantity of sugar. *Tins* means cases made of tin; *coppers* means coins made of copper; *irons*, fetters made of iron; *slates*, tiles made of slate; *sugars, teas, calicoes, wines*, mean different sorts or varieties of these commodities, and in these plural forms the nouns are common nouns.

77. A Collective Noun is one which denotes a number of things regarded as forming a whole. Such nouns as *mob, regiment, flock, congregation*, are collective. Both plurals and collectives denote a number of things: *boys, cricketers, soldiers, sailors*, are plurals. But collectives denote a number of things **taken in the aggregate** and viewed as forming a **single group;** *school, team, army, crew,* are collectives. Collective nouns are mostly common: there are several *schools, teams, armies, crews.* Sometimes however we use them in a restricted sense as applicable to only one object. Thus, if I say 'The Queen opened Parliament,' the common collective noun *parliament* has its application narrowed down to one assembly, just as the common noun *queen* has its application narrowed down to one person.

Collective nouns are also called **Nouns of Multitude,** and in using them we sometimes think of the **individuals** included in the group rather than of the **group as a whole.** Hence these nouns are found with either singular or plural predicates. We may say 'Parliament was unanimous,' if the thought uppermost in our minds is the assembly as a whole, but we may say 'Parliament were all sixes and sevens,' if we are thinking of the assembly as divided into different parties.

78. Abstract and Concrete Nouns.

Consider the qualities of the boy sitting opposite. You say he is handsome or plain, clever or stupid, industrious or lazy, thin or fat, tall or short, and so on. To these qualities we give names and speak of the handsomeness or plainness, cleverness or stupidity, etc., of the boy. Not that the qualities can actually exist apart from the boy, or from some other subject which possesses them. We cannot separate the boy's stupidity or fatness and say 'There is the boy, and here I have got his stupidity.' But though **the qualities have no separate and independent existence,** we can **consider them separately.** We can **abstract** our thoughts from the boy's other qualities and can think and speak of his stupidity; and then, abstracting our attention from the other points of interest which he presents, we can think and speak of his fatness. The names of the qualities which we isolate from the rest by this process of abstraction are called **Abstract Nouns**: the names of the things which possess the qualities are called **Concrete Nouns.**

A Concrete Noun is the name of a thing regarded as possessing attributes.

An Abstract Noun is the name of an attribute or quality of a thing.

For many qualities or attributes no abstract names exist. If a boy is brown-haired or first man out of the eleven, he has the qualities of brown-hairedness and of first-man-out-of-the-elevenness; but when there is seldom occasion to speak of qualities, such qualities have not received names, especially if the names would be long and awkward. We can speak of *squareness* and *redness ;* not of *oblongness* and *vermilionness.*

79. **Many nouns are abstract in one sense and concrete in another.** When we say ' His industry

is remarkable,' the word *industry* is abstract; it denotes a quality or attribute. But when we say 'The cotton industry is carried on in the north,' *industry* is concrete. We can use it in this latter sense in the plural and speak of 'the cotton and iron industries.' Now an abstract noun while it remains abstract cannot be used in the plural. It seems, no doubt, as if it could be so used sometimes. Thus the Prayer-Book has the expression 'negligences and ignorances.' But these plurals signify acts or instances of negligence and ignorance, and the words have become concrete. If we say 'Beauty is a perishable gift,' *beauty* is an abstract noun; if we say 'The baby is a little beauty,' it is concrete. *Length* is abstract when we speak of 'the length of the course;' it is concrete when we say that 'Oxford won by two lengths.'

80. Modes of formation of Abstract Nouns.

(*a*) Most abstract nouns are formed from adjectives by adding *-ness*, as good-*ness*, white-*ness*; some are formed by adding *-th* or *t*, as tru-*th*, slo-*th*, from *true*, *slow* and heigh-*t* from *high*: these forms are of English origin. Abstract endings from a foreign source are seen in cruel-*ty*, honest-*y*, brav-*ery*, grand-*eur*, just-*ice*.

(*b*) Some are formed from verbs, as possess-*ion*, instruct-*ion*, enjoy-*ment*, err-*or*.

(*c*) Some from nouns, as priest-*hood*, bond-*age*, serf-*dom*, friend-*ship*, hat-*red*, slav-*ery*.

QUESTIONS.

1. Take these names and say of each whether it is Proper, Singular, Common, Collective, Abstract, Concrete:—*island, Somerset House, hope, a Nero, fleet, the last Chancellor of the Exchequer, truth, universe, chloroform, friendship, nobility.* Give the reason for your answer in each case.

2. State what nouns we get from the following names (*a*) of persons: —*Augustus Caesar, Captain Boycott, Epicurus, Dr Guillotin, James II.* (Lat. *Jacobus*), *Colonel Negus, Philip of Macedon, Simon Magus, Duns Scotus:* (*b*) of places:—*Bayonne, Calicut, Canterbury, Damascus, Milan, Spain.*

3. The following nouns are names of materials, but they can be used in the plural. When so used, what meanings do they bear?— *paper, tea, stone, wood, sand, salt.*

4. What is a noun? Is the paper on which you are writing a noun? Shew that the second part of your answer is consistent with your definition.

5. Give examples of *collective nouns* and of *names of materials.* When are collective nouns treated as singular, and when as plural? Do names of materials ever admit of a plural?

6. What Collective Nouns denote groups composed of the following individuals?—oxen, books, birds, bees, thieves, cut flowers, musicians, singers in a church, cricketers, hunting-dogs, legislators.

7. Define an Abstract Noun, and give the derivation of the term *abstract.* Form an Abstract Noun from (1) an Adjective, (2) a Verb, (3) a Common Noun.

8. Write sentences in which the following Nouns are used respectively as Concrete and Abstract :—*age, youth, fiction, poetry, painting, belief, scholarship, royalty.*

9. State whether the italicised Nouns are used as Abstract or as Concrete in the following sentences :—' He contributed liberally to many a *charity.*'—'*Charity* begins at home.'—' *Necessity* is the mother of *invention.*'—' Men's *necessities* have led to many *inventions.*'—' The *form* of this goblet makes it a great *curiosity.*'—' *Curiosity* is one of the *forms* of feminine *bravery.*'—' *Life* is a *time* of *trial.*'—' For some *time* before his *trial* he underwent great *hardship* in prison.'—' They suffered many *trials* and *hardships* in their *lives.*'—' Hasty *resolutions* seldom speed well.'—' The native hue of *resolution* is sicklied o'er with the pale cast of *thought.*'—' Fancy scatters *thoughts* that breathe and words that burn.'—' *Thought* is free.'—' Towards *government* by the wisest does bewildered Europe now struggle.'—' Before parliament met, the *government* had resigned.'—' The *nobility* in some countries form an exclusive *society.*'—' The test of a man's *nobility* is the small pleasure he has in others' *society.*'—' As *reason* is a rebel unto faith, so is *passion* unto reason.'—' There is no *reason* why you should fly into such a *passion.*'

10. Assign each of the nouns in italics in the following sentences to its proper class. Give reasons for your answers.

(a) The *Terror* sailed yesterday.

(b) The *nobility* opposed the Crown.

(c) At the *noise* of the *thunder* she lost *courage*.

11. Give instances of the conversion (a) of Abstract into Concrete Nouns, (b) of Proper into Common.

12. Substitute for the following phrases equivalent expressions :—
'Some *Cromwell* guiltless of his country's blood,'—'a *Paul* in faith,'—'a second *Hercules*,'—'a new *Timon*,'—'a fat *Adonis*,'—'a financial *Napoleon*,'—'a *Nimrod* of to-day,'—'a modern *Sappho*,'—'a *Daniel* come to judgment.'

13. Mention the Abstract Nouns connected with the following—

(a) Adjectives :—*high, weary, decent, cruel, just, true, gentle, plural, brave, honest, sublime, wise*;

(b) Verbs :—*enchant, forbear, abstain, steal, wed, gird, grow, know, depart*;

(c) Nouns :—*child, glutton, hate, horseman, hero.*

CHAPTER IX.

INFLEXION OF NOUNS.—I. GENDER.

81. Nouns are **inflected,** that is to say, they undergo **a change of form,** to indicate **Gender, Number,** and **Case.** In English however these distinctions are often made without any inflexion.

82. Sex is a **natural distinction** which we find existing in the sentient creatures around us; they are male or female. **Gender** is a **grammatical distinction** which we make in **words,** corresponding, in English, to the natural distinction in the sentient creatures. Words are masculine or feminine according as the objects to which they are applied are male or female. The names of the things around us which are without sex,—and such names form by far the largest portion of the nouns in our vocabulary,—are said to be of **neuter** gender, *i.e.* of neither masculine nor feminine gender. Some nouns are used to denote objects of either sex, such as *parent, sovereign, painter, attendant.* These nouns are said to be of **common** gender.

83. Comparing gender **in English** with gender as we see it **in Latin** or German, we note these **points of difference.**

i. In English, **gender corresponds with sex.**

Males are denoted by masculine nouns, females by feminine nouns, inanimate things by neuter nouns. In Latin or German, inanimate things are often denoted by masculine or feminine nouns. *Mons* the Latin for 'mountain' is masculine; *res*, 'a thing,' is feminine; *animal*, 'an animal,' is neuter. In German *Löffel*, 'a spoon,' is masculine; *Gabel*, 'a fork,' is feminine; *Messer*, 'a knife,' is neuter. French has no neuter; consequently all its nouns are of the masculine or of the feminine gender. Our method in Modern English is simpler and more rational.

To a very limited extent the correspondence of gender with sex in English is interfered with (1) by Personification, a figure of speech under which we refer to inanimate objects as if they were endowed with life and sex. Things associated with the idea of strength or destructiveness are treated as males, and their names are masculine: *e.g. death, time, fear, war*. Things associated with the idea of grace, or of fertility, are personified as females, and their names are feminine : *e.g. moon, mercy, nature, earth*. But very often we do not personify these objects at all: we use *he* or *she* to refer to them when we become melodramatic or rhetorical, but in our ordinary moments we employ the neuter pronoun *it*. Nor could it be considered a breach of grammatical propriety, if we spoke of a *ship* as *it*.

Again (2) we often disregard the sex when we are speaking of children and the lower animals, and use the pronoun *it*. So the distinction of masculine and feminine is of very narrow application in English.

2. Another point of contrast between English and Latin or German is this. These languages possess inflexions marking gender in the adjectives : our adjectives have no inflexions of gender, number, or case. We say *good man, good woman, good thing.* Hence for a foreigner learning English there are only two points requiring attention in reference to gender; one, to use the feminine form of a noun, where one exists, to denote a female ; the other, to use *he, she, it, his, her, its,* correctly, according as the reference of these pronouns or adjectives is to a male, a female, or an inanimate object.

84. Gender is the form of a noun or pronoun

corresponding in English to the sex of the thing named.

We have in English **three ways** of making a distinction in language corresponding to the difference of sex in the objects themselves :

1. By Inflexion.
2. By Composition.
3. By using an entirely different word.

85. (1) **Gender marked by Inflexion.** The suffixes, *i.e.* the terminations, or endings, of words indicating gender may be classified thus :

Of English origin $\begin{cases} \text{-ster, in } spinster \\ \text{-en, in } vixen \end{cases}$

Of Foreign origin $\begin{cases} \text{-ess, Norman French, } countess \\ \text{·trix, Latin, } testatrix \\ \text{-ine, Greek, } heroine; \text{ German, } land\text{-}gravine \\ \text{-a, Italian or Spanish, } signora, infanta \end{cases}$

86. Remarks on these forms.

The native English suffixes *-ster* and *-en* survive with their feminine force only in the words *spinster* and *vixen*. *Spinster* properly signifies a female *spinner*, but now means 'an unmarried woman.' In proper names, such as *Webster* and *Brewster* (feminines respectively of *weaver* and *brewer*) the form still exists, as it does in the words *tapster*, *maltster*, but the signification of the suffix has disappeared. In *trickster*, *youngster*, *gamester*, it is employed with an idea of depreciation or contempt. So completely has the original force of the ending been lost that to the feminine forms *songster* and *seamster* we have added the inflexion *-ess*, making *songstress* and *seamstress*, words which are open to the twofold objection that they are (*a*) double-feminines, (*b*) hybrids, *i.e.* they contain elements borrowed from different languages, the original words being of English origin and the suffix *-ess* coming from the French.

In *vixen* two things are to be noticed : (*a*) the appearance of *fox* in the form *vox* : to this day a Somersetshire labourer uses *v* in place of *f* in many words ; the Authorised Translation of the Bible preserves for us the word *wine-fat*, which has now been ousted by the form *wine-vat*, belonging to the Southern dialect of English: (*b*) the modification of the root vowel from *o* to *i*: this is due to Umlaut. See p. 50.

Foreign endings.—The use of the suffix *-ess*, borrowed from the French *esse*, is the only method of formation which is employed when we make a new feminine word at the present day: so, *authoress*, *doctress*. Occupations once reserved to men are now thrown open to women. If we wish to mark the female sex of the persons following these occupations, we must either use compounds and say *lady-doctor*, *lady-lawyer*, or manufacture inflected forms and say *doctress*, *lawyeress*.

This French suffix is freely added to nouns of English extraction, without any regard being paid to the fact that the resulting forms are hybrids: *e.g. goddess, shepherdess.*

Frequently, when this ending is attached to a word, there is an omission of a vowel or of a syllable: *e.g. actress, empress, governess, negress, sorceress. Abbess = abbotess. Duchess* comes from the French *duchesse.* The feminine of *marquis* or *marquess* is *marchioness.* The root of this word occurs in *marches*, meaning 'boundaries' or 'confines': 'Lord of the *Marches*.' In *mistress* we have the feminine of *master* with the vowel weakened as in the pronunciation of *Mr.* From *mistress* we get the abbreviated form *Miss.*

The remaining suffixes do not exemplify *English* modes of formation of feminine nouns at all. The words which contain them are borrowed directly from foreign languages and therefore illustrate no process of English grammar.

87. (2) **Gender marked by composition.** When we make a new word by **joining together two or more existing words**, we call the process **composition** and the resulting word a **compound.** Thus *he-goat, cock-sparrow, maid-servant* are **compounds**: each part of the words has a meaning by itself. Compare with these the word *authoress*, formed from *author* by adding *-ess.* Now *-ess* has a force only when added to another word; by itself it is without any meaning; it is a mere suffix, not a word. We call such a word as *authoress* a **derivative.**

The distinction marked by these two processes of Inflexion and Composition may be said to come under our definition of gender as 'the *form* of a word which corresponds to a difference of sex.' *Authoress* and *he-goat* are modifications of *author* and *goat*, marking a change in their meaning. The indication of gender by Inflexion is a genuine gram-matical process, but we can bring the compound forms also within the

6—2

four corners of the definition. The remaining method is not a grammatical process: in such pairs of words as *brother, sister; boy, girl; bull, cow*, the difference of gender is marked, not by a modification in the *form* of one of the words, but by the use of words wholly unconnected with each other.

88. (3) **Gender marked by the Use of Different Words.** As examples of these correlatives, or pairs of words not grammatically connected, take the following in addition to those given above:—*boar, sow; buck, doe; bullock* or *steer, heifer; colt, filly; drake, duck; earl, countess; drone, queen-bee; gaffer, gammer; gander, goose; hart, roe* or *hind; monk, nun; ram, ewe; sire, dam; wizard, witch; sloven, slut; bachelor, maid* or *spinster.*

These words deserve notice:

Drake was once *end-rake*; the *end* was the significant part, meaning *duck*, as *Ente* does in German to-day, and the *rake* was a mere suffix, meaning 'lord' or 'male.' Thus two-thirds of the important part, the root, have been lost, and one-third, a single letter, has been kept, with the whole of the masculine ending. It is as if the word *actress* were decapitated and reduced to *tress.*

Lord is *loaf-ward*, 'bread-guardian': *lady* contains the same root *loaf*, and possibly meant originally 'loaf-kneader.'

Gaffer is a corruption of 'grandfather,' *gammer* of 'grandmother.'

Sir = sire = senior; madam = mea domina, 'my lady.'

Wizard comes from Old Eng. *wīs*, 'wise,' with suffix *-ard* added, not from the English *witch*, though both words have originally the same root.

Woman = wife + man, not 'wife *of* man,' but 'wife-person.'

89. It is evident that in almost all cases **the feminine is formed from the masculine.** In the following words this order is reversed:

Bridegroom, the masculine of *bride*, was originally *bryd-guma*, or 'bride's-man,' in German *bräutigam. Guma* meant 'a man' in Old English.

Gander comes from the same root as *goose*, the German for which is *gans*. The *d* has crept in between the *n* and the last syllable, as in *tender* and *gender* (Latin *tener, gen-er-is*).

Widower has been formed from *widow.*

QUESTIONS.

1. Give the feminine form or word corresponding to *mayor, bull-calf, murderer, milkman, ogre, peacock, marquis, testator, czar, sultan, fox, earl.*

2. Give the masculine form or word corresponding to *roe, hind, nun, countess, landlady, doe-rabbit, abbess, traitress, margravine, spinster, bride, lass.*

3. Write the feminine words corresponding to *hero, giant, sorcerer, ram, stag,* and the masculine words corresponding to *duck, heifer, goose, empress, executrix.*

4. Give two examples under each of the following heads:—

(1) Nouns of common gender:

(2) Nouns in which the termination *-ster* is without a feminine force:

(3) Nouns in which the masculine has been formed from the feminine:

(4) Feminine Nouns without corresponding masculines.

[Only a few examples of (4) are to be found; *e.g. brunette, dowager, milliner, laundress, shrew, virago.*]

5. If we personify the objects indicated by the following names, which of them should we speak of as *she?—Earth, Sun, Moon, Night, Death, Love, Nature, Winter, War, Justice, Time, Liberty.*

CHAPTER X.

90. Number is an inflexion which shows whether we are speaking of one thing or of more than one.

When we speak of one thing, the form of the noun is singular ; when of more than one thing, the form of the noun is plural. In Greek there was a dual number with separate inflexions, used when two things were spoken of, and English once had a dual number in the personal pronouns. But the absence of a dual from modern English is not a matter for regret. It is enough to distinguish between one and more than one ; to distinguish between one, two, and more than two, is a needless refinement.

91. The ways of forming plurals in English nouns are shown in the following classified scheme, which should be learnt by heart :—

Table of Plural Forms.

I. **Add -s** to the singular.

II. **Add -es** to the singular of—

1. Nouns ending in a sibilant, viz., *s, z, sh, x, ch.*
2. Nouns ending in *f* or *fe,* if of English origin and preceded by *l* or by a long vowel ; change *f* into *v.*
3. Nouns ending in *y* preceded by a consonant ; change *y* into *i.*
4. Some nouns ending in *o.*

III.   **Archaic** or **Old English** forms:

1.   Add *-en, ox-en.*
2.   Add *-er, child-(e)r-en.*
3.   Change the vowel: *men, geese.*

IV.   **Foreign** forms:

1.   Ancient; *seraphim, phenomena, appendices.*
2.   Modern; *banditti, mesdames.*

92.   Remarks on the Table of Plural Forms.

I.   The ordinary mode of forming a plural in modern English is to add *-s* in writing: thus a new word like *telephone* or *cablegram* takes *s.* If however a word is borrowed directly from a foreign language, it may retain the form of the plural which it had in that foreign language. Such a word is then said to be 'imperfectly naturalized'; it has not yet become an English subject.

Observe however that though we add *s* in writing, we often add *z* in pronunciation.   We have seen that if a surd *s* is added to a word ending in a sonant, either the inflexion *s* or the last letter of the noun must be altered.   Both sounds must be sonant or both must be surd; otherwise it is difficult to pronounce them in the same syllable. Thus we write *slabs, pods, hogs,* but we pronounce these words *slabz, podz, hogz.*   To pronounce them *slaps, pots, hocks,* preserving the true sound of the *s,* would be to obscure the nouns themselves.

II.   This inflexion in *s* is a survival of the older form of the plural in *-es.*

1.   The inflexion *es* as a separate syllable is necessarily retained to make the plurals of nouns ending in a sibilant sound.   For if we add *s* to words with *s, z, sh, x,* or *ch,* for their last letter, such as *gas, topaz, bush, box, church,* the *s* thus added cannot be pronounced.   As we have seen, *x* is an abbreviation of *ks,* so words ending in *x* really end in *s.*   The *ch* of which we speak here is the *ch* of *arch, beech,* and is really a compound of *t+sh,* so the sibilants enumerated above are reducible to three, viz., *s, z, sh.*   The hard *ch* of *monarch* and the *ch* of the Scotch *loch* take *s.*

2.   For the formation of plurals of nouns ending in an *f* sound, it is impossible to state concisely a rule which shall cover all instances. The rule, as we have stated it, is rather complicated, yet some words evade it.   The following nouns illustrate the rule: *leaf, loaf, calf, wife, wolf, self,* for these words are of English origin and the vowel is long, or, if short, the *f* is preceded by *l.*   On the other hand, the long vowel sound *oo* in *roof, hoof,* is not followed by *-ves*: these words take *s.* *Staff,* though of English origin and with long vowel, has for its plural

both *staves* and *staffs*. *Strife, safe, brief, chief, proof,* take *s* conformably with the rule, as they are not of English origin, but come from the French. But *beef* is exceptional in making *beeves*, as it is a French word. *Wharf, dwarf, scarf, turf,* are found with plurals in both forms, *fs* and *ves*.

3. There is hardly anything in the nature of an exception to the rule respecting nouns ending in *y*. A word like *soliloquy*, which makes its plural in *ies*, looks as if it were an exception, but it really follows the rule, for the combination *qu* has the force of *kw*, which is a consonantal sound. Perhaps the only established exception is *flys*, meaning 'carriages,' and inn-keepers can scarcely be blamed for refraining from advertising '*Flies* on hire.' Some words in *ey* are occasionally found with their plural in *ies*, *e.g. monies*, but it is better to spell them according to the rule.

4. With regard to nouns in *o*, it is difficult to discover any principle which determines whether their plurals are in *s* or in *es*. Many of our words in *o* are of Italian origin, and these take *s*, as do all nouns in *io*. The nouns in *o* which take *es* are usually of earlier introduction. *Cargo, echo, hero, potato, negro,* take *es*: *canto, solo, alto, piano, folio, oratorio,* take *s*.

Observation and practice are required to enable us to form the plurals of nouns in *f* or in *o* correctly. Rules are of little or no use for the purpose. Still it is our business in dealing with grammar to search out the principles, if such there are, on which the rules are based, although the rules when we get them may be insufficient guides.

III. Old English forms, other than *es* and *s*, which survive in modern English are few.

1. *Oxen* is the only modern English word which presents us with the form *en* simply. *Chicken* is not a plural form, though it is used as such in country districts. *Kine* is a double plural: *cow* in Old English modified its vowel to form the plural and became *cy*, as *mouse* becomes *mice*, and the plural inflexion *en* was also added. *Swine* however is not the plural of *sow*. In Old English several neuter nouns of one syllable, such as *swine, sheep, deer, folk,* underwent no change of their singular form when they were used in the plural number.

2. *Child-er-en* is a double plural, the *er* being one sign of the plural and the *en* another. No other word preserves for us the inflexion *er* with a plural force. *Brethren* is a double plural, *brother* having already modified its vowel to mark the plural, before *en* was added. But the -*r*- in *brethren*, unlike the *r* in *children*, belongs to the original word, and is not an inflexion.

3. There are only six nouns, in addition to the double forms mentioned above, which change their vowel to mark the plural: *man, foot, tooth, goose, mouse, louse.*

IV. To those who know Latin and Greek, foreign plural forms seldom present any difficulty. People who have learnt no Latin sometimes make the plurals of neuter nouns wrong and talk of *animalculæ* or *effluviæ* instead of saying *animalcula* and *effluvia*. Most of these nouns from dead languages can now be used with English plural forms: we can say *formulas, memorandums, dogmas,* as well as *formulæ, memoranda, dogmata. Cherubim* and *seraphim* are Hebrew plurals, but it is only in the language of religion that we use these forms. We speak of babies as 'plump little cherubs,' not 'plump little cherubim,' and say of a chorus of girls that they sing 'like seraphs,' not 'like seraphim.' The forms *cherubims, seraphims,* are double-plurals.

93. The following paragraphs contain illustrations of various kinds of **anomaly** in the **number of nouns.** *Anomaly* means 'unevenness,' or irregularity.'

(1) Some nouns are used in the Plural **without change of form.**

The following are examples: *deer, sheep, swine, score, yoke* ('five *yoke* of oxen'), the names of several sorts of *fish,—salmon, trout, cod*: also *grouse, brace, hundredweight, gross.*

(2) A few nouns **appear to be Plural but are really Singular.**

In the following words, the *s* is not a sign of the plural but is a part of the original word.

Alms: in O. E. *ælmesse,* borrowed through the Latin from the Greek root which we preserve in the word '*el*eemosynary.'

Eaves: in O. E. *efese.*

Riches : we took our noun from the French *richesse,* though we had the adjective *rich* in English.

Owing to a mistaken notion respecting the *s* in these words, they are treated as plurals : 'If riches increase, set not your heart upon *them.*'

(3) Some nouns **Plural in form are sometimes treated as Singulars.**

News always takes a singular verb and a singular demonstrative adjective : 'This news is not true,' not 'These news are not true.' Yet *news* is a translation of the Medieval Latin *nova,* and means literally 'new things.' *Small-pox* is a plural in disguise, for *pox* is really *pocks* : we have the singular in *chicken-pock.* Yet we never use a plural verb with *small-pox.*

Tidings, means, amends, pains, odds, wages, are treated sometimes as singular, sometimes as plural. To decide whether we are acting more in accordance with usage if we regard them as singular or as plural, we should place a verb after them and also observe whether they are more appropriately qualified by *this* or *these*, *much* or *many*. Does it sound more natural to say 'This odds is too great,' or 'These odds are too great'? to say 'Much pains has been taken,' or 'Many pains have been taken'? The usage of different people may vary.

Mathematics, physics, statics, and several similar words are plural forms taken from Greek adjectives. A century ago they were followed by a verb in the plural, and *politics* continues to take a verb in the plural. But, with the exception of the word *politics,* these nouns are now used as singular words.

(4) Some nouns change their meaning in the Plural.

Domino means 'a mask,' *dominoes* 'a game': *vapour* means 'steam,' *vapours* 'ill-humour': *compass* 'a mariner's compass,' *compasses* 'instruments for measuring': *vesper* 'evening,' *vespers* 'evening service': *good* means 'benefit,' *goods* means 'chattels.'

(5) A few nouns have two forms of the Plural with different meanings, the ordinary form being plural and the anomalous form having a collective force.

Pennies means separate coins, *pence* is collective: 'Can you give me six pennies for this sixpence?' *Brother* has the collective plural *brethren,* meaning members of the same community. *Die,* 'a stamp,' makes a plural *dies,* 'stamps,' and a collective *dice,* 'cubes' used in gambling. *Cloth* makes *cloths,* signifying different kinds or different pieces of cloth, and also *clothes,* the collection of one's garments. *Fish* has for its plural *fishes*: 'The multitude were fed with a few *fishes*'; but for its collective *fish*: 'He brought home a large basket of fish.' The word *pea* has lost the *s* in the singular by mistake: in the French *pois* it is still visible. But in its reduced form it has a plural *peas,* 'This pod contains six peas,' and a collective *pease,* as in 'pease pudding.'

Index and *genius* have different plural forms, neither of which is however collective. *Indexes* means 'more than one table of contents'; *geniuses* 'more than one person of genius.' But *indices* means certain 'algebraical signs,' and *genii* 'fabulous spirits.'

(6) Some nouns have no Plural.

This is because their meaning excludes the idea of plurality. We saw that abstract nouns, while they remain abstract, cannot be used in the plural. Many of these nouns do occur in the plural, but they have then ceased to be abstract and have become concrete general names. Observation alone will show us which nouns are used in this double way and which are not. *Hope, hardship, joy, colour*, are abstract nouns which we use as concretes when we speak of *hopes, hardships, joys, colours*. On the other hand, *manhood, indolence, goodness, courage,* are always abstract and singular.

We noticed also that though the names of many substances or materials are used in the plural number, signifying different kinds or different portions of the material, there are some names of this description which custom forbids us to use in this way. *Granite, gold, potash, bread, hemp,* are never plural. The names of some diseases also are always singular, *e.g. gout, consumption, rheumatism.*

(7) Some nouns have **no Singular.**

These nouns denote things composed of separate parts, and the complex character of the object makes the plural form appropriate. *E.g. scissors, tweezers, trousers, entrails.*

(8) **Plural of Compound nouns.**

i. When the combination of parts is so complete that we regard the compound as a single word, the sign of the plural is added at the end of the compound, although the last part of the word may be an adjective. Thus we say *spoonfuls* when the words form a compound, but *spoons full* when they are taken separately.

ii. But when the fact of composition is brought prominently before us by hyphens, as in *brother-in-law, man-of-war, maid-of-honour, groom-of-the-chambers,* the principal noun and not the qualifying adjunct usually takes the inflexion. Our practice however in this matter is by no means uniform. In spite of the hyphen in *attorney-general,* we speak of two *attorney-generals,* not *attorneys-general,* though these officials are not *generals* but *attorneys.* Again, *lady superintendent* becomes *lady superintendents,* not *ladies superintendent,* though the words are unconnected even by a hyphen. Notice that the *'s* of the possessive case is added at the end of the compound word. Thus we should say 'I have three *brothers-in-law,* and I am staying at my eldest *brother-in-law's* house.'

iii. In a very few instances, both parts of the compound take the sign of the plural: *men-servants, lords-justices, knights-templars.* We may regard this as apposition.

iv. In a few instances, in which the noun comes before the adjective, only the noun takes the sign of the plural: *courts-martial, knights-errant.*

v. Nouns compounded with *man* form their plural in *men,* with the exception of *Norman.* Notice however that several proper nouns with this ending are not compounds of *man* at all, and their plurals are therefore formed in *s. German* probably comes from a Keltic word which signifies 'one who shouts.' *Brahman, Ottoman, Turcoman, Mussulman,* are unconnected with *man.*

(9) How shall we form the **Plural** of (*a*) **Miss Brown**, and of (*b*) **Mr Smith** ?

(*a*) We may say (1) The *Miss Browns*, or (2) The *Misses Brown*, or conceivably, though as a fact we never do say so, (3) The *Misses Browns*. The usual form is the first, ' The *Miss Browns*,' in which we must regard *Miss-Brown* as a complete compound, like *spoonful*, which takes the sign of the plural at the end. The second form, ' The *Misses Brown*,' corresponds in its type to *courts-martial*, *Miss* being regarded as the noun, and *Brown* dwindling away to an adjective in its force. In the third form, ' The *Misses Browns*,' we have a mode of expression analogous to *lords-justices*, the two nouns being in apposition and each of them taking the inflexion.

(*b*) Similarly we may say in practice either ' The Mr Smiths,' or ' The Messrs (Messieurs) Smith.' The grammatical justification of these alternative forms the reader can supply for himself.

QUESTIONS.

1. Write the plurals of *German*, *Dutchman*, *Norman*, *story*, *storey*, *octavo*, *roof*, *reef*, *cuckoo*, *buffalo*, *formula*, *radius*, *crocus*, *datum*, *axis*, *appendix*, *genus*, *series*, *virtuoso*, *criterion*, *madam*, *dilettante*.

2. Write the plurals of *jay*, *journey*, *difficulty*, *colloquy*, *chief*, *staff*, *quarto*, *die*, *cloth*, *half*, *son-in-law*, *Miss Williams*.

3. Write the plurals of *butterfly*, *shelf*, *wharf*, *ox*, *man-of-war*, *oasis*, *index*, *simile*, *automaton*, *stratum*, *focus*, *caucus*, *terminus*, *cargo*, *portmanteau*.

4. Show how the addition of the plural sign -*s* entirely alters the meaning of some English nouns.

5. Greek adjectives supply us with the forms *logic*, *dynamic*, *optic*, *metaphysic*, *rhetoric*, *physic*, *politic*. To which of these is an *s* added to make the name of a science ?

6. Write the plurals of *strife*, *topaz*, *solo*, *echo*, *Mary*, *fife*, *bureau*, *elk*, *species*, *ellipsis*, *rhinoceros*, *hippopotamus*.
Mention some nouns about whose plural forms there is variety of usage, and some which have been taken for plurals though really singulars.

7. The following nouns have two meanings in the plural but only one in the singular. Give their plural meanings:—*custom*, *spectacle*, *manner*, *effect*.

8. The following nouns vary in meaning according as they are singular or plural. What meaning has each of them in the plural? *salt*, *force*, *iron*, *content*, *draught*, *beef*.

9. With each of the following nouns should a verb be used in the singular or the plural number?—*alms, banns, optics, poultry, scissors, salmon, sheep, sixpence, thanks.*

Give a reason for your answer when you can.

10. Mention three English nouns which have two plural forms, the one with a collective, the other with a distributive force.

11. Are the verbs right in these sentences?

The innings *was* finished at six o'clock—A gallows *has* been erected inside the prison—The tidings *are* false—The barracks *has* been burnt down—The odds *is* 7 to 2—The alms *is* distributed on Sunday—A summons *has* been issued.

12. Are the following words strictly of the singular or of the plural number?—*eaves, tidings, alms, news, riches, means.*

Mention some nouns which have only a singular form, and some which have only a plural form.

13. In what number would you put the verb which is to agree with *news, ethics, summons, the odds, gentry, fish, firearms, tongs*?

14. Give examples of nouns which have (1) a plural inflexion without a plural sense, (2) a plural sense without a plural inflexion.

15. State and illustrate the rules for the formation of the plural of compound nouns.

16. Form the plural of *pailful, forget-me-not, spendthrift, lord-lieutenant, runaway, poet-laureate, hanger-on, maid-in-waiting, will-o'-the-wisp, four-in-hand, valet-de-chambre, envoy extraordinary, minister plenipotentiary.*

17. Write the plurals of the following compound nouns:—*man-servant, maid-servant, man-of-all-work, passer-by, looker-on, onlooker, castaway, prince-consort, lord justice, camel-driver.*

18. Is there anything wrong in speaking of 'a curious phenomena,' 'two octopi,' or in saying 'A rich strata of gold has been struck'?

CHAPTER XI.

INFLEXION OF NOUNS.—III. CASE.

94. IF we examine the following sentences, we shall see that they contain various assertions about a thing called a *town*, which stands in different relations to other things called *enemies, walls,* or *circumstances.* ' *The town* admitted *the enemy.*' ' *The enemy* took *the town.*' 'The walls *of the town* were destroyed.' 'This circumstance was beneficial *to the town.*' 'The enemy were driven away *from the town.*' Thus, in the first sentence we say that the town did something to the enemy,—not, of course, the word *town* to the word *enemy*; what occurred was done by a thing to a thing, not by a word to a word. In the second, we say that the town occupied a different relation towards the enemy, and the enemy did something to the town. Now, when we employ language to record these events,—when we make assertions about these things,—we use **nouns** to name the **things** and **verbs** to make our **statements**, and we may then say that just as the **things stand in different relations to other things and to acts**, so our **nouns stand in different relations to other nouns and to verbs.** There is an indefinite number of these relations, expressed in English for the most part by prepositions. We can say *in the town, through the town, across, down, up, over, under, round the town,* and so on, marking in every instance some fresh relation.

Next let us write these sentences in Latin and notice the different method by which that language represents these various relations. *Urbs admisit hostes. Hostes ceperunt urbem. Moenia urbis diruta sunt. Haec res urbi utilis erat. Hostes urbe sunt expulsi.* Here we find the relations expressed by **inflexions**, whereas in English they were expressed by **prepositions**, or by the **position** of the nouns in the sentence. When we said that the town did something to the enemy, we put the word *town* before the verb and the word *enemy* after it, and we reversed their places when we said that the enemy did something to the town. But a Roman was not tied down as we are to a fixed order of subject and object in his sentence : *urbs* would show itself as subject and *urbem* as object, whatever place they might occupy. Again, *urbis, urbi, urbe,* inflected forms of *urbs,* express the relations of *urbs* to the other words in the sentence, whilst the prepositions *of, to, from,* express the same relations of *town.*

If the student has obtained some notion of the meaning of the word **relation** (which is one of the vaguest words in the language), he will find but little difficulty in what remains to be said on the subject of case.

95. Case is the form of a noun, or pronoun, which shows its relation to other words in the sentence.

As we have said above, the relations in which a noun can stand are very many, but we do not call the expression of these relations by means of prepositions **cases** : if we did, we should have as many cases as we have prepositions. It is only when the relation is marked by the **form** of the noun that we can properly speak of case. *Urbis, urbem, urbe,* are cases in Latin : *town, town's,* are cases in English : but *of a town, to a town, from a town,* are no more cases than *ad urbem, ex urbe, contra urbem,* are cases.

96. How many cases have we then in English **nouns** and **pronouns?**

In answer to this question, let us write out the declension of *town* and *he*.

	Sing.	*Plur.*		*Sing.*	*Plur.*
Nom.	town	towns		he	they
Poss.	town's	towns'		his	their
Obj.	town	towns		him	them

It is clear that the pronoun *he* is better off than the noun in its supply of case-inflexions. *He, his, him,* are three genuine cases, just as much as *urbs, urbis, urbem,* are genuine cases. But it is otherwise with the noun. *Town,* nominative, is indistinguishable in form from *town,* objective. The **form** of the word *town* does not show its relation to the rest of the sentence : the **position** of the word, or its **context,** shows its relation. We must not however interpret our definition too rigorously. If we found ourselves without the means of drawing the fundamental distinction between subject and object, because of the absence of an inflexion, parsing and analysis would be reduced to absurdity. The fact is, the definition suits an inflexional language like Latin much better than it suits a non-inflexional language like English. Even in Latin there are many nouns in which the strict application of the definition would land us in confusion. Neuter nouns of the Fourth Declension, like *cornu,* have an inflexion only in the genitive of the singular number, *cornus*: all the other singular forms are the same as the nominative. Yet we speak of the accusative, dative, and ablative cases of *cornu,* and in like manner **we speak of the nominative and objective cases of English nouns,** though there is but **one form** to express **two relations.**

97. The **Nominative** case is the form of a noun when it stands as **subject** of a verb.

' *The town* admitted the enemy : ' ' *The town* was taken.'

In each of these sentences the subject is *town,* though in
the first sentence *town* represents the doer of the action,
in the second, it stands for the thing to which the action is
done.

When the noun represents a thing spoken *to,* we may
call its case the **Vocative,** or the **Nominative of
Address.** 'Waiter!' 'Come here, John!' 'O death! O
grave!' are examples.

The **Objective** case is the form of a noun when it
stands as **object** of a verb, or **follows a preposition.**
'The enemy took *the town :*' 'The enemy are in *the town.*'
Town is said to be in the objective case, in the former
sentence because it represents the object which the enemy
took, in the latter because it comes after the preposition
in.

Some verbs take two objects : 'Give *me the book :*'
'He told *us a story :*' 'She taught *him music :*' 'Get *them a
cab.*' In these sentences, *me = to me, us = to us, him = to
him, them = for them.* These words *me, us, him, them,* are
called **Indirect** Objects ; *book, story, music, cab,* are called
Direct Objects. Formerly a dative case with distinct inflexions was used in English to express Indirect Objects,
but through the loss of these distinct inflexions the dative
and the accusative case assumed the same form in nouns,
while in the pronouns the dative forms *whom, him, them,* took
the place of the accusatives. We cannot understand the
impersonal verbs *methought, meseems,* unless we remember
that the *me* in these words is a survival of a true dative case.

The **Possessive** Case is the form of a noun when
it stands for a thing **to which something else belongs
or with which it is connected.**

The King's crown: the King's execution. The noun
King assumes the form *King's* because it stands for a thing
(*e.g.* Charles I. or Louis XVI.) to which a crown belongs, or
with which an execution is connected.

This relation may be expressed by the inflexion *'s* or by the preposition *of*. We may say *the King's crown, the King's execution*, or *the crown of the King, the execution of the King*. The form *King's* is a possessive case : the expression *of the King* is no case at all, any more than *to, from, by, with, in, round the King* are cases.

The **apostrophe** before the *s* is **no part of the inflexion or case** : it is merely an **orthographical device** to show that a letter, *e*, has been thrown out, or turned away. (*Apostrophe* means 'a turning away.') In *Wednesday* the *e* is still present : *Wednes-day = Wodin's day*.

98. *Formation of the Possessive case.*—To form the possessive case singular add *'s*.

To form the possessive case plural add *'s* if the plural does not already end in *s* : if it already ends in *s*, add the apostrophe only.

So, sing. *town, town's*; plur. *towns, towns'*. Thus in sound *town's, towns, towns'* are indistinguishable. But if we add the *'s* to a singular noun ending in the singular in an *s* sound, or sibilant, we pronounce the *'s* as a separate syllable : thus *actress's* is pronounced just like *actresses* or *actresses'*.

The possessive singular of a noun ending in a sibilant is frequently formed by adding the apostrophe without the *·s*, in order to avoid the recurrence of the *s* sound : but no hard and fast rule can be laid down. We say 'Jesus' brothers,' 'Sophocles' tragedies,' 'for goodness' sake,' 'for conscience' sake.' But we more commonly sound the *s* and write 'St James's Square,' 'Mr Jones's,' 'St Thomas's Hospital,' in accordance with the pronunciation.

Compound nouns take the possessive inflexion *s* at the end of the word : *son-in-law's, man-of-war's*. When we use several words to form a name, we put the *s* after the last, treating the name as a compound word, though it has no place in the vocabulary as such. Thus we say '*The prime minister of England's* residence,' 'I got this at *Marshall and Snelgrove's*,' 'He is in *Price, Waterhouse & Co.'s* office.'

Even nouns in apposition are dealt with in the same fashion. When one noun is used to explain another, it is put in the same case, generally in the same number, and if possible in the same gender. In the expressions *Queen Victoria, Turner the baker*, the noun *Victoria* explains *queen*, and *baker* explains *Turner*. But when we use these expressions in the possessive case, we almost invariably drop the apposition and convert the two nouns into a compound. We might indeed say 'This is *Victoria's*, the *queen's*, crown:' 'I buy my bread at *Turner's*, the *baker's*, shop': these forms illustrate apposition and are perfectly grammatical. But as a fact we should all say 'This is *Victoria the queen's* crown,' 'I buy my bread at *Turner the baker's* shop.'

The reader may find the following examples of the declension of nouns of some service in recalling to his mind the details contained in this section.

	Sing.	*Plur.*		*Sing.*	*Plur.*
Nom. Obj.	ox	oxen		mouse	mice
Possess.	ox's	oxen**'s**		mouse's	mice's

	Sing.	*Plur.*
Nom. Obj.	conscience	consciences
Possess.	conscience's,	consciences**'**
	or conscience'	

	Sing.	*Plur.*
Nom. Obj.	son-in-law	sons-in-law
Possess.	son-in-law's	sons-in-law's

	Sing.	*Sing.*	*Sing.*
Nom. Obj.	James	Henry VIII.	The last of the barons
Possess.	James',	Henry VIII.'s	The last of the barons'
	or James's		

99. Can we always use at pleasure the **inflected form** of the **possessive** in *'s* or the **preposition** *of*?

No: a few trials will show that the preposition *of* can always be employed, but that there are narrow limits to the use of *'s*. We can say either 'the boy's cap,' or 'the cap of the boy,' 'the horse's bridle,' or 'the bridle of the horse,' 'nature's forces,' or 'the forces of nature,' 'friendship's garland,' or 'the garland of friendship.' But we cannot say, 'the ink's colour,' 'grammar's laws,' 'the kettle's lid,' 'the station's platform.'

Speaking generally we may say that the **inflected form** in *'s* is reserved for the **names of living things** and of **personified objects**, though our usage does not entirely conform to this principle: we use the form in *'s* in such phrases as 'a year's absence,' 'a month's delay,' though there is no personification to justify these idioms.

100. A quaint error was formerly prevalent that this 's was a corruption of *his* : that *John's book* was a degenerate form of *John his book*. In the Prayer-Book we find the expression '*Jesus Christ his sake*.' Whatever may be the origin of phrases of this form, two considerations disprove the theory that the 's of the possessive was a corruption of *his* :

1. Old English presents us with the possessive form in *es*, but shows no trace of an original *his* from which it was alleged according to this theory to have been developed.

2. How can the *s* of the word *his* itself be explained on this theory? If *s* = *his*, whence did we get the first *his*?

101. The beginner may find it helpful in determining the case of the nouns in a sentence if he asks the following questions :

To discover the—

Nominative, put *who?* or *what?* before the verb. 'The enemy took the town.' 'Who took the town?' 'The enemy.' 'The town was taken by the enemy.' 'What was taken?' 'The town.'

Objective : (*a*) **Direct Object,** put *whom?* or *what?* before the verb and its subject. 'The enemy took the town.' 'What did the enemy take?' 'The town.'

(*b*) **Indirect Object,** put *to* or *for whom* or *what?* 'Give me the book.' 'What do you give?' 'The book :' this is the direct object. 'To whom do you give it?' 'To me.' 'Me' is the indirect object.

Possessive, look for the sign of inflexion 's.

QUESTIONS.

1. Name the case of each noun in the following sentences :—
John killed Thomas. Thomas was killed by John. Thomas, the coachman's brother, was killed by John the gardener. Thomas the coachman's brother was killed by John. Call me a friend. Call me a cab. The people chose Balbus consul.

2. *Wolsey the chancellor.* Preserve the apposition of these nouns and make three sentences in which they occur respectively in the Nominative, Possessive, and Objective cases. How should we form the Possessive in common use?

3. Write the possessive case singular and plural, (where the meaning of the noun admits a plural), of *goodness, Socrates, Burns, Debenham and Freebody, his sister Mary, his sisters Mary and Rose, hero, goose, the Prince of Wales, the Duke of Beaufort, child, sheep, footman, Norman, Englishman.*

4. Give the feminine of *songster, marquis, beau*; the masculine of *witch, roe, slut*; the plural of *sheep, sheaf, cargo, cameo.*

5. How did the termination *es* or *s* come to be the usual mark of the plural in English nouns?

Mention other ways of forming the plural, and give examples.

Is there anything anomalous in the use of the words *brethren, riches, chickens*?

[In Old English, nouns had several plural suffixes, the commonest of which was *-an*: another common ending was *-as*. It was formerly supposed that the extension of *-as* (which became *-es*) was due to French influence. The plural in *-es* is now known, however, to have been in general use before French had exercised any influence on our language.]

6. How does the possessive case differ both in form and in use from the old genitive? State and illustrate the rules for its use in the singular and in the plural.

[Our possessive inflexion *'s* has come to us from the Old English termination *es*, which was the genitive ending of some masculine and neuter nouns, but not of feminine nouns, nor of nouns in the plural. The *s* in plurals like *oxen's, mice's*, has been attached through the influence of nouns with plurals regularly formed in *s*, as such nouns have the *s* in the possessive, *sons', duchesses.'* The uncontracted *es* is still visible in Wedn-*es*-day and is sounded in many words ending in a sibilant, such as *duchess', Thomas', ass's*. One of the old genitive plural endings is preserved in Wit-*ena*-gemot, 'meeting of wise men.' The absence of the *s* from *Lady-day, Friday*, is due to the fact that feminine nouns in Old English did not take this inflexion.

The relations expressed by the old genitive were much more numerous than those expressed by the modern possessive. The possessive inflexion is now generally limited to names of living beings and of personified objects. The preposition *of* enables us to express the relations indicated by the old genitive: *e.g.* partitive relation, 'door of the house,' 'half of his fortune'; adjectival relation, 'act of mercy,' 'man of virtue'; objective relation, 'love of money.'

For a fuller treatment of this question the student may consult Bain's *Higher English Grammar*, pp. 79—82, and 135—7.]

7. Give the definition and derivation of the word *Case.*

How many Cases are there in English? Name them and describe their uses.

[The Latin grammarians represented the nominative by a perpendicular and the other cases by lines falling away from it. This symbol

Nom. Obj. Poss.   Dat.   Abl. explains the origin of some of our terms connected with case : thus, 'case' itself is from the Latin *casus*, 'a falling' : '*oblique* cases' are 'slopings-away' from the nominative : when we enumerate the cases of a noun, we *decline* it or give its *declension*, that is, its 'fallings.']

8. Insert the apostrophe where it is usually placed in the following phrases :—*Socrates wife, the captains son, for conscience sake, their whos and their whiches, the Officers Widows and Orphans Fund.*

9. Write the possessive case in the plural of the feminine form corresponding to *bachelor, nephew, gander, sultan, fox, peacock, earl, host, billy-goat, jackass, husband, abbot, widower, marquis, drake.*

10. State and illustrate the rules for the formation of the possessive case of Nouns, singular and plural.

Define the relations expressed by the following phrases, and state which, if any, contain true possessive cases : *in Reason's ear, what a love of a baby!, a day's journey, a man of feeling, my money's worth.*

11. Addison says,—'The single letter *s* on many occasions does the office of a whole word and represents the *his* or *her* of our forefathers.' Criticise this statement.

CHAPTER XII.

ADJECTIVES.

102. An Adjective is a word which is used with a noun to limit its application.

The name *sheep* is applicable to all sheep. If we join the word *black* to the noun *sheep*, the name *black sheep* is applicable only to those sheep which possess the quality of blackness. The **application** of the name *sheep* has been **limited** to a smaller number of things. In like manner, if we say *some sheep, twenty sheep,* or *these sheep, those sheep,* we narrow, or restrict, or limit, in every instance the application of the noun. We can make this limitation in other ways: we can say 'the sheep which won the prize at the show,' or 'the squire's sheep,' restricting the application of the word *sheep* by the use of a subordinate clause, or by the use of a noun in the possessive case. But a subordinate clause is not an adjective, though it may be so used as to have the force of an adjective, and *squire's* is a noun in the possessive case, though it limits the application of the word *sheep* like an adjective. *Squire* or any other noun in the possessive case does the work of an adjective, but it is only when it is in the possessive case that it performs this function. *Squire* is not an adjective, nor is its possessive *squire's* an adjective.

103. **Adjectives and verbs resemble each other** in this respect, that they **express attributes** or **qualities of things,** but there is a **difference in their way of doing it.** In the expression 'the prosperous merchant,' prosperity is assumed as an attribute of the merchant : in the sentence 'The merchant prospered,' prosperity is declared to be an attribute of the merchant. In the expression ' the victorious army,' the connexion of victory with the army is implied : in the sentence ' The army conquered,' this connexion is formally stated. So again, when we say 'the black sheep' we assume, or imply, or take for granted the connexion of the attribute blackness with the thing a sheep. When we say ' The sheep is black,' we explicitly state this connexion. The word *black* in the former case is said to be used *attributively,* in the latter case *predicatively,* since it forms, together with the verb *is,* the predicate of the sentence.

104. Bearing in mind that the function, or special work, of an adjective is to limit the application of a noun, let us **arrange adjectives in groups,** or **classes,** according to the **kind of limitation** which they effect.

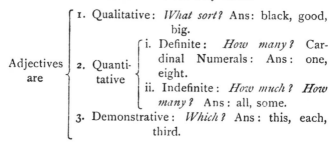

Adjectives are
- 1. Qualitative : *What sort?* Ans: black, good, big.
- 2. Quantitative
  - i. Definite : *How many?* Cardinal Numerals : Ans : one, eight.
  - ii. Indefinite : *How much? How many?* Ans : all, some.
- 3. Demonstrative : *Which?* Ans : this, each, third.

This classification is open to criticism, but for practical purposes it will probably serve our ends better than one more exhaustive. A few words are required to meet objections and to remove difficulties. These questions may be asked :—

1. Why are such words as *big, great, large, small,* placed among *qualitative* adjectives? Do they not mark *quantity*?

They mark size, but not amount : they indicate the dimensions of the thing, but not how much of it we refer to.

2. Where are the Ordinal Numerals, *first, second, third, etc.*?

Their place is among the Demonstrative adjectives, which point out a thing by marking its relation to ourselves or to some other thing. What is *this* to me is *that* to you, and *vice versâ.* A thing is *fifth* in relation to other things which are fourth and sixth. The word *fifth* answers the question *Which?* not the questions *How many?* or *How much?*

3. If we say 'blind Milton,' 'patriotic Hampden,' 'the resounding ocean,' do these adjectives limit the application of the nouns?

No, for the nouns already name objects which are single or individual. 'Milton' or 'Hampden' is the name of one thing: there is only one ocean. We must understand these expressions as condensed forms of saying 'Milton who was blind,' 'Hampden who was patriotic,' 'the ocean which is resounding.'

4. Why should *all* and *half* be classed as Indefinite?

Because they are clearly lacking in numerical definiteness. *All* may be five or fifty: the same thing is true of *half.* They express a definite proportion, but not a definite number.

On the other hand *none* and *both* must be placed amongst the Definite Quantitative Adjectives, for though *all* is Indefinite, since it does not express how many, *none* is as Definite as possible, since it expresses the absence of any. *Both,* again, means two, but two taken together.

105. The student may find it helpful towards a clear understanding of the classification of adjectives, if he reads the examples given below in their respective groups.

1. Adjectives of Quality : *thick, wise, sad, tall, magnificent, modern, holy, native, senior.*

2. Adjectives of Quantity :

(i) Definite ; Cardinal Numerals, *one, two, fifty, no, none, both.*

(ii) Indefinite ; *many, any, some, all, few, half, several, most.*

3. Demonstrative Adjectives:

(i) The so-called Articles, *an* or *a* and *the.*

(ii) Pronominal Adjectives (*i.e.* Adjectives derived from Pronouns or having the force of Pronouns) of various kinds: *this, what, any, each, his.* These we shall deal with in Chapter xiv.

(iii) The Ordinal Numerals, *first, twentieth, thousandth.*

106. Some Adjectives are used as Nouns.

(*a*) 'The *good,* the *true,* the *beautiful,*' may be substituted for 'goodness, truth, beauty.' We describe these words as Adjectives employed as Abstract Nouns.

(*b*) 'The *wise,*' '*rich* and *poor,*' signify 'wise people,' 'rich and poor people.' We describe these words as Adjectives employed as Concrete Nouns.

(*c*) Several adjectives have become nouns so completely that they take a plural and a possessive inflexion. Thus, we say *Romans* (*e.g.* 'Friends, *Romans,* countrymen, lend me your ears'; 'this is a *Roman's* part'; 'the *Romans'* bane'), *Germans, Catholics, Stoics, Liberals, Jacobites, seniors, elders, betters, ancients, blacks, whites,* 'form *fours!*' 'things are all *sixes* and *sevens,*' *others.*

107. Remarks on the Forms of the Numerals.

1. Cardinals indicate the number of things spoken of. They answer the question *How many?*

One appears with a negative prefix in *none—no one*: in the possessive case as an adverb in *once,* (a similar use of the possessive case is seen in the adverbs *twi-ce, thri-ce*): in the adverbs *only,* literally, 'one-like,' and *alone, i.e.* 'all one'; and as a noun in the plural, 'her little *ones.*'

Two was originally the feminine and neuter form of which *twain* was the corresponding masculine.

Five has lost before the *v* an *n* which is kept in German *fünf,* Latin *quinque.*

Ten supplies the ending *-teen* to numerals from 13 to 19, and *-ty* to multiples of 10 up to 90.

Eleven is composed of parts signifying 'one-left,' *i.e.* one over when we have counted ten. Its constituents are clearly seen in the Gothic *ain-lif.*

Twelve means 'two-left,' *i.e.* two over ten. The form in Gothic was *twa-lif.*

Dozen is from *douze*, Latin *duodecim.*

Score is from a Scandinavian word, signifying 'a notch' or 'cut': it is used now as a verb signifying 'to keep an account.' As a noun it sometimes means 'twenty,'—perhaps because twenty was the number of notches marked on one tally or stick,—and sometimes means an indefinite number: 'He made a good score.'

Million is from the Latin *mille*, 'a thousand,' with an augmentative suffix *-on*, signifying 'a big thousand,' just as *balloon* signifies 'a big ball' and *trombone* 'a big trumpet.'

2. Ordinals indicate the position in a series of the things spoken of.

First is the superlative of *fore*, 'most in front,' the *o* being altered by Umlaut. See p. 50.

Second is from the Latin *secundus*, 'following,' from *sequor*, 'I follow.' Our native word was *other.*

Third was once *thrid*, retained in the word *Riding= Thriding= Thirding*, 'a little third,' of Yorkshire. This transposition is called metathesis. See p. 51.

It should be noticed that with the exception of the words *second, dozen, million, billion, &c.*, our numerals are of English origin.

3. Multiplicatives indicate how many times the thing spoken of exceeds some other thing. They are formed by adding *-fold* to the Cardinals: *e.g. twentyfold, hundredfold.*

108. The so-called Articles. The words *the* and *an* or *a* are **Demonstrative adjectives.** In parsing, we may describe *the* as a demonstrative adjective commonly called the definite article, and *an* or *a* as a demonstrative adjective commonly called the indefinite article.

In Old Eng. *the* was an indeclinable relative, used later as a demonstrative adjective, declined in three genders, singular and plural. *That* was its neuter singular.

An is another form of the numeral adjective *one*. The *n* is thus part of the root. We have not added *n* to *a*, but have dropped the *n* before words beginning with a consonantal sound.

109. Points of interest connected with the words *the* and *an* or *a* are discussed in the following paragraphs.

1. Do *the* and *an* differ so widely from **Adjectives** as to justify grammarians in regarding them as forming a **separate Part of speech ?**

Let us inquire, first, in what respects they resemble the adjectives *that* and *one*, and secondly, in what respects they differ from the adjectives *that* and *one*.

In the first place, what are the points of similarity?

(1) They resemble *that* and *one* in their force: 'the book' is a weaker form of 'that book,' 'a book' of 'one book.'

(2) They are connected with *that* and *one* in their origin: *that* was the neuter of *the*, *an* was the older form of *one*.

On the other hand, what are the points of difference?

(1) *That* and *one* are used as adjectives and as pronouns, *the* and *an* are used only as adjectives. Thus we can say 'Give me *that* book,' 'Give me *one* book,' using *that* and *one* as adjectives, or we can say 'Give me *that*,' 'Give me *one*,' using *that* and *one* as pronouns or substitutes for nouns. But although we can say 'Give me *the* book,' 'Give me *a* book,' using *the* and *a* as adjectives, we cannot say 'Give me *the*,' 'Give me *a*,' using *the* and *a* as pronouns.

(2) An ordinary adjective can be used either attributively, as in the expression, 'the black horse,' or predicatively, as in the expression, 'The horse is black.' Now the Articles can be used only attributively. We can say 'Sovereignty is *one* and indivisible,' but we cannot say 'Sovereignty is *an* and indivisible.' We can say 'John is lazy: James is *that* also,' but we cannot say 'James is *the* also.'

But this restriction about the use of *the* and *an* affords quite insufficient reason for constituting a new Part of Speech which shall consist of these two words. For there are other adjectives which do not admit of being used to form predicates. We cannot say 'This is *my*, that is *your*,' any more than we can say 'This is *the*, that is *an*.' But this peculiarity does not prevent us from calling *my* and *your* adjectives. Why then should *the* and *an* be differently regarded?

2. When is *an* used instead of *a* ?

Before words beginning with a vowel, or a silent *h*, as in *heir, honest*; but words beginning with a *y*, or with a *u* which has the sound of *y* before it, take *a*: thus we say '*an* utter failure,' but '*a* useful machine.' To speak of '*an* university' sounds rather pedantic. Words beginning with an aspirate, however, if accented on the second syllable, commonly take *an*: thus we speak of '*an* habitual offence,' '*an* historic character,' '*an* heroic incident,' although, we say '*a* habit,' '*a* history,' '*a* hero.'

3. What are the chief uses of *the*?

(*a*) to point out a thing: 'Give me *the* book,—not *the* red one, *the* black one.'

(*b*) to specify objects which are well known to us: 'Let us have a walk in *the* garden'; '*the* village,' '*the* church.'

(*c*) to indicate things of which only a single specimen exists: '*the* Alps,' '*the* Atlantic,' '*the* Thames.' Hence also with superlatives, '*the* meanest of mankind,' '*the* highest point,' as these are singular objects.

(*d*) to signify a class, with nouns in the singular number or with adjectives: '*the* horse,' '*the* ant'; '*the* rich,' '*the* wise.'

(*e*) in colloquial language with emphasis on the word *the*, to give the force of a superlative: 'Here comes *the* cricketer,' meaning 'the best cricketer.'

(*f*) as an adverb with comparatives: '*the* more *the* better.' This signifies '*by that* much the more *by so* much the better,' like the Latin *quo* and *eo*. *The* is here a survival of the Old English ablative or instrumental case, *thi*, from the definite article or demonstrative pronoun *the*.

4. What are the chief uses of *an* or *a*?

(*a*) to signify *one*: 'three men in *a* boat', 'two of *a* trade': 'In *a* year or two he will come down to *a* shilling a day.'

(*b*) to signify *any one*: 'If *a* body meet *a* body:' '*A* horse is a vain thing for safety.'

(*c*) to signify *some one*, or *a certain one*: '*A* policeman told me there was *a* fire:' 'He has *a* great liking for sport.'

QUESTIONS.

1. Give the derivation and definition of the term adjective.

Distinguish the different kinds of adjectives in the sentence:—'Every man did that which was right in his own eyes.'

Give one example of each kind of adjective not represented in the preceding sentence.

[Adjective is from Latin *adjectivum*, 'what can be added on.']

2. Is it right to say that an Adjective marks the quality of a *Noun*?

3. What is an adjective? Point out the adjectives in the lines:

> ' And his droop'd head sinks gradually low—
> And through his side the last drops, ebbing slow
> From the red gash, fall heavy, one by one,
> Like the first of a thunder-shower.'

4. Refer to its class each Adjective in the following stanza:

> ' Far different we,—a froward race:
> Thousands, though rich in Fortune's grace,
> With cherished sullenness of pace
>   Their way pursue,
> Ingrates who wear a smileless face
>   The whole year through.'

5. Refer to its class each Adjective in the following sentences:—

> ' My mind to me a kingdom is,
> Such perfect joy therein I find.'

' Second thoughts are best.'—' No road is long with good company.'—
' That civility is best which excludes all superfluous formality.'—' Most
things have two handles and a wise man will lay hold of the best.'—
' What truly great thing has ever been effected by the force of public
opinion?'—' Few of the many wise apophthegms which have been
uttered, from the time of the Seven Sages of Greece to that of Poor
Richard, have prevented a single foolish action.'

6. Limit the application of the nouns *thoughts, mutton, music,* by
prefixing to each (1) a Qualitative, (2) a Quantitative, (3) a Demonstrative Adjective.

7. Form Adjectives from the following Nouns:—*slave, tempest,
clay, sense, man, quarrel, sore, gold, wretch, care, right, thought, fire,
silver, courage.*

Attach each Adjective to a suitable noun.

[More than one Adjective can be formed from some of the above
words. From *sore* we obtain *sorry.*]

8. Write short sentences to illustrate the use of an adjective
(*a*) attributively, (*b*) predicatively, (*c*) as an abstract noun.

9. The following Adjectives are used as Nouns in the plural.
Supply the appropriate Noun which may be understood with each
word:—*eatables, valuables, incapables, unmentionables, vitals, italics,
sundries, greens, empties, brilliants.*

Add any more examples which occur to you.

10. (*a*) Some Adjectives are used as Nouns:

    (*b*) Some Nouns are used as Adjectives:

    (*c*) Some Adjectives are used only predicatively.

Construct three sentences to illustrate each of these statements.

[The use of Nouns as Adjectives is exemplified in such combinations as 'iron bar,' 'village church,' 'church bell,' 'railway bridge.' Instances abound. Adjectives used only predicatively are not numerous. See § 247. Other examples are *akin, alive, athirst, aware, awry.*]

11. Would you put *a* or *an* before each of the following words?— *union, year, hypocrisy, hotel, urn, hour, harangue, history, historian, usurper.*

12. Distinguish between the use of the Definite and of the Indefinite Article. Explain the use of the Article in '*a* burnt child shuns *the* fire,' 'twice *a* day,' '*the* red flag.'

[Note here that we might have expected '*a* fire' rather than '*the* fire,' as a burnt child shuns not only the fire at which it was once burnt, but any fire.

In 'twice *a* day,' although *a* has the form of the article now, it is a corruption of the preposition *on*, meaning *in*.]

13. Explain the uses of *the* and *a* in the following phrases:

    (*a*) The more the merrier.

    (*b*) The lazy Scheldt.

    (*c*) A penny a piece.

CHAPTER XIII.

INFLEXION OF ADJECTIVES.

110. ONE result which the Norman Conquest produced upon our language was this : the inflexions marking gender and case disappeared from our adjectives and, with the exception of *these* and *those*, the plurals of *this* and *that*, the inflexions marking number followed them. The adjective in English is thus in striking contrast with the adjective in Greek, or Latin, or German. In these languages the adjective is declined : with us it is invariable as regards gender, number, and case. Thus the **only inflexion of adjectives** which survives in modern English is that of **Comparison.**

111. What do we mean by the **Comparison of Adjectives ?**

We saw that adjectives might be classified in three groups as Qualitative, Quantitative, or Demonstrative. A qualitative adjective indicates the presence of some quality in the thing of which we are speaking. If we say 'The sheep is black,' we assert that the sheep has the quality called *blackness*, or in other words that blackness is an attribute of the sheep. Now many qualities are variable in the amount or degree in which they are present. Blackness admits of different shades : height, weight, speed, cleverness, are qualities which admit of far greater differences of degree than blackness. We observe the varying extent to which these different qualities are presented to us by making a comparison of the objects, and we record the results of our observation by modifying the adjectives which are attached to the names of these objects. This modification is called Comparison of Adjectives.

An Adjective in the Positive Degree expresses the presence of a quality without reference to the extent to which that quality is present in something else.

An Adjective in the Comparative Degree expresses the presence of a quality to a greater extent than that to which it is present in something else, or in the same thing under other circumstances.

An Adjective in the Superlative Degree expresses the presence of a quality to a greater extent than that to which it is present in anything else with which we make the contrast.

Thus we say 'John is younger but taller than his brother : Mary is the cleverest of the three children.'

112. Do all Adjectives admit of Comparison ?

Clearly not. The **Demonstrative** Adjectives,—*this, that, a, the, first, second,*—express no quality which varies in amount. Then again of the **Quantitative** Adjectives, those which are *definite*, like the Cardinal Numerals and *none, both,* have meanings which do not admit of variations of degree. And it is only a few of the indefinite adjectives of quantity which admit of comparison. We can compare *many, much, little, few,* but not *any, all, some, half, several.*

Nor is it possible to form comparatives of all even of the **Qualitative** Adjectives : for—

(i) The adjective in the positive degree may already express the presence of the quality in the greatest conceivable extent : thus, *extreme, universal, full, empty, top, infinite, perfect,* if literally used cannot be compared. When we say 'This glass is *emptier* than that,' 'Yours is a more *perfect* specimen,' we are evidently employing the words *empty* and *perfect* in an inexact sense.

(ii) The adjective may denote the presence of a quality which does not vary in its amount: e.g. *wooden, circular, monthly, English.*

113. Formation of Comparatives and Superlatives. There are **two** ways of forming the degrees of comparison:

1. Add to the Positive *-er* to form the comparative and *-est* to form the superlative, in the case of all words of one syllable and some words of two syllables, especially those in *-er, -le, -y*, as *clever, able, merry.*

2. Use the adverbs *more, most* before the Positive.

The substitution of *more* and *most* for the inflexional forms *-er* and *-est* began through Norman French influence, but has been extended during the last two centuries on the grounds of euphony. Such forms as *honourablest, ancienter, virtuousest*, are not only disagreeable to the ear but also awkward to pronounce.

Notice the following changes of spelling when the inflexions marking comparison are added :

i. If the positive ends in *-e*, cut off the *-e: e.g. grav-er, larg-er.*

ii. If in *y*, change the *y* to *i* if a consonant precedes, as *drier, merrier*, but retain the *y* if a vowel precedes, as *gayer, greyer.* (This is similar to the rule determining the spelling of plurals of nouns in *-y*.) Note that the adjective *shy* keeps the *y*.

iii. Monosyllabic words ending in a consonant preceded by a short vowel double the consonant to show that the vowel is short : *hotter, thinner, redder.* A few other adjectives, not monosyllabic, exhibit the same orthographical change: *crueller, hopefuller.*

114. The following comparisons are **irregular,** that is to say, they do not conform to the general rules stated above ; in many instances deficiencies have been supplied by borrowing words from other adjectives : defect is one kind of irregularity.

Positive.	Comparative.	Superlative.
Good	better	best
Bad	worse	worst
Little	less	least
Much, many	more	most
Nigh	nigher	nighest, next
Near	nearer	nearest
Fore	former	foremost, first
Far	farther	farthest
[Forth]	further	furthest
Late	later, latter	latest, last
Old	older, elder	oldest, eldest
Hind	hinder	hindmost, hindermost
[In]	inner	inmost, innermost
[Out]	outer, utter	utmost, uttermost
[Up]	upper	upmost, uppermost
Rathe	[rather]	

The positive forms in brackets are adverbs: corresponding adjectives exist only in the comparative and superlative.

115. Remarks on the Irregular Comparative Forms.

Better comes from a root which we have in the word *bootless*, meaning 'of no good'; and in *to boot*, meaning 'to the good.' *Best=bet-est.*

The stems of *worse* and *less* end in *s*, and the comparative suffix, which was originally -*s* before it became -*r*, has been merged in the *s* of the stems. Thus *worse* and *less* were not obviously comparative forms, and consequently we get the double comparatives *worser, lesser*.

Less, least are not formed from *little*.

More, most are connected etymologically with *mickle*, not with *many*.

Near is really the comparative of *nigh*: the *r* is the sign of comparison: so *nearer* is a double comparative. In Old Eng. the positive was *neah*.

Last is from *latest*, as *best* from *betest*. We use *latter* and *last* of order in a series, *later* and *latest* of time.

Elder, eldest show a modification of the vowel of the positive which is common in German comparative forms. With reference to the double set of forms, *elder, eldest, older, oldest*, observe that (1) *elder* is no longer used to express comparison with *than*: we cannot say 'He is elder than his brother': (2) the use of *elder* is restricted to persons: we cannot say 'This is the elder of the two horses:' (3) *elder* can be used as a substantive, 'Respect your *elders*:' *older* is always an adjective.

Rathe as a positive adjective meant 'early.' Milton speaks of 'the *rathe* primrose.' We preserve only the comparative *rather*, which we use as an adverb: 'I would *rather* go'=I would *sooner* go than not go, if I had the choice.

Hindmost, inmost, utmost, etc. These words in *-most* require particular attention. At first sight one would naturally suppose them to be compounds of *most*, as this explanation would exactly suit their meaning as superlatives. But we can trace their forms back to an earlier period of the language and satisfy ourselves that they did not arise by the combination of *most* and *hind*, *most* and *in*, etc. In Old English, several adjectives, which have comparatives and superlatives formed from adverbs, contain the letter *-m-* which was a superlative suffix. To this was added the superlative ending *-est*, making *mest*, which was confounded with *most*. Thus these words are really double superlatives. (But *most* the superlative of *much* is not formed in this way. It is derived from a positive root *mag-*, meaning 'great,' by adding *st*.)

Foremost is really a double superlative of *fore*, containing the two superlative inflexions *-m-* and *-st*. But the fact that the *-m-* represented an earlier superlative suffix was forgotten, and from *forem-ost*, as if it were a simple superlative, the comparative *form-er* was coined. Hence the word *former* breaks up into these elements; root *fore*, superlative suffix *-m-*, comparative suffix *-er*.

First represents the superlative of *fore*, *fore-st*, the vowel of the root being changed by Umlaut.

Further is a comparative of *fore*, formed by adding a comparative suffix *-ther*. It was wrongly looked upon as a comparative of *forth* to which the regular comparative ending *-er* had been added, and, owing to this mistaken notion, the *th* was retained in the superlative *furth-est*.

Farther and *further* are used indiscriminately now, but their meanings were originally different; *farther* meant 'more distant, more far away,' *further*, 'more in front, more to the fore.' Yet we see no contradiction at the present day in saying 'Stand further off,' 'He is coming farther this way.'

Hind occurs as an adjective in 'the *hind* quarter,' '*hind* wheel.'

Utter is used as a comparative in the law-courts in the phrase 'the *utter* bar,' in contrast with the 'inner bar.'

116. Examples of Double Comparatives are seen in *nearer, lesser, worser:* examples of **Double Superlatives** in *foremost, inmost, upmost*, etc. Such expressions as *more better, more braver, most worst, most unkindest* are frequently met with in Shakespeare and other Elizabethan writers. When we use such expressions as *chiefest* or *most universal*, we are employing adjectives which are double superlatives in meaning though not in form. But this arises from our laxity in the choice of words: we use *chief* as if it meant the same as *important*, and *universal* as if it meant the same as *general*.

117. Superlatives are sometimes employed to denote the presence of a quality in a high degree, without any suggestion of comparison. When a mother writes to her son as 'My dearest boy,' she does not mean that his brothers occupy a lower place in her affections: 'dearest' signifies in such a case 'very dear.'

118. There are some comparative adjectives which we cannot use with *than*. Thus the following adjectives which have been borrowed directly from the Latin in the comparative form do not admit *than* after them: *senior, junior, exterior*, (which take *to* after them); *major, minor, interior*. The following adjectives of English origin have the same characteristic; *elder, inner, outer, latter*. We can say *older than, later than*, but not *elder than, latter than*.

QUESTIONS.

1. Adjectives of two syllables having certain terminations may be compared without the use of *more* and *most*. Specify three of these terminations, and mention adjectives which contain them.

2. Give the comparative and superlative degrees of *sad, gay, free, nigh, bad, old, hateful, happy, out, awry, fore, late, sly, holy, far, virtuous, dry, complete, big, honourable*.

3. Make sentences which illustrate the difference in our use of *oldest, eldest; latest, last; nearest, next; farthest, furthest*.

4. Which of the following Adjectives, when employed in their strict sense, cannot be compared?—*common, universal, supreme, monthly, triangular, despotic, absolute, inevitable, unique, European, eternal, boundless*.

5. Describe the origin and formation of the words *first, second, eleven, thirteen, twenty, million*.

CHAPTER XIV.

Pronouns.

119. A Pronoun is commonly defined as **a word used instead of a noun.** The definition has these merits: it is short, it is easily understood, and it calls attention to the useful service which most Pronouns perform in saving the repetition of a noun. Thus, for example, if no pronouns existed, instead of saying 'John gave Mary a watch on *her* birthday, and *she* lost *it*,' we should have to say 'John gave Mary a watch on *Mary's* birthday, and *Mary* lost *the watch.*'

120. But have all pronouns this property of serving as substitutes for nouns?

A good deal of ingenuity must be exercised if we are to bring within the scope of the definition (1) the Personal Pronouns of the First and Second Persons, and (2) the Interrogative Pronouns.

(1) For if the pronouns *I* and *you* were abolished, and nouns were put in their places, we should have to recast our sentences entirely and make all our statements in the third person.

(2) Again, when we ask '*Who* broke the window?' what is the noun for which we are to say that the pronoun *Who* serves as substitute? We must maintain that the pronoun *Who* here stands for the noun which the answer supplies, but this seems rather far-fetched. For suppose that the reply to the question is not 'Brown,' or 'the boy,' but 'I don't know,' where is the noun?

The ordinary definition is exposed to the further objection that it overlooks the essential difference between Noun and Pronoun. The essential difference is this. A Noun has a uniform meaning of its own. It always indicates an object of the same kind. The meaning of a Pronoun, on the contrary, varies with every change in its application. (See § 73, 3, p. 70.) If I read the words, 'A horse ran away,' I know, not indeed what particular horse ran away, but the particular class of objects to which the thing that ran away belonged. If, on the other hand, I read the words, 'It ran away,' *it* may signify a horse, or a dog, or a traction-engine, or. anything else, according to the context. *I* means Jones when Jones speaks, Zeus when Zeus speaks, a horse or a tree when horses and trees speak, as they do in fables. In certain situations anything can be *I, you, he, this,* or *that*, but only one set of things can be *horses.* Pronouns admit of universal application : the objects which they denote are infinitely various. Nouns, on the contrary, identify things as belonging to particular groups. In short, Pronouns indicate ; Nouns name.

A Pronoun might therefore be defined as a word which denotes a thing, not by its own name but by its relation to something else. This statement, however, unless accompanied by some such explanation as we have given above, would convey very little meaning to anybody. The student will probably prefer to fall back upon the ordinary definition of a Pronoun as a word used instead of a noun, and provided that he understands in what respects the definition is defective, no harm will result if he follows his preference.

121. Pronouns are of different kinds.

(1) Some are used exclusively as substitutes for nouns : *e.g. he, who.* We cannot say, 'He man' or 'Who boy.' In such expressions as, 'I, the master,' 'You, the pupil,' 'He, John,' we have a noun in apposition with the pronoun : *John* explains *he*; *he* does not limit the application of *John.*

(2) Others are used both as substitutes for nouns and as adjectives limiting nouns: *e.g. that, what.* In the sentence, 'I like *that* book,' *that* is an adjective: in ' I like *that,*' it is a substitute for a noun (though we might also regard it as an adjective with a noun understood, just as we understand the noun 'horse' to be implied with the adjective 'black' in the sentence 'I like the white horse better than the *black*'). In the sentence ' *What* did he do?' *what* takes the place of a noun: in ' *What* work did he do?' it is an adjective limiting the meaning of *work.*

(3) A few so-called pronouns are used only as adjectives, but they are usually dealt with under the head of pronouns because they are connected with pronouns in their origin: *e.g. my, your.* Thus we can say, ' *My book* is lost,' but not ' *My* is lost'; 'Lend me *your book,*' not 'Lend me *your.*'

Keeping these distinctions in view, we may arrange the various classes of Pronouns in the following manner:

TABLE OF PRONOUNS.

Used only as Nouns.	*Used as Adjectives also.*
I. PERSONAL—I, we: thou, you, ye	
II. DEMONSTRATIVE—he, she, it, they	this, these; that, those
III. REFLEXIVE—myself, yourself, himself	
IV. RELATIVE—that, who	what, which
V. INTERROGATIVE—who	what, which
VI. INDEFINITE — anybody, anything, aught, somebody, something	one, any, certain, other, some
VII. DISTRIBUTIVE — everybody, everything	each, every, either, neither

Used only as Adjectives.

VIII. POSSESSIVE—my, our; thy, your; her, its, their.

The Possessives *ours*, *yours*, *hers*, *theirs*, are used when no noun follows them, and in this respect they resemble nouns, but their force is purely adjectival. The same remarks apply to *mine* and *thine* in modern diction. *His* admits of use either with or without a noun following.

The Distributive pronoun *every* is now used only as an adjective, except occasionally in legal phraseology.

122. Definitions of the different kinds of Pronouns.

1. **Personal.**

The Pronoun of the First Person is used in the singular to denote the speaker alone, and in the plural to denote the speaker and others with whom he is associated.

The Pronoun of the Second Person is used of the person or persons addressed.

2. A **Demonstrative** Pronoun is one which points out a thing.

3. A **Reflexive** Pronoun denotes the object of an action when the object is the same as the doer of the action.

4. A **Relative** Pronoun is one which refers to some other nouns or pronoun and has the force of a conjunction.

5. An **Interrogative** Pronoun is one by means of which we ask a question.

6. An **Indefinite** Pronoun is one which does not point out precisely the object to which it refers.

7. A **Distributive** Pronoun is used when there are more things than one, to denote that the things are taken separately.

8. A **Possessive** Pronominal Adjective denotes that the noun which it limits is the name of a thing belonging to some other thing.

With the exception of the word Relative, the adjectives by which the kinds of pronouns are described convey a clearer notion of their characteristic features than these definitions will afford. The student should carefully notice the Examples of Pronouns given in the Table under their respective heads and observe the appropriateness of the names by which the various classes are distinguished.

We will now consider the different classes in detail.

123. I. The **Pronouns** of the **First, Second,** and **Third Persons** are declined thus:

	Pronoun of 1st Person		Pronoun of 2nd Person		Pronoun of 3rd Person			
	Sing.	*Plur.*	*Sing.*	*Plur.*		*Sing.*		*Plur.*
					M.	*F.*	*N.*	
Nom.	I	we	thou	ye, you	he	she	it	they
Obj.	me	us	thee	ye, you	him	her	it	them
Possess.	my	our	thy	your	his	her	its	their
	mine	ours	thine	yours		hers		theirs

124. Remarks on these Pronouns.

(1) There cannot be a plural of *I* at all, strictly speaking. *We* does not mean *I + I*, as *horses* means *horse + horse*: there is in the nature of things for each of us only one *I*. *We* signifies really *I + you*, or *I + they*.

(2) Why should the pronouns denoting the 1st and the 2nd Person have no distinctions of Gender, while the pronoun denoting the 3rd Person possesses a set of inflexions to mark Gender?

Because when *I* am addressing *you*, our sex is not a matter of doubt, as we are both of us present; but when we are speaking of a third thing, it is desirable for greater certainty to indicate whether it possesses sex or not, and what sex, as it may be absent.

(3) The Pronoun of the Third Person is sometimes called a Personal pronoun, but it is better to class it with the Demonstratives. *She* was not originally the feminine of *he*: *she* was the feminine of the Old English definite article or demonstrative adjective, which supplied us also with our forms of the plural number, *they, their, them*[1].

The *t* in *it* is a sign of the neuter, like the *d* in *illud*. *Its* is a modern word, occurring rarely in Shakespeare, at the beginning of the 17th century, and frequently in Dryden, at the end of it. It appears once in the Authorized Version of the Bible (*Levit.* xxv. 5) as it is now printed, but not in the original edition of 1611. *His* was formerly the genitive case of both *he* and *it*: 'If the salt have lost *his* savour.'

(4) The forms of these Pronouns in the Possessive case are used no longer as Personal Pronouns, but only as Possessive Adjectives. Thus *my* and *thy* are equivalents of the Latin *meus* and *tuus*, not of *mei* and *tui*. *Pars mei* must be rendered 'a part of me,' not 'my part;' 'forgetfulness of you' is not expressed by saying 'your forgetfulness,' nor 'envy of them' by saying 'their envy.' Passages may be found however in Shakespeare, or in the Authorized Version of the Bible, in which *my, our, your, their*, &c., are used as true genitives of the Personal Pronouns. When Shakespeare writes 'at *your* only choice,' 'to all *our* sorrows,' the meaning is 'at the choice *of you* alone,' 'to the sorrow *of us* all.' Similarly, 'Be not afraid of *their* terror' (1 Peter iii. 14) means 'Be not afraid of the terror *of them*,' and 'In *thy* fear will I worship' (Psalm v. 7) means 'In the fear *of Thee* will I worship.' These forms

---

[1] In Old English the Pronoun of the Third Person was declined in the nominative case thus: masc. *he*, fem. *heo*, neut. *hit*. Of these forms we have retained *he* and (*h*)*it*, but have borrowed the feminine *she* from the feminine *seo* of the Demonstrative, masc. *se*, fem. *seo*, neut. *þæt* ('that'). The colloquial *'em*, as in 'Give it *'em*,' is a survival of *hem*, the old dative plural of *he*, not a corruption of *them*.

belong to the Personal Pronouns by origin, but have become purely adjectival in force. We have therefore enclosed them in brackets.

(5) *Thou* is used only in addressing God and in the flights of poetry or rhetoric. But half-a-century ago the Quakers employed *thou* and *thee* in ordinary speech. In the Elizabethan age *thou* and *thee* expressed affection or contempt, as is the case with *tu* in French and *du* in German to-day. The plural *you* is now used exclusively, whether we are addressing several individuals or only one. Sovereigns adopt this plural style in their manifestoes when speaking of themselves and say 'We' for 'I.' Editors of newspapers express their opinions in the same fashion, frequently with effects which are droll rather than impressive.

In an older stage of our language, *ye* was reserved for the nominative and *you* for the objective: ' *Ye* have not chosen me, but I have chosen *you*.' *Ye* occurs now only in the diction of poetry.

(6) The dative *me* survives in *methinks, meseems*, 'woe is *me*,' and as the indirect object, *e.g.* ' do *me* a service '; here *me* is equivalent to ' for me ' or ' to me.'

125. II. Demonstrative Pronouns.

This and *that* are employed to denote the latter and the former, like the Latin *hic* and *ille*,—*this* the one nearer to us, *that* the one farther away.

That is by origin the neuter of the definite article or demonstrative adjective : the *t* is a sign of gender as in *it* and *what*.

Those is used as the plural of *that, these* as the plural of *this* : *these* and *those* are really forms of the plural of *this*.

126. III. Reflexive Pronouns.

Myself, ourselves, yourself, yourselves, himself, herself, itself, themselves, oneself.

(1) 'Take care of yourself,' 'They killed themselves.' In such sentences we have the *reflexive* use of these pronouns : the action performed by the doer passes back to him, so both the subject and the object of the sentence stand for the same person.

(2) 'Take care yourself,' 'They themselves killed **it.**' In such sentences we have the *emphatic* use of these pronouns : there is nothing reflexive in their meaning here.

127. The compounds of *self* present difficult problems which are rendered still more obscure by research into their forms at earlier stages of the language. Let us take the words *myself*, *ourselves*, *himself*, and *themselves*, and see if, keeping our heads clear of historical details, **we** can give a satisfactory account of the words as they exist to-day.

In the first place, what part of speech is *self*?

A noun : we speak of 'love of *self*'; 'a sacrifice of *self*'; we say '*Self* makes demands on one's time.' Nouns take inflexions to mark the plural ; *self* becomes *selves*. Nouns are limited in application by adjectives: *my* and *our* are possessive adjectives. There is no particular difficulty in understanding how the word *myself* came to be used both for reflexive and for emphatic purposes. If *self* means 'one's own person,' 'I myself did it' is a way of saying 'I did it of my own person': 'I hurt myself' is a way of saying 'I hurt my own person.' Thus far all is fairly simple.

But then by analogy we should expect the forms *hisself* and *their-selves*. Is there any way of explaining the forms *himself* and *them-selves*?

In the first place, *self* must still be regarded as a noun, for it forms a plural *selves*. In the second place, *him* and *them* are pronouns, or the equivalents of nouns, in the objective case. Now the relation of the nouns *him* and *self*, *them* and *selves*, not being one of dependence, (for if it were, one of the words would be in the possessive case, which it is not), must be one of apposition. Therefore the entire words must be composed of two nouns in the objective case standing in apposition. And this explanation fits in very well with the reflexive use of *himself*, *themselves*, 'He struck *himself*,' 'They hurt *themselves*,' where nouns in the objective case are required. But then we can also say emphatically 'He *himself* did it,' 'They *themselves* said so,' using *himself* and *them-selves* as subjects. Here the explanation breaks down. We can assume, if we like, that people lost sight of the original objective force of these words and came to use them as nominatives, just as we use *me* as a nominative, when we say 'It's *me*.'

Applying these conclusions to the forms *one's self* and *oneself* we may say that both can be justified : the former shows us *one's* in a relation of dependence on the noun *self*, and therefore in the possessive case ; the latter exhibits the two words *one* and *self* in apposition.

This is the simplest explanation which we can offer of these compounds of *self*, as we find them existing now. The reader must not suppose however that the earlier history of these obscure forms affords any foundation for this mode of treating them.

128. IV. Relative Pronouns.

The characteristic feature of the Relative Pronouns is this: **they have the force of conjunctions.** Thus, the sentence 'I met the policeman *who* said there was a disturbance' contains two sentences rolled into one: 'I met the policeman. He told me there was a disturbance.' 'This is the book *that* you lent me' may be resolved into 'This is the book. You lent it me.' The name *relative* is not a happy one, as it does not call attention to this connective function. These pronouns might more appropriately be called **conjunctive** or **connective pronouns.** Several other pronouns might with equal reason be called relative in this sense, that they relate or refer to an antecedent: thus, in the sentences 'I saw John : he was looking very well,' 'Here are your pens : they are all broken,' *he* refers to *John*, and *they* refers to *pens*, but *he* and *they* have no power to unite the sentences in which they occur with the sentences which precede them : this power belongs to the so-called Relative Pronouns alone. If we substitute *who* and *which* for *he* and *they*, the two sentences become in each case a single sentence: 'I saw John *who* was looking well,' 'Here are your pens *which* are all broken'. The name Relative Pronoun is established too securely among grammatical terms, however, to allow us to replace it by another more suitable word : the student must therefore pay particular attention to the concluding part of the definition of a Relative Pronoun as one which refers to some other noun or pronoun and *has the force of a conjunction.*

The noun or pronoun to which the Relative refers is called the **antecedent,** *i.e.* that which goes before. The relative usually comes after the noun or pronoun to which it refers, but the order of the clauses containing the relative and antecedent is sometimes inverted. Thus 'Whom I honour, him I trust' is equivalent to 'I trust him whom

I honour :' *him* is the antecedent, though the relative *whom* precedes it.

The relative is often omitted when, if expressed, it would be in the objective case. Thus 'The man I met told me so' is an elliptical form of expression for 'The man whom I met;' 'I have lost the book you lent me' is elliptical for 'the book which you lent me.' ,Similarly, 'the man you gave it to' is a condensed way of saying 'the man whom you gave it to', or 'the man to whom you gave it'; 'the book I asked for' represents 'the book which I asked for', or 'the book for which I asked'; 'the day I came' stands for 'the day which I came on', or 'the day on which I came'. But this omission of the relative can occur only when the relative is in the objective case : we cannot suppress the relative, if it is in the nominative or possessive. Thus from the sentence 'The man *who* met me told me so' we cannot leave out *who*, nor from the sentence 'The man *whose* horse ran away was thrown off' can we leave out *whose*.

The antecedent is sometimes omitted. Thus we may say 'Who breaks, pays.' When *what* is used as a relative, the antecedent is always omitted : 'I understand *what* you mean.' It is contrary to modern idiom to insert *that* in such a sentence before *what*.

The Relative Pronouns are *that, who, what, which, as.* As a relative, *that* is always used as a noun. Beginners who find it puzzling to determine whether, in any sentence, *that* is a Demonstrative or a Relative, may find help in applying tests such as these : (1) Try *who, whom*, and *which*, and notice whether by the use of any of these words the sense is preserved. If so, *that* is a Relative. Thus 'The man *that* met me,' 'The man *that* I met,' 'The man *that* I spoke to,' might be expressed with *who* in the first sentence, *whom* in the second and third. (2) Try *this* instead of *that* : if sense is made, though not precisely the same sense, *that* is a Demonstrative. Thus in the sentence 'Lend me *that* book : *that* is the only one *that* I haven't read,' the reader will be able to identify the first *that* as a demonstrative adjective limiting the noun book ; the second *that* as a demonstrative pronoun ; and the third *that* as a relative. It is true that the substitution of *which* for the second *that* would still make sense, and the application of the first of our two tests might therefore lead to the mistaken description of this word as a relative. But this error will be corrected by the use of the second test which shows that *this* can replace *that*. The difficulty of identifying *that* is increased by the fact that it is also a conjunction. If we meet with *that* in a context where *who, whom,* and *this,* will none of them make sense as its substitute, the word must be a conjunction. The reader can experiment upon the sentences ' He said *that* you were here,' 'I work *that* I may live.'

129. V. The following are both **Relative and Interrogative Pronouns.**

Who is used only as a noun : we cannot say *who man.* It has three cases, *who, whom, whose,* in singular and plural.

What is the neuter of *who* and can be used both as noun and adjective *What* is used as an Interrogative in '*What* did he say?' Here it has the force of a noun. '*What* remark did he make?' Here it is adjectival. It is used as a Relative in '*What* they took they kept.' Here it has the force of a noun. '*What* towns they took they kept.' Here it is adjectival.

What is not declined. When used as a noun it is neuter, but as an interrogative adjective it can be used with names of persons: 'What man, what woman, what child would believe this statement?'

Which is equivalent to *why+like* (*i.e.* 'in what way like'), as *such* is to *so+like.* It can be used as noun or adjective, both as Interrogative and as Relative. '*Which* will you have?' '*Which* book will you have?' 'Take *which* you please,' 'Take *which* book you please.'

There is a slight difference in our use of *which* and of *who* or *what* as interrogatives. *Which* implies that the choice is restricted to a known group of things. Thus we say '*What* shall we have for dinner?' when the selection is unlimited, but 'There's only turbot or salmon to-day; *which* shall we have?' as the selection is to be made from a definite number.

Which as a Relative pronoun is no longer used of persons, though it was so used formerly: *e.g.* 'Our Father, *which* art in heaven.'

From *who, what, which*, we have formed compound relatives *whosoever, whichsoever, whatsoever. Whosoever* is declined as follows:

Nom. *whosoever*, Obj. *whomsoever*, Possess. *whosesoever*.

130. The differences in our use of *that* and of *who* or *which* as relative pronouns must be carefully noted.

(1) *That* is used of persons and things, whilst *who* is used of persons only and *which* of things.

(2) *That* cannot follow a preposition: if *that* is used as the relative, the preposition is tacked on at the end of the sentence. Thus 'The man *in whom* I trusted' becomes 'The man *that* I trusted *in*;' 'The house *of which* you told me' becomes 'The house *that* you told me *of*;' 'The means *by which* he did it' becomes 'The means *that* he did it *by*.'

(3) *That* has a restrictive force which renders it unsuitable sometimes as the substitute for *who* or *which*. I can say 'My sister *that* is abroad is ill,' because I may have several sisters, and the clause introduced by *that* limits the application of the noun to one of the number. But I cannot say 'My mother *that* is abroad is ill,' because the restrictive *that* would suggest that I have more mothers

than one, which is absurd. I must say 'My mother *who* is abroad,' which signifies 'My mother, and she is abroad,' the word *who* having a **coordinating** force in uniting two coordinate statements, 'My mother is ill,' 'My mother is abroad.'

131. *As* and *But* occur with the force of **Relative Pronouns.**

As is the correlative of *same* and *such*: 'Mine is not the same *as* yours,' 'His behaviour is not such *as* will secure for him many friends.' We still hear *as* used for *whom* or *that* in rural districts: 'The man *as* I saw,' 'The man *as* told me.' These are vulgarisms now, but they were good English once. *As* is entitled to a place among the relative pronouns.

But has the force of a relative pronoun in certain negative construc-tions. Thus in 'There is nobody *but* thinks you mad,' '*but* thinks' means 'who does not think:' in 'Who is there *but* hopes for happi-ness?' '*but* hopes' means 'who does not hope.' We are not however to call *but* a relative pronoun here, though it serves as the substitute for one: it is a conjunction, and there is an ellipsis of a pronoun which should follow it: 'There is nobody but *he* thinks you mad,' ' Who is there but *he* hopes for happiness?'

132. VI. Indefinite Pronouns.

One is an indefinite pronoun: it is used vaguely, re-ferring not to any particular individual, but to persons or things generally: '*One* hears strange rumours of a rupture in the party.' It has a possessive case, *one's*: '*One* must be sure of *one's* ground.' Two views have been held respecting the origin of this word: (1) that it is simply the cardinal numeral, used as a pronoun; this is probably the right view: (2) that it is from French *on*, as in '*on* dit,' '*one* says,' where *on* = *homme* = Latin *homo*, 'man,' just as in German we have the equivalent expression '*man* sagt.' *One* has the meaning 'a certain' in such expressions as '*one* Simon a tanner.'

Any contains the numeral *one* in its root *an*.

Aught contains the word *whit*,—preserved in our expres-sions 'not one whit,' 'not a whit,'—meaning 'thing.'

Naught or *nought* is *ná-wiht*, 'no whit': of *nought* the adverb *not* is merely a shortened form.

133. VII. Distributive Pronouns.

Each represents 'aye-like,' *i.e.* all alike. It can be used both as noun and as adjective: 'Give one to *each*,' 'Give one to *each* boy.'

Every is a corruption of 'ever-each,' and is used only when more than two are referred to. It is not employed in modern English as a noun, but must always be followed by a noun.

Either contains as its elements 'aye-whether': in its constituent part *whether*, the suffix *-ther* marks duality or comparison, as in *other, further*. *Either* means 'one of two,' but sometimes occurs with the meaning 'each of two;' *e.g.* 'on *either* side of the river was there the tree of life.' (Rev. xxii. 2). Its negative is *neither*.

Each other and *one another* are used after a transitive verb to express **reciprocity of the action.** When we say 'They hate *each other*,' we mean that the feeling is mutual. *Each other* is used of two agents and objects, *one another* of more than two. The construction of the two parts of these compound expressions is different : *each* and *one* stand for the agents or subjects, *other* and *another* for the objects; thus—

'They hate each (*subject*) the other (*object*),'
'They hate one (*subject*) another (*object*),'

each and *one* being in apposition with the subject *they*. But the grammatical relation of these Reciprocal Pronouns has been lost sight of in common use. If we still recognised their original construction, we should say 'They gave a present each to the other,' or 'one to another,' instead of saying, as we do, 'They gave a present to each other,' or 'They gave presents to one another.'

134. VIII. **Possessives.**

The forms *my, thy, its,* were dealt with when we discussed the pronouns of the First, Second, and Third Persons. *Mine* and *thine* contain a genitive inflexion *n*: this *n* has been dropped in *my* and *thy,* which are shortened forms of *mine* and *thine,* just as *a* is a shortened form of *an.* The *r* in *our, your, their,* is a genitive plural inflexion.

Our, your, their, her, give rise to secondary forms *ours, yours, theirs, hers,* containing *s* which was originally an inflexion of the genitive singular only. They are thus double genitive forms, just as *brethren* is a double plural, *nearer* a double comparative, and *inmost* a double superlative.

It has already been pointed out that in modern speech we employ the Possessives belonging to the two groups with this difference:

We use *my, thy, her, its, our, your, their,* if a noun immediately follows them:

We use *mine, thine, hers, ours, yours, theirs,* if the noun which they limit does not follow them:

His is used in both ways, but *its* only when followed by a noun.

Thus we say 'Give me *my* book and take *yours,*' not 'Give me *mine* book and take *your.*' But we say 'This is *his* book' and 'This book is *his.*'

In the diction of poetry, *mine* and *thine* occur with nouns following them, if the nouns begin with a vowel-sound: '*mine* eye,' '*mine* ear,' '*thine* honour.'

135. Before leaving the subject of Pronouns, the reader should notice how inflexions, which have disappeared from nouns and adjectives, have survived in words belonging to this part of speech. *Hi-m* preserves the form of the dative singular, *the-m* the form of the dative plural; the *r* in *our, your, her,* is a sign of the genitive; the *t* in *it, what, that,* marks the neuter gender.

QUESTIONS.

1. Rewrite the following sentence without using any of the Pronouns:—'The policeman accompanied the prisoner's sister to his house and told her that she was to let him know if she received any further annoyance from her brother or his confederates.'

2. Refer to its class each of the Pronouns in the following sentences:—

'Who steals my purse steals trash; 'tis something, nothing;
'Twas mine, 'tis his, and has been slave to thousands;
But he that filches from me my good name
Robs me of that which not enriches him
And makes me poor indeed.'

'Who shall be true to us,
When we are so unsecret to ourselves?'

'Whatsoe'er thine ill
It must be borne, and these wild starts are useless.'

'And I myself sometimes despise myself.'

'What everybody says must be true.'—'Some that speak no ill of any do no good to any.'—'Their sound went into all the earth.'—'One may be sure of this, that one must be something to do something.'— 'What is my life if I am no longer to be of use to others?'—'Eat such things as are set before you.'—'Whether of them twain did the will of his father?'—'Anything for a quiet life.'—'That which each can do best, none but his Maker can teach him.'—'He is a wise man who knows what is wise.'—'That is but an empty purse that is full of another's money.'

3. How far may *he, she,* and *it,* be correctly classed as Personal Pronouns? In what respect do they differ from *I* and *thou?*

[When a speaker says *I* or *thou*, the persons to whom he refers are clearly identified. The meaning of *he*, on the contrary, would be as indefinite as possible, unless the previous remarks enabled us to limit the application of the word.]

4. Define Pronoun and Reflexive Pronoun.

Name the other classes of Pronouns and give one example of each.

Place in their proper classes *ours, that, which, each.*

5. Distinguish between the use of a Personal and a Relative Pronoun. Illustrate your explanation by reference to the two sentences: 'My brother who came is gone,' 'My brother came, but he is gone.'

6. State the rule of syntax respecting the agreement of the Relative Pronoun.

Give two illustrations of the omission of the Relative, and make a sentence in which *but* is used with the force of a Relative.

7. Write three short sentences in which the nominative, possessive, and objective cases of *who*, used as a *Relative* Pronoun, respectively occur.

8. ' A gate which opened to them of *his* own accord' (Acts xii. 10). Why is *his* used here?

9. Enumerate some of the principal uses of the word *one*.

10. Point out anything faulty in the following sentences:

' You may take either of the nine.'

' There goes John with both his dogs on either side of him.'

' Between every stitch she would look up to see what was going on in the street.'

[*Every* is distributive and singular. It must have been at least ' every two stitches' or ' every stitch and the next' (or 'the last') that she looked *between*.]

11. In the following sentences, to what class of Pronouns does the italicised word belong?
    (*a*) ' I believed *what* you told me.'
    (*b*) ' She asked *who* told him.'
    (*c*) ' I don't know *what* we have to learn by heart.'
[In (*a*) *what* is Relative : ' I believed *that which* or *the thing which* you told me.' But in (*b*) *who* is Interrogative, not Relative. The sentence means, ' She asked *the question*, Who told him?' not, ' She asked *the man* who told him.' In (*c*) *what* may be either Relative or Interrogative, according to the meaning. Suppose that for his Latin lesson a boy has to write an exercise and to commit to memory Horace's Fifth Ode. If he says, ' I've done my exercise, but I don't know what we have to learn by heart,' he may mean, ' I've done my exercise, but I don't know *that* (namely, the Fifth Ode) *which* we have to learn by heart.' In this case, *what* is Relative. Or he may mean, ' I've done my exercise, but I don't know the answer to the question, *What* have we to learn by heart?' meaning, ' I don't remember the number of the Ode which was set.' In this case, *what* is Interrogative.]

CHAPTER XV.

VERBS.

136. A Verb is a word with which we can make an assertion.

We make assertions about things. The word which stands for the thing about which we make the assertion is called the subject of the verb, or the subject of the sentence. As the names of things are nouns, the subject must be a noun or its equivalent, such as a pronoun, a verb in the infinitive mood, or a noun-clause. Thus we may say

Error (*Noun*)
It (*Pronoun*)
To err (*Infinitive*)
That one should err (*Noun-clause*)
} is human.

When we make an assertion about a thing, we are said in grammatical language to *predicate* something about the thing. As no assertion can be made without the use of a verb, the verb is called the Predicate of the subject, or of the sentence in which it occurs.

What is asserted is either **action** or **state**. *Action* is asserted when we say 'The prisoner stole the watch,' 'The watch was stolen by the prisoner,' 'The prisoner ran away.' *State* is asserted when we say 'The prisoner was glad,' 'The prisoner continued unrepentant,' 'The prisoner slept soundly.'

137. The action denoted by some verbs is conceived as being directed towards, or passing over to, a certain object. When we say 'The boy kicked the dog, and the dog scratched him,' we assert actions the effects of which were not confined to the agents performing them: the boy's action passed beyond the boy, and the dog's action passed beyond the dog. But when we say 'The boy sat down and cried, and the dog barked and ran away,' we assert actions which terminated with the agents performing them. This distinction is expressed by the words *Transitive* and *Intransitive:* it is of the greatest importance.

A Transitive Verb is one which indicates an action directed towards some object.

An Intransitive Verb is one which indicates (1) an action not directed towards some object, or (2) a state.

The student may occasionally be puzzled to determine whether a verb is used transitively or intransitively, for many verbs are used in both ways, though not of course in both ways at the same time. He must ask himself whether the action expressed by the verb produced an effect upon something outside the doer (or, in the case of a reflexive verb, upon the doer itself). He will usually find a word representing the object to which this action passed, but occasionally the object is not mentioned. The verb *kicked* is clearly transitive when *the dog* comes after it to indicate its object, and so is *scratched* when it is followed by *him*. But how are we to describe these verbs when we say 'The boy lay on the floor and kicked and scratched'? If we mean that he kicked and scratched people at large, the verbs are both transitive, though the recipients of the actions are not specified. But do we necessarily mean this? If the verbs signify that he merely threw his legs and arms about in the fruitless endeavour to reach an object, *kicked* and *scratched* are not transitive verbs here any more than *walked* or *ran* would be, though they become so, if we suppose that an object is implied.

138. As we shall have occasion to make frequent mention of the word Object in connexion with Transitive Verbs, the reader must notice that this term has unfortunately to do a double duty, standing sometimes for the *thing* affected by an action and sometimes for the *word* which represents this thing. The following definition may help the student to keep his mind clear of confusion arising from this ambiguity :

The Object of a verb is the word which stands for the thing which is the object of the action denoted by the verb.

It would be a concise description of a **Transitive** Verb to say that it is a **Verb that can take an Object.**

139. Intransitive Verbs are used as Transitives in these ways:

1. A verb, usually intransitive, is occasionally employed with a transitive force:

Ordinarily Intransitive.	Used Transitively.
The horse *walks*.	I *walked* my horse.
I will *run* there.	I will *run* the boat aground.
The ship *floats*.	He *floated* the ship.
Birds *fly*.	The boys are *flying* their kites.
The mother *rejoiced*.	The mother *rejoiced* her son's heart.

2. **Prepositions following Intransitive Verbs** may be regarded as forming with them **compound verbs which are Transitive.** Thus 'I laughed (intrans.) at him,' where the preposition *at* takes an objective case *him*, becomes 'I laughed-at (transitive) him,' where the *him* is the object of the verb. The passive construction can then be employed, and we can say 'He was laughed-at.' So, 'We arrived at this conclusion' becomes in the passive 'This conclusion was arrived-at': 'They came to this decision' becomes 'This decision was come-to.'

3. **Prepositions prefixed to some Intransitive Verbs** make them **Transitive.** Thus the intransitive *lie* becomes the transitive *overlie; stand, understand; run, outrun; weep, beweep; moan, bemoan.*

4. From a few Intransitive Verbs, **Transitive derivatives** are formed called **Causatives,** signifying to cause or produce the action indicated by the original verb: thus from *sit* we obtain *set,* meaning to 'make to sit'; from *lie, lay*; from *fall, fell*; from *rise, raise*; from *drink, drench.*

The student must be on his guard against supposing that an Intransitive is Transitive whenever a noun follows it. A noun of kindred meaning to that of the verb accompanies many Intransitives, not as an *object* but as an *adverbial modification.* In Latin Grammar this construction is called the **Cognate Accusative:** *ludum ludere,* 'to play a game,' *vitam vivere,* 'to live one's life,' are examples in both languages. 'To run a race,' 'to walk a mile,' 'to dream a dream,' 'to fight a good fight,' 'to sleep the sleep of death' are illustrations of this construction. We describe these nouns as **Cognate Objectives.**

140. Conversely, **some Transitive Verbs are used Intransitively.** Compare the following:

Transitive.	Intransitive.
He broke the glass.	The glass broke.
They moved the chair.	The chair moved.
I slammed the door.	The door slammed.
He opened the lid.	The lid opened.
The sun melted the snow.	The snow melted.
We reformed the criminal.	The criminal reformed.

Some writers regard these intransitive uses as apparent rather than real, and consider the verbs to be Reflexives with an object *itself* understood.

141. **Verbs of Incomplete Predication.** Many intransitive verbs make no sense as predicates, unless they are followed by some noun, adjective, or verb in the infinitive mood. To say 'He is,' 'They can,' 'We became,' 'You will,' 'She seems,' is meaningless until we add some word to complete the sense. Thus we give significance to these

incomplete assertions, if we say 'He is good,' 'He is captain,' 'He is killed,' 'He is come,' 'They can speak French,' 'We became rich,' 'We became partners,' 'You will win,' 'She seems vexed.' Such verbs are called Verbs of Incomplete Predication, and the word or words which are added to make sense are called the **Complement** of the Predicate. The verbs *grow*, *look*, *feel*, in some of their uses are intransitives of this kind.

Certain transitive verbs require, always or in some of their uses, a similar complement. If we say 'The king made a treaty,' the sense is complete: but if we say 'The king made Walpole,' the sense is incomplete until we add the complement 'a peer,' or 'angry,' or 'continue minister.' The verb 'called' is a complete predicate in the sentence 'The master called his valet,' meaning 'summoned him to his presence': it is an incomplete predicate if it signifies 'applied a name to him,' until the name is added; 'The master called his valet a thief,' or 'lazy'. 'I think you' requires 'a genius,' 'a fool,' 'clever,' 'mad,' to complete the sense.

The name *Neuter* is applied in some books to Intransitive verbs generally, in others to Intransitive verbs of incomplete predication. As there is this ambiguity in its meaning, the best course is to dispense with its use altogether.

142. Auxiliary and Notional Verbs. When we come to the conjugation of the verb, we shall see that most of the different forms are made by means of other verbs, which are therefore called Auxiliaries (from Lat. *auxilium*, 'help,' because they help to conjugate the verb). The different parts of the verbs *be, have, will, shall, may,* are employed as Auxiliaries, and when so employed are the substitutes for inflexions of which in our English conjugation very few survive. Thus 'I shall have written' is in Latin expressed in one inflected form, *scripsero*, 'you were being loved,' *amabamini*.

But the verbs *have*, *will*, *shall*, *may*, possess meanings of their own which are dropped when the words are used as auxiliaries. 'He *will* do it' may mean 'He is determined to do it,' as well as 'He is going to do it.' In the former case *will* is not an auxiliary, in the latter it is. *Have* signifies *possess* when I say 'I have a bicycle,' but it is merely auxiliary when I say 'I have lost my bicycle.' *May* means permission in 'You may try if you like;' it is auxiliary when we say 'You won't find out, though you may try your best.' Verbs which are used *with a meaning of their own*, and not merely as *substitutes for inflexions* in the conjugation of other verbs, are called **Notional** Verbs.

143. An Impersonal Verb is one in which the source of the action is not expressed.

A true Impersonal Verb therefore has no subject. Only two examples of true Impersonals occur in modern English, *methinks* and *meseems*, and these belong to the diction of rhetoric rather than to every-day speech. *Me* is a dative case: hence it cannot be the subject. The meaning of the two Impersonals is the same, viz. 'It seems to me.' *Thinks* in *methinks* comes from the Old English *thynkan*, 'to seem,' which was a different verb from *thencan*, 'to think.'

'It rains,' 'it freezes,' and similar expressions are commonly called Impersonal, but they have a grammatical subject, *it*. If we are asked however, 'What rains?' 'What freezes?' we cannot specify the thing for which the *it* stands: the grammatical subject represents no real source of the action.

QUESTIONS.

1.   Write sentences to illustrate the transitive use of the following verbs:—'We are resting.'—'Don't push.'—'How you squeeze !'—'Forty feeding like one.'—'They are pressing for payment.'—'The shadows lengthen.'—'The days draw in.'—'Times change.'—'How it pours !'—'The meat will keep.'—'We mean to remove next spring.'—'The king recovered.'

2.   Write sentences to show that the following verbs may be used both transitively and intransitively :—*strike, shake, stop, roll, boil, survive, wake, burst, upset, grow.*

3.   Distinguish the terms *Transitive, Intransitive, Active, Passive.*

State which of these terms you would apply to the verbs in the following sentences respectively, and point out any peculiarities of construction:—*they are arrived, they ran a race, he overeats himself, the book is selling well, he swam the river, he lay down.*

4.   Refer to its class (as Transitive, Intransitive, Verb of Incomplete Predication, Impersonal, Notional or Auxiliary) each Verb in the following sentences:—'It will rain tomorrow.'—'I will do it my own way.'—'They will not succeed.'—'You may call if you like, but he may not be at home.'—'He feels his way.'—'He feels ill.'—'The bonnet became a hat.'—'The bonnet became the lady.'—'You shall not go out.'—'We shall not go out.'—'He grows barley.'—'He grows stout.'

5.   Give instances of verbs which can be used (1) both transitively and intransitively, (2) both as complete predicates and as incomplete.

CHAPTER XVI.

144. VERBS undergo changes of form to mark differences of Voice, Mood, Tense, Number, Person.

As inflexions have almost entirely disappeared from English verbs, we have recourse to auxiliary verbs and pronouns to express these differences. *Amaverimus, amabimur* are inflexions of the Latin verb *amo: we shall have loved, we shall be loved*, their English equivalents, are not inflexions of the verb *love*; the required changes in the meaning of the verb are effected by the use of auxiliaries. *Amo* has over a hundred of these inflexions: *love* has seven, viz., *love, lovest, loves, loveth, loved, lovedst, loving*, and of these seven, the three forms *lovest, loveth, lovedst*, are no longer employed in ordinary speech.

Voice is the form of a verb which shows whether the subject of the sentence stands for the doer or for the object of the action expressed by the verb.

Mood is the form of a verb which shows the mode or manner in which the action is represented.

Tense is the form of a verb which shows the time at which the action is represented as occur-

ring and the completeness or incompleteness of the action.

Number is the form of a verb which shows whether we are speaking of one thing or of more than one.

Person is the form of a verb which shows whether the subject of the sentence stands for the speaker, for the person addressed, or for some other thing.

We shall treat of these modifications of the verb in order.

145. I. Voice.

In English there are two Voices, an Active and a Passive Voice.

The **Active Voice** is that form of a verb which shows that the subject of the sentence stands for the doer of the action expressed by the verb.

The **Passive Voice** is that form of a verb which shows that the subject of the sentence stands for the object of the action expressed by the verb.

Thus in 'Brutus stabbed Caesar,' *Brutus*, the subject of the sentence, represents the doer or agent of the act of stabbing expressed by the verb : *stabbed* is in the active voice. In 'Caesar was stabbed by Brutus,' *Caesar*, the subject of the sentence, represents the object or recipient of the act of stabbing : *was stabbed* is in the passive voice.

Now as the subject of the sentence, when the verb is in the passive, stands for the object or receiver of the action, it is clear that, unless the action denoted by the verb passes on to some object, the passive construction will be impossible. Accordingly, only Transitive verbs admit of a passive use.

The parts of the auxiliary verb *be* are used with the perfect participle of a transitive verb to form the passive voice: 'I *am* injured,' 'You *were* beaten,' 'He *is* captured,' 'They will *be* assisted,' 'We have *been* turned out.'

146. The reader may easily be misled by such forms as 'I *am* come,' 'You *are* arrived,' 'He *is* gone,' 'They *are* fallen,' in which the verbs are intransitive, and their perfect tenses therefore are not passive, though they look as if they were. In 'I am injured,' 'You were beaten,' the participles *injured* and *beaten* are passive : in 'I am come,' 'You are arrived,' the participles *come* and *arrived* are active. There is a slight difference of meaning between the forms 'He is arrived,' 'He is gone' and 'He has arrived,' 'He has gone.' 'He *has* gone' lays stress on the action, 'He *is* gone' calls attention to the fact that he continues in a certain state, namely that of absence. We can say 'He *has* come and gone,' but not 'He *is* come and gone,' as *is* becomes unsuitable in connexion with *come*, when he no longer continues here, but *is* gone.

147. **Verbs** which take a **double object** admit of **two forms of passive construction** according as one object or the other is made the subject of the passive verb. A few illustrations will make this clear.

Active.	Passive.
He told me a story.	A story was told me by him.
	I was told a story by him.
You granted him permission.	Permission was granted him by you.
	He was granted permission by you.
They awarded him a prize.	A prize was awarded him by them.
	He was awarded a prize by them.

The reader may construct further illustrations for himself, using the verbs *promise, ask, refuse, show, offer, forgive,* for the purpose.

The secondary forms, in which the Indirect Object, originally in the dative case, becomes the subject, are harsh in sound and illogical in their nature, but there is much of *laisser-aller*, or 'go-as-you-please,' about English syntax, and we find such expressions even in good writers.

This object after the passive verb is called the **Retained Object.** Whether it is the Direct or the Indirect Object that is thus retained the reader can easily determine, by shifting the position of the two objects in the equivalent sentence expressed in the active voice and noticing which of the two requires a preposition when it comes last. The object which requires a preposition is the Indirect Object. So, 'I forgive you your fault,' becomes 'I forgive your fault *to* you'; 'I will allow you your expenses,' 'I will allow your expenses *to* you'; 'I have got you the book,' 'I have got the book *for* you.' In each example *you* is the Indirect Object.

148. There is a curious use of certain transitive verbs in the active form with a passive meaning. In Latin Grammar, verbs of active form and passive meaning are called **Quasi-passive**: *vapulo*, 'I am beaten,' *exulo*, 'I am banished,' are examples. Some of our English Quasi-passive verbs express sensations: we say of a thing that it '*feels* soft, *tastes* nice, *smells* sweet,' whereas it is really we who feel, taste, and smell the thing. In like manner we say that a sentence '*reads* badly,' that a book '*sells* well,' and that a house '*lets* readily.'

149. II. Mood.

The Moods, or changes of form assumed by a verb to show the different ways in which the action is thought of, are four in number:

(i) The **Indicative** Mood contains the forms used (1) to make statements of fact, (2) to ask questions, and (3) to **express suppositions in which the events are treated as if they were facts.**

(ii) The **Imperative** Mood contains the form used to **give commands.**

(iii) The **Subjunctive** Mood contains the forms used to represent actions or states **conceived as possible** or **contingent, but not asserted as facts.**

(iv) The **Infinitive** Mood is the form which denotes actions or states **without reference to person, number, or time.**

150. (i) **Uses of the Indicative Mood.** The Indicative Mood is used (1) to state facts; 'The man stole the watch,' 'He will be punished': (2) to ask questions; 'Which man stole the watch?' 'Will he be punished?' (3) to express suppositions in which the conditions are dealt with as if they were facts; 'If it is fine to-morrow (the condition may be fulfilled, or it may not, but assuming that as a fact it is,) we will go for a pic-nic.'

151. (ii) **Use of the Imperative Mood.** Commands must be addressed to the person who is to obey them. The person addressed is the second person. Accordingly the Imperative Mood can be used only in the second person singular and plural. Such expressions as '*Go we* forth together,' or '*Let us go* forth together,' in which we utter a wish or exhortation respecting the first person, are not instances of the Imperative mood : they are substitutes for it. *Go we* is subjunctive : *let us go* is a circumlocution, or roundabout form of expression, which contains an imperative of *let* in the second person and an infinitive *go* : expanded it becomes *you let*, or *allow* (imperative) *us* (object) *go*, or *to go* (infinitive).

152. A tense which is expressed by a single word is called a **Simple Tense** : a tense which is expressed by the help of an auxiliary verb is called a **Compound Tense.**

English verbs contain only two simple tenses in the Indicative and Subjunctive moods, namely, the Present and the Past Indefinite. The verb *to be* possesses a fairly complete set of distinct forms in the two tenses of these moods, but in other verbs a difference of inflexion is seen only in the 2nd and 3rd persons singular of the present subjunctive as compared with the indicative. Now as the 2nd person singular is used to-day exclusively in the language of prayer and of poetry, the difference of form between the indicative and the subjunctive mood can be detected in ordinary speech only in the 3rd person singular of the present tense, so long as we confine ourselves to the simple tenses. *Thou stealest, He steals*, are indicative forms : *If thou steal, if he steal*, are subjunctive forms. But as we no longer employ *thou* in the language of every-day life, the sum-total of inflexional differences in the simple tenses, according as the mood is indicative or subjunctive, is represented by the forms *he steals* and *if he steal.*

153. The student should make a careful study of the tenses conjugated below :

		To Be				To Steal	
		INDICATIVE	SUBJUNCTIVE		INDICATIVE		SUBJUNCTIVE
		Present *Past*	*Present* *Past*		*Present* *Past*		*Present*
Sing.	1.	am was	be were	steal	stole		steal
	2.	art wast	be wert	stealest	stolest		steal
	3.	is was	be were	steals	stole		steal
Plur. 1, 2, 3.		are were	be were	steal	stole		steal

There are no separate forms for a Past Tense in the subjunctive of any verb except the verb *to be*. Consequently, to illustrate the uses of the subjunctive we have recourse to this verb. In other verbs the inflexions are reduced to two, one of which, as we said, has no place in ordinary speech, while the use of the other is passing away from modern English. The subjunctive mood has decayed till it is almost dead. It is really alive only in the Past Subjunctive of the verb *to be*, especially in its 1st person singular. A speaker who employed the Present Subjunctive of *to be*, and said, quite correctly, 'If I *be* there, I shall see him,' would be supposed by many people of average education, (unless their education had included the facts of English Grammar,) to be making the same blunder as a labourer makes when he says 'I *be* here; I *be* just going home.' Let the reader ask himself whether he would be more likely to say 'I shall play tennis this afternoon, if it *be* fine,' subjunctive, or 'if it *is* fine,' indicative: 'I shall stay in, if it *rain*,' subjunctive, or 'if it *rains*,' indicative. There is a quaint formalism about the employment of the subjunctive which makes us avoid it in every-day conversation.

154. (iii) **Uses of the Subjunctive Mood.** There are cases however in which we still use the subjunctive mood, and there are other cases in which its use would be legitimate, though it has been ousted from its place by the indicative. We still say 'If I *were* you,' not 'If I *was* you,' and we ought to say 'If he *were* you,' though 'If he *was* you' is to be heard quite as often. Of these actual or possible uses a book on Grammar must take cognisance.

The **Subjunctive Mood** may be employed to express

(1) **a wish**: 'O that I *were* dead !' '*Perish* idolatry !' 'God *save* the Queen !' or **an exhortation**: '*Go* we forth,' '*Tell* me he that knows.' This latter use of the subjunctive is almost obsolete, even in poetry. We should now say 'Let us go,' 'Let him tell.'

(2) **a purpose**: 'Work lest thou *lose* the prize,' 'Mind that the letter *be* written.'

(3) **uncertainty**: 'I'll tell him so, whoever he *be*.'

(4) **supposition**: 'If I *were* you, I would go.'

There is thus a scarcity of inflected forms in the Subjunctive, and we manifest a growing reluctance to use those which we still possess. Of the ten or twelve tenses with which the Subjunctive mood is credited in the Conjugation of an Active Verb, as set out in many works on English Grammar, some are identical in form with the tenses of the Indicative, and others which differ, differ only in the form of the auxiliary. If we are asked whether any particular tense-form, which is identical in appearance in both moods, is subjunctive or indicative in a certain context, the answer will be suggested, if we substitute for the tense-form in question an equivalent expression compounded with the verb *to be*, as the verb *to be* marks the difference between subjunctive and indicative by a variation in its inflexions. Thus, suppose we wish to determine the mood of *spoke*, in ' The master asked who *spoke*'; if we convert *spoke* into *was speaking* we see that the mood is indicative. Again, supposing we are asked the mood of *told*, in 'I should not believe him even if he *told* the truth,' if *told = was telling*, the mood is indicative, if *told = were telling*, the mood is subjunctive. Similarly, 'I *could* do it if I *liked*' resolves itself into 'I *were* able to do it if I *were* willing': it would be impossible to replace *could* by *was able*, so we may say that *could* is used with the force of the subjunctive here; but as 'if I liked' might be replaced by either '*were* willing' or '*was* willing,' we may regard *liked* either as subjunctive or as indicative.

155. Finite and Infinite forms of the Verb. Thus far we have dealt with those parts of the verb which are called **finite**. When we say 'I ran,' the action expressed by the verb is **limited** in various ways. Thus it is limited as regards **number** ; it is one person who ran. It is limited as regards **person** ; it is *I*, not *thou* nor *he*, that ran. It is limited as regards the **time** when the running took place ; the running is not occurring now, nor is it going to occur in the future ; it occurred in the past. A verb, with the action which it denotes thus limited or restricted as regards person, number, and time, is said to be a **finite verb**, because *finite* means 'limited,' 'bounded,' 'restricted,' (from Latin *fines*, 'boundaries').

Now the verb can also be used in various forms without these limitations, and it will then express merely the idea of the action (or state) without denoting that the action is done by one agent or by more than one, or by any particular agent at all, or at any particular time[1]. These forms belong

[1] On this point see Question 28 at the end of this chapter.

to what is called the **Verb Infinite**, that is to say, the verb unlimited, unrestricted, unbounded.

156. The **Verb Infinite** contains the **Infinitive Mood**, the **Gerund**, the **Verbal Noun**, and the **Participles**.

(iv) The **Infinitive Mood** commonly occurs in modern English with *to* before it, but there are many verbs which are followed by an infinitive without *to* : the verbs *may, can, shall, will, must, let, do*; verbs expressing sensation, *see, hear, feel, need*; and the verbs *make* and *dare* are examples. Thus we say 'I may, can, shall, will, must *do* it,' not '*to do* it': 'Let him *do* it,' not '*to do* it': 'You do *think* so,' not '*to think* so': 'We saw, heard, and felt it *shake*,' not '*to shake*': 'They made him *tell*,' not '*to tell*': 'You need not *go*,' not '*to go*': 'I dare *say* this,' though the *to* is admissible here, 'I dare *to say* this.' But after several of these verbs in the passive, *to* is inserted: 'He was seen *to take* it and made *to return* it.'

The Infinitive mood is equivalent to a Noun. It resembles a noun in this respect, that it can be used as the **subject or object** of a verb :

'*To read* improves the mind': *to read* is here subject.

'He likes *to read*': *to read* is here object.

The infinitive resembles a noun in this respect also, that it can **follow certain prepositions**: 'I want nothing *except* to live quietly,' 'He has no hope *but* to escape punishment,' 'You care for nothing *save* to make money.'

157. Simple and Gerundial Infinitive. In an earlier stage of the language, *to* was not used with the simple infinitive any more than it is now used with infinitives which follow the verbs mentioned above. The infinitive had an inflexion which showed what part of the verb it was, and the preposition *to* was prefixed to the dative case of this infinitive in order to mark purpose. Thus in 'I came to see him,' where *to* signifies 'in order to' and expresses purpose, *see* would have appeared in the dative with *to* prefixed in Old English, but in 'I wish to see him,' where *to* does not signify 'in order to' and no purpose is expressed, *see* would have appeared without *to*, in the objective case of the infinitive. We may still discriminate between these uses of the infinitive, though the inflexion has vanished, and the preposition *to* has been attached to the simple infinitive. When the infinitive is employed with the meaning that something is purposed to be done, or that it is fit or necessary to be done, and in cases in which the gerund preceded by *to*, *for*, or similar prepositions, would express the same meaning, we call it the Gerundial Infinitive. The following examples illustrate its use:

' They came *to tell* me.' ' He that hath ears *to hear*, let him hear.' ' He is much *to be pitied*.' ' These troubles are hard *to bear*.' ' These troubles are hard *to be borne*.' ' This is sad *to tell*.' ' Here is water *to drink*.' ' I have a house *to let* and a horse *to sell*.'

158. Verbal Forms in -ing. We now come to the forms in -ing, which are a cause of great perplexity to beginners. Beginners are disposed to describe every form in *-ing* as a present participle. We shall here deal with these forms as we find them existing at the present day and shall give them such names as are in keeping with the functions which they perform in modern English. And this we shall do without touching upon any questions connected with their origin and history[1].

Let us take the sentence—

(1) ' *To heal* the sick is a noble work.'

In what other ways can we make this assertion, employing some form in *-ing* of the verb *heal* for our subject and leaving the rest of the sentence unchanged?

We can say—

(2) ' *The healing of* the sick is a noble work,'—and

(3) ' *Healing* the sick is a noble work.'

And whether we say *to heal*, or *the healing of*, or *healing*, the meaning is the same as if we said ' The cure of the sick.'

---

[1] For the historical aspect of the subject the student is referred to my *Key to Questions*, p. 61, Q. 19. Our modern Verbal forms in *-ing* were originally either Verbal Nouns or Present Participles: they were never Infinitives, Simple or Gerundial.

Now *cure* is a noun. So it is clear that these various forms of the verb *heal* are equivalent to nouns. We have seen that *to heal* is the simple infinitive. In *the healing of, healing* is evidently a noun : it takes the article before it, and it is followed by a noun dependent on it in the possessive case. Thus only *healing* in the third sentence remains for consideration. What are we to call it?

(*a*) Some say a noun. But is it exactly like an ordinary noun? No, for it takes an objective case after it instead of being followed by a possessive.

(*b*) Some say an infinitive. '*Healing* the sick' means just the same as '*to heal* the sick': 'to heal' is infinitive, therefore *healing* is infinitive.

(*c*) Some say a gerund. The Gerund in Latin grammar is a verbal noun, occurring in certain cases, and possessing this peculiarity that, although a noun, it governs another noun, just as the verb from which it is formed governs a noun. This description seems to agree very well with the character of the word *healing* when we say '*Healing* the sick is a noble work,' for *healing* is followed by *the sick* in the objective case.

Now if a person chooses to call *healing* in this context an Infinitive, or a Noun, or a Gerund, he is at liberty to do so, and it really is a matter of small importance which name he selects ; for the Infinitive is a noun, and the Gerund is a noun. But as we already have two forms of the Infinitive with *to* on our hands, there is an advantage in not pressing the name 'Infinitive' into service to describe the form in *-ing*. And as we already have another form of the verbal noun, with *the* before it and *of* after it, there is an advantage in refraining from calling this form in *-ing* also a noun ; so we may as well agree to call it a Gerund, and we will give its definition thus :

A Gerund is a verbal noun in -ing which, when formed from a transitive verb, can take after it an object.

159. Entirely different from all these noun-forms is the **Participle in -ing. Participles are adjectives.** To confound one of the preceding forms with a participle in *-ing* is to confound a noun with an adjective, a name of a thing with a word which limits the application of the name; and this is a very serious confusion indeed.

A Participle is a verbal adjective. The active participle of a transitive verb differs from an ordinary adjective in taking an object.

Thus in the sentence 'I saw a doctor *healing* his patients,' *healing* refers to 'doctor,' limiting the application of the name, and at the same time takes an object *his patients*, just as the verb in its finite forms would take as an object *his patients: e.g.* 'He healed his patients.'

Why are beginners inclined to describe every verbal form in *-ing* as a participle?

Because, as a fact, we do make use of a large number of present participles in the conjugation of our verbs. All the tenses expressing incomplete action are formed by the aid of this participle in *-ing*; 'I am writing,' 'You were speaking,' 'He will be waiting,' 'They will have been searching,' are examples, and the reader will realise on reflexion that they illustrate a very common form of expression. Except in conjugating the imperfect tenses of our verbs, however, the participle in *-ing* is not largely used. Thus, though we might possibly say 'Meeting Smith and hearing you were in town, I came to see you,' yet we should be more likely to say 'I met Smith and heard you were in town, so I have come to see you.'

The Participle in *-ing* is an active participle. It is usually called the Present Participle, and we shall give it this name, though it would be more properly termed the Imperfect or Incomplete Participle, as it denotes not time but unfinished action,—action still in progress: *writing, healing.*

Our other Participle is the Perfect Participle, denoting action which is completed and no longer in progress. This is usually called the Past Participle, and we shall employ the ordinary though less accurate name for it. It ends in *-en, -n, beaten, shown,* or *-ed, -d, -t, healed, loved, slept.* If the verb is a transitive verb, this Participle is passive.

160. Notice these points connected with the Participles:

(i) The Passive Participle combined with the verb *have* forms tenses of the active verb : thus, ' He has stolen the watch,' ' I had eaten my dinner.' The explanation of the construction is this : ' He has stolen the watch' was once expressed thus, ' He has (or holds, or possesses) the watch stolen,' *stolen* being originally in agreement with *watch.* So, ' I had eaten my dinner' was once ' I had (or held, or possessed) my dinner eaten.' Then came a time when the real force of *have* in this connexion was lost, its notional meaning disappeared, and it became a mere auxiliary, so that no contradiction was apparent, as it would formerly have been apparent, in saying ' I have lost my watch,' though it is obvious that, if the watch is lost, we cannot correctly say ' I have (or hold, or possess) my watch lost,' as in such a case I hold or possess it no longer.

(ii) We have adopted this use of *have* with the Past Participle of intransitive verbs, and we say ' I have been,' ' I have stood,' ' I have dreamt,' ' I have slept,' though we cannot say ' I am been,' ' I am stood,' ' I am dreamt,' ' I am slept.' The Participle of intransitive verbs is Perfect, or Past, but it is not Passive.

161. The results of this discussion of the Verb Infinite may be summarized in a convenient form thus ;

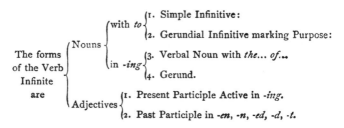

The forms of the Verb Infinite are

- Nouns
  - with *to*
    - 1. Simple Infinitive:
    - 2. Gerundial Infinitive marking Purpose:
  - in *-ing*
    - 3. Verbal Noun with *the... of...*
    - 4. Gerund.
- Adjectives
  - 1. Present Participle Active in *-ing.*
  - 2. Past Participle in *-en, -n, -ed, -d, -t.*

162. Illustrations of these forms.

1. **Simple Infinitive :** '*To work* hard is the way *to get* on.' 'I can go.' 'We heard him *call*.' 'Better *dwell* in the midst of alarms 'Than *reign* in this horrible place.'

2. **Gerundial Infinitive :** 'The sower went forth *to sow*.' 'Bread *to eat*,' *i.e.* 'for eating.' 'Ears *to hear*,' *i.e.* 'for hearing.'

3. **Verbal Noun :** 'They brought flowers for *the decorating of* the altar.' '*The writing of* the book was a protracted task.' '*The hunting of* the fox is a national pastime.'

4. **Gerund :** '*Seeing* is *believing*.' '*Seeing* a conjuror is one thing and *believing* him is another.' 'I am fond of *seeing* a conjuror.' 'We were prevented from *seeing* the conjuror.' 'They asked about *seeing* the conjuror.'

5. **The Participle in -ing.** 'The company sat *watching* the conjuror *performing* his tricks.' 'They are *watching* the conjuror.' '*Seeing* the conjuror there, I went in.'

6. **The Participle in -en, -d, -t.** 'This is *stolen*.' 'He has *stolen* it.' 'This is *mended*.' 'He has *mended* it.'

Compound Gerund Forms. It should be noticed that we use combinations of the Gerunds of the verbs *have* and *be* with Participles, as we use the simple Gerunds: the following are examples of these compound gerund forms : 'I was afraid of his *having gone* away.' 'The master charged him with *having been wasting* his time.' 'My *having been struck* explains my *being* exasperated.'

Observe that in compound nouns the form in -ing is frequently gerundive. Thus a *walking-stick* is a stick *for walking*, a *fishing-rod* is a rod *for fishing*. If these forms in *-ing* were participles, a *walking-stick* would be a stick that walked and a *fishing-rod* a rod that fished, just as a *talking-fish* is a fish that talks and a *laughing-hyæna* a hyæna that laughs.

163. III. Tense.

Tense marks (i) the **time** at which we represent an action as occurring. Now time is either Present, Past, or Future. So far therefore as the time alone of an action is taken into account, we shall have three Tenses: *I write, I wrote, I shall write.*

But tense marks not only the time at which the action is described as occurring, but also (ii) its **completeness or incompleteness** at that time. An action must be either finished, done, completed, perfect, at any particular time, or it must be unfinished, not yet done, incomplete, imperfect, still in progress, at that time. But though the action itself must be either finished or not finished, we may speak of it **without reference to its character as finished or not finished,** and our mention of the action in this aspect will then be undetermined or **indefinite.**

Hence, as we may indicate that an action belongs to present, past, or future time, and may also describe it at each of those times (1) as in a finished condition, or (2) as in a progressive condition, or (3) may leave the fact of its being already finished or still in progress undetermined or indefinite, we shall have nine distinct tenses in which these differences are expressed. The following table presents these **nine Primary Tenses** in an intelligible form.

Time	Imperfect, Incomplete, Unfinished, Progressive, Continuous	Perfect, Complete, Finished	Indefinite
Present	I am writing	I have written	I write
Past	I was writing	I had written	I wrote
Future	I shall be writing	I shall have written	I shall write

164. Remarks on the Tenses.

1. **The Perfect Continuous Tenses.** There is an additional set of tenses, by which we indicate that an action has been, had been, or will have been going on, and also that it still is, was, or will continue to be, in progress. Thus we may say 'I have been writing all the morning,' which signifies that my writing has been going on in the past and is not yet over but still continues. 'I have written all the morning' would imply that my writing was now completed or done. Similarly, 'I had been waiting an hour when he met me' means that my waiting was still in progress and had lasted some time when he arrived. 'I shall have been travelling for six hours when I reach Bristol' means that my journey will have lasted for six hours and will not yet be finished when I arrive at Bristol. These tenses are called—

Present Perfect Continuous	. .	I have been writing
Past Perfect Continuous	. . .	I had been writing
Future Perfect Continuous	. .	I shall have been writing

2. **Other so-called Tenses.** We may have occasion to describe an action as about to begin, and to do this may use the verb *go* in combination with the principal verb, and say 'I am going to write.' In some books on grammar, 'I am going to write,' 'I was going to write,' 'I shall be going to write,' are called Intentional Tenses, or Paulo-post-future Tenses. They are however not tenses at all. Compound Tenses are formed only by the assistance of the auxiliary verbs, and *go* is not an auxiliary verb. We express an action as on the point of beginning equally well when we say 'I am about to write,' but no one proposes to call this form of expression a tense. In Latin there was a class of derivative verbs called Inceptives, which marked the fact of the commencement of an action by their suffix *-sco: e.g. pallesco,* 'I turn pale,' *calesco,* 'I grow warm,' *silvescit,* 'it runs to wood.' The verbs *turn, grow, run,* in these connections express the beginning of the act, but we do not regard them as contributing to the formation of Inceptive tenses.

On similar grounds we must reject the so-called Emphatic Tenses formed by using the verb *do* : 'I *do* think so,' 'He *did* say that,' '*Do* tell me.'

3. **Modes of Tense Formation.** With the exception of the Present Indefinite and the Past Indefinite, all our tenses are formed by the use of auxiliaries. The Past Indefinite undergoes inflexion to mark the change of time: 'I wrote,' 'I walked.' It is sometimes called the Preterite, or Aorist.

A glance down the columns of Imperfect and of Perfect Tenses will enable the reader to see the principle on which these tenses are formed. The Imperfect Tenses are formed by combining some part of *be* with the Present Participle. The Perfect Tenses are formed by combining some part of *have* with the Past Participle.

The Future tenses are formed by the verbs *shall* and *will* with the infinitive mood.

4. **Perfect and Imperfect.** The student must be careful to understand that the words Perfect and Imperfect refer to the character of the action as regards completeness, and not to its time. In the Latin Grammar he finds *amabam* described as 'Imperfect,' and as *amabam* means 'I was loving' he gets the notion that an Imperfect Tense is necessarily a Past Tense. Again, *amavi* is called 'Perfect,' and one of the renderings given of it is 'I loved'; hence he gets the notion that a Perfect Tense is necessarily a Past Tense. Now *Perfectum* means 'finished,' 'completed': *Imperfectum* means 'unfinished,' 'incomplete.'

To gain a clear conception of this distinction, let us suppose that a boy walks from one side of the room to the other. How should we describe his action? We should say 'He *is walking* across the room': the action is in progress: it is unfinished, or Imperfect. But it is going on at this moment and is therefore rightly described as Present Imperfect. When he has finished walking across the room, we say 'He *has reached* the other side,' 'He *has walked* across the room.' Does this necessarily imply that the action is past? As soon as the action is finished, it is certainly past. But in saying 'He has reached the other side,' we are thinking rather that he is there now, than that the action belongs to past time. The action is ended, but it is only just ended, and its consequences continue present with us. If the action and its consequences are over and done with, the Perfect Tense is no longer appropriate. We should not say 'I have written a letter last week,' but 'I wrote a letter': the action took place some time ago. 'I have written a letter' signifies that my letter has just now been completed, and here it is.

5. **Advantages of our Mode of Tense Formation.** By the aid of auxiliary verbs, we are able to express distinctions of time and completeness with a minuteness and accuracy to which other languages are unable to attain. *Amat* in Latin means both 'he loves' and 'he is loving': *amavi* means 'I have loved,' which is Present Perfect, and 'I loved,' which is Past Indefinite, or Aorist.

6. The **Uses of the Present Indefinite** should be noted:

(1) This tense occasionally expresses an action going on at the present time, but it does this very rarely: 'How fast it *rains*!' 'He *wins* in a canter,' 'The kettle *boils*.' Generally we should use the Present Imperfect even in such expressions as these, and in most cases it would be impossible to employ the Present Indefinite to denote an action in progress at the present time. We say 'What *are* you *writing*?'

not 'What *do* you *write*?' 'I *am writing* my exercise,' not 'I *write* my exercise.'

(2) It expresses an action which is habitual, as 'He *goes* to town every morning,' and a general truth, as 'Water *boils* at 212°.'

(3) It expresses a future action, as '**I** *go* to town next week.'

(4) It expresses a past action in graphic narrative. 'The Greeks *maintain* their ranks; the Persians *press* on; Leonidas *falls*, and the battle *rages* fiercely.' This is called the Historic Present: it gives a vivid representation of an occurrence, and is frequently used in the conversation of persons of lively imagination.

(5) It introduces quotations: 'Shakespeare *says*,' 'Xenophon *describes*,' 'The Bible *tells* us,' 'Montaigne *remarks*.'

165. IV. Number.

There are two numbers in verbs. When the subject of the verb is in the singular, the verb is in the singular; when the subject is in the plural, the verb is in the plural.

166. V. Person.

Although we have an inflexion marking the Second Personal Singular, *lov-est*, *loved-st*, these forms occur only in the language of prayer and of poetry, not in ordinary speech.

The form of the Third Person Singular Present Indicative, *lov-eth*, is also obsolete in conversation and is used only when an archaic diction is employed for the purpose of solemnity, real or affected. The suffix *-s* is the only inflexion of Person which survives in common use.

The Personal endings were originally Personal Pronouns. The suffix of the First Person, *-m*, is still visible in *a-m*. This *-m* is the *m* of *me*. Compare the Latin su*m*, ame*m*.

To trace the Pronouns in their disguises as endings of the Second and Third Persons Singular of the verb would lead us into very obscure by-paths of philology. The reader must pursue this inquiry at a later time.

167. Weak and Strong Verbs. According to their mode of forming the Past Tense, verbs are called Weak or Strong.

A **Weak Verb** formed its Past Tense by adding *-d* or *-t* to the present : *e.g. loved, dreamt.*

A **Strong Verb** formed its Past Tense by change of vowel and without the addition of a suffix.

The Past Participle of a Weak Verb is of the same form as the Past Tense : *I walked,* (I have) *walked.*

The Past Participle of a Strong Verb (1) sometimes ends in *-en,* (2) sometimes has a different modification of the vowel from that of the Past Tense, and (3) sometimes is of the same form as the Past Tense : *I drove,* (I have) *driven ; I sprang,* (I have) *sprung; I stood,* (I have) *stood.*

168. Suppose that a verb forms its Past Tense in *-d* or *-t* and also changes its vowel : are we to call it Weak or Strong ?

In such a case, look at the Past Participle. If this is formed in *-en,* then probably the verb is Strong. But if it is not formed in *-en,* we can tell whether the verb is to be classed as Weak or Strong only by tracing it back to an earlier period and discovering how it was originally conjugated. The safest practical guide is the formation of the Past Tense in *-d* or *-t.* Verbs with a Past Tense formed in this manner are with very few exceptions Weak Verbs. The following are however Strong Verbs, though their Past Tense ends in *-d* or *-t,* for this *-d* or *-t* is in these instances a part of the present stem and not an inflexion of the past tense: *beat, bid, bind, bite, burst, fight, find, get, grind, hold, let* ('to allow'), *seethe, shoot, sit, slide, stand, tread, wind.*

169. The following points connected with these two conjugations deserve notice:

(*a*) The verbs which belong to the Strong conjugation are old verbs and of English origin. Their number is just over a hundred and, with the exception of a few to which a prefix has been attached, they are monosyllabic words. All words newly introduced make their Past Tense and Past Participle in *-ed,* as *telegraphed, boycotted.* Many verbs once Strong have become wholly or partially Weak : thus *climbed, crowed, cleft, helped* take the place of *clomb, crew, clove, holp* as forms of the Past Tense, and *shaped, shaved, melted, swelled* are used as Past Participles in lieu of or alongside of the forms *shapen, shaven, molten,* *swollen.* For a verb originally Weak to have become wholly or partially Strong is a rare occurrence: *dig, hide, wear* are examples of this unusual process.

(*b*) Some of the Strong Verbs originally formed their Past Tense by reduplication: we see this mode of formation at work in Latin perfects like *te-tendi, tu-tudi, spo-pondi, fe-felli.* Perhaps *did,* past tense of *do,* is formed by reduplication. If so, it is the sole surviving example of the process. The obsolete verb *hight* exhibits reduplication in the recurrence of the *h.* The Gothic *hai-hait,* past tense of *hait-an,* 'to call,' shows the reduplication more clearly. *Hight* means 'was called': 'This grisly beast, which by name Lion *hight,*' means 'This grisly beast, which was called Lion.'

Strong Verbs are classified in seven conjugations. Those verbs whose past tenses indicate a process of reduplication at a remote period form one group, and the remaining verbs fall into six groups according to the character of their vowel changes. Taking a verb which is typical of each group, Dr Sweet names the seven conjugations as follows: (1) Reduplicative or *Fall*-class: (2) *Shake*-class: (3) *Bind*-class: (4) *Bear*-class: (5) *Give*-class: (6) *Shine*-class: (7) *Choose*-class. These classes may be easily remembered by Professor Skeat's couplet:

'If e'er thou *fall,* the *shake* with patience *bear*;
    Give; seldom *drink*; *drive* slowly; *choose* with care.'

Here *drink* corresponds to *bind* and *drive* to *shine.*

(*c*) The -*d* or -*t* of Weak Verbs has been regarded by some writers as an abbreviated form of *did*: thus *I walk-ed, thou walk-edst* were supposed to be corruptions of *I walk-did, thou walk-didst.* This conjecture is no longer considered plausible.

(*d*) It is interesting to notice how certain Strong Past Participles are still preserved as Adjectives used in particular phrases, though the Participle proper has assumed the Weak form. Thus, we say '*cloven* hoof,' not *cleft* (but '*cleft* palate '); '*graven* image,' not (*en*)*graved*; '*molten* metal,' not *melted*; '*rotten* timber,' not *rotted*; '*sodden* earth,' not *seethed.*

(*e*) In like manner when two forms of the Past Participle exist, both Strong or both Weak, in some cases one form is preferred for use as the Adjective. The following are instances of this:

As Adjectives	As Participles
A *drunken* man	The man is *drunk.*
Ill *gotten* gains	He has *got* his gains ill.
A *sunken* ship	The ship has *sunk.*
My *bounden* duty	I was *bound* to do it.

The duplicate forms given above belong to verbs of the Strong Conjugation. The following are instances of a similar distinction in Weak Verbs:

A *dread* foe	The foe was *dreaded.*
A *lighted* candle	The candle was *lit.*
Roast meat	The meat was *roasted.*
On *bended* knee	His knees were *bent.*

(*f*) The following orthographical modifications, or changes in spelling, in the inflexion of verbs should be noticed.

1. An *e* at the end of the verb is dropped before another vowel: so, *love, lov-ing; shape, shap-ing, shap-en.* (Notice, however, *singeing* from *singe,* to avoid confusion with *singing* from *sing.*)

2. To verbs ending in a sibilant, *es* is added in the 3rd person singular of the present indicative and sounded as a distinct syllable: so *pass-es, push-es, touch-es.*

3. After a consonant, *y* becomes *ie* when *-s* or *-d* follows: so, *rel-ies, rel-ied:* but after a vowel, *y* is kept: so, *play-s, play-ed.* (Compare the formation of plurals of nouns in *-y, e.g. lady, boy;* and of comparatives of adjectives in *-y, e.g. merry, gay.*)

4. A final consonant, preceded by an accented short vowel, is doubled before *e* and *i,* to mark the pronunciation as short: so, *shop-p-ing, bid-d-en, excel-l-ed, prefér-red;* but *díffer-ed, óffer-ed.*

170. In the following lists of Strong and Weak Verbs, with their Past Tense and Past Participle, the student will find only those about the principal parts of which he is likely to feel any uncertainty. For convenience of reference the arrangement is alphabetical: a distribution of Strong and Weak Verbs in classes, according to their mode of forming their Past Tense and Past Participle, is of no value except to those whose researches carry them back to the earlier stages of our language. In the Questions at the end of this chapter, many of the verbs omitted from these lists will be found. The reader should test his knowledge of their principal parts and mark those in which he makes any mistake. He will get at the Past Participle most easily by thinking of it in its combination with *I have* to form the Present Perfect tense: thus, supposing that he is asked to give the principal parts of *spring,* he may blunder in the

principal parts, if he tries mechanically to repeat *spring,
sprang, sprung,* and may say *spring, sprung, sprang,* but if
he thinks of the forms as he is in the habit of using them,
I spring, I sprang, I have sprung, it is much less likely that
he will go wrong.

The forms given below in brackets are those less frequently used, or
used only in special phrases.

The letter *W.* prefixed to forms in the list of Strong Verbs indicates
that those forms are Weak.

171. List of Strong Verbs.

Pres.	Past	P. Part.
abide	abode	abode
awake	awoke	awoke
	W. awaked	awaked
bear	bore	born
(carry)	bore	borne
behold	beheld	beheld (beholden)
bid	bade, bid	bidden, bid
bind	bound	bound (bounden)
blow	blew	blown
chide	chid	chidden, chid
choose	chose	chosen
cleave	clave	cloven
	W. cleaved	cleft
crow	crew	
	W. crowed	crowed
dig	dug	dug
	W. (digged)	(digged)
draw	drew	drawn
drink	drank	drunk
eat	ate	eaten
fly	flew	flown
forbear	forbore	forborne
forget	forgot	forgotten
forsake	forsook	forsaken
get	got	got (gotten)
grow	grew	grown
hang	hung	hung
	W. (hanged)	(hanged)
hew	hewed	hewn, hewed

Pres.	Past	P. Part.
lade		laden
	W. laded	laded
lie	lay	lain
mow		mown
	W. mowed	mowed
rise	rose	risen
rive	*W.* rived	riven
seethe	sod	sodden
	W. seethed	seethed
sew	*W.* sewed	sewn, sewed
sow	*W.* sowed	sown, sowed
shake	shook	shaken
shear	(shore)	shorn
	W. sheared	sheared
shine	shone	shone
shew	*W.* shewed	shewn
show	*W.* showed	shown
shrink	shrank	shrunk (shrunken)
sit	sat	sat
slay	slew	slain
slide	slid	slid (slidden)
sling	slung	slung
slink	slunk	slunk
smite	smote	smitten
stride	strode	stridden
strive	strove	striven
swear	swore	sworn
swell		swollen
	W. swelled	swelled

Pres.	Past	P. Part.	Pres.	Past	P. Part.
tear	tore (tare)	torn		W. waked	waked
thrive	throve	thriven	wear	wore	worn
throw	threw	thrown	weave	wove	woven
tread	trod	trodden (trod)	win	won	won
wake	woke	woke	wring	wrung	wrung

172. List of Weak Verbs.

The following verbs show a departure from the regular formation of the Past Tense and Past Participle in -*d* or -*t*.

Pres.	Past	P. Part.	Pres.	Past	P. Part.
bend	bent	bent	kneel	knelt	knelt
bereave	bereft	bereft	lay	laid	laid
	bereaved	bereaved	lean	leaned	leaned
beseech	besought	besought		leant	leant
betide	betid	betid	learn	learned	learned
bleed	bled	bled		learnt	learnt
blend	blended	blent	leave	left	left
		blended	light	lighted, lit	lighted, lit
breed	bred	bred	make	made	made
cast	cast	cast	pen (confine)	penned	penned, pent
catch	caught	caught	pen (write)	penned	penned
clothe	clothed	clothed	put	put	put
	clad	clad	read	read	read
dream	dreamed	dreamed	rend	rent	rent
	dreamt	dreamt	rid	rid	rid
dwell	dwelled	dwelled	set	set	set
	dwelt	dwelt	seek	sought	sought
flee	fled	fled	shoe	shod	shod
flow	flowed	flowed	speed	sped	sped
gird	girded	girded	weep	wept	wept
	girt	girt	work	wrought	wrought
have	had	had		worked	worked

Help was a strong verb: the past participle *holpen* occurs in the A.V. 'He hath holpen his servant Israel.'

Clave, cloven, are from *cleave*, 'to split': *cleaved, cleft*, from *cleave*, 'to cling to.' But *clave* was sometimes used for *cleaved* (Ruth, i. 14), and *cleft* for *cloven*.

Wrought from *work* shows transposition of consonants.

Go (P. Part. *gone*) supplies its Past Tense *went* from *wend*, which is now inflected as a Weak verb, *wended*.

Yclept is from an Old Eng. verb meaning 'to call.' The *y* is a corruption of the prefix *ge-*, which occurs in the P. Part. in modern German.

173. Conjugation of the Verb.

The collection of all the forms of a Verb, by which we mark its Voice, Mood, Tense, Number, and Person, is called its Conjugation.

We have already seen that our supply of inflexions is quite insufficient to mark many of the distinctions of voice, mood, and tense, which we wish to express. In conjugating our verbs we therefore make use of other verbs called Auxiliaries. These Auxiliary Verbs will be discussed in the next chapter, but as the reader possesses a practical knowledge of his own language, it will be no embarrassment to him, if we complete our treatment of the verb generally, by inserting at this point illustrations of the conjugation of a verb, although to do this will involve the employment of those Auxiliaries to the treatment of which we are to come later on.

First we will give the conjugation of a Weak and of a Strong Verb containing all their simple forms (that is, those not made by the aid of auxiliary verbs), both inflected and uninflected. The reader should notice (1) that the conjugation when confined to the simple forms is of very limited extent, and (2) that the inflexions of Strong verbs are the same as those of Weak verbs except in the Past Tense and Past Participle. Take as the Weak verb *want,* and as the Strong verb *break*[1].

[1] Low's *English Language,* pp. 129, 148.

Verb Finite.

PRESENT.

	INDICATIVE.		SUBJUNCTIVE.	
Sing. **1.**	want	break	want	break
2.	want-est	break-est	want	break
3.	want-s	break-s	want	break
Pl. **1, 2, 3.**	want	break	want	break

PAST.

Sing. **1.**	want-ed	broke	[wanted	broke
2.	want-edst	brok-est	wanted	broke
3.	want-ed	broke	wanted	broke
Pl. **1, 2, 3.**	want-ed	broke	wanted	broke]

IMPERATIVE.

2 *Sing.*
2 *Pl.* } want, break

Verb Infinite.

INFINITIVE : (to) want, break
GERUND : want-ing, break-ing
PARTICIPLES { PRESENT: want-ing, break-ing
{ PAST : want-ed, brok-en

Next let us take the conjugation of the verb *break*, making use of Auxiliaries. To bring out, where possible, the distinction between Indicative and Subjunctive forms, the Third Person Singular of each Tense is given, *he* or *it* being understood as a subject.

INDICATIVE.

TENSE.		ACTIVE.	PASSIVE.
Present	Indefinite	breaks	is broken
	Imperfect	is breaking	is being broken
	Perfect	has broken	has been broken
	Perfect Contin.	has been breaking	
Past	Indefinite	broke	was broken
	Imperfect	was breaking	was being broken
	Perfect (Pluperf.)	had broken	had been broken
	Perfect Contin.	had been breaking	
Future	Indefinite	will break	will be broken
	Imperfect	will be breaking	(will be being broken)
	Perfect	will have broken	will have been broken
	Perfect Contin.	will have been breaking	

SUBJUNCTIVE.

TENSE.		ACTIVE.	PASSIVE.
Present	Indefinite	break	be broken
	Imperfect	be breaking	be being broken
	Perfect	have broken	have been broken
	Perfect Contin.	have been breaking	
Past	Indefinite	broke	were broken
	Imperfect	were breaking	were being broken
	Perfect (Pluperf.)	had broken	had been broken
	Perfect Contin.	had been breaking	
Future		No future tenses	

IMPERATIVE—Present: ACTIVE: break,   PASSIVE: be broken

INFINITIVE.

TENSE.		ACTIVE.	PASSIVE.
Present	Indefinite	(to) break	(to) be broken
	Imperfect	be breaking	(be being broken)
	Perfect	have broken	have been broken
	Perfect Contin.	have been breaking	

PARTICIPLES.

ACTIVE.	PASSIVE.
breaking	being broken
having broken	broken
having been breaking	having been broken

QUESTIONS.

1. Give the Past Tense and Past Participle of the following Strong Verbs:—*arise, beat, begin, bite, break, burst, climb, cling, come, do, drive, fall, fight, find, fling, freeze, give, go, grave, grind, heave, help, hold, know, melt, ride, rise, run, see, shave, shoot, sing, sink, speak, spin, spring, stand, steal, sting, stink, strike, swim, swing, take, wind, write.*

2. Give the same forms of the following Weak Verbs:—*bring, build, burn, buy, cost, creep, cut, deal, dwell, feed, feel, gild, hit, hurt, keep, knit, lead, leap, let, lose, mean, meet, put, rap, rid, rot, say, sell, send, set, shed, shred, shut, sleep, slit, smell, spell, spend, spill, spit, split, spread, sweat, sweep, teach, tell, think, thrust, wend, wet, whet.*

3. Give the Present Participle and Past Participle of the Verbs to which the following Preterites belong:—*saw, sawed, sewed, sued, sat, set, sod, sold, fell, felled, laid, lay, raised, rose, rang.*

4. Show from forms still in use that *melt, mow, swell, shear*, were once of the strong conjugation.

Write the Past Participles of *shoe, light, work, knit, speed.*

5. Give the Past Tense and Past Participle of each of the following verbs:—*fall, fell, hoe, sing, knot, ride, know, jump, go, tear, bear, steal, sit, sling, wring.*

6. Give in two columns the 1st person singular of the Present and of the Past Tense Indicative of the verbs to which the following participles belong:—*flown, lain, eaten, forsaken, set, clad, shown.*

7. Write the Present Participles of *die, dye, lie, forget, credit, acquit, sever, differ, infer, stop, hope, worship, marvel, singe, grieve.*

8. Give in two columns the 1st person singular of the Present Indicative and the Past Participle of the verbs to which the following Past Tenses belong:—*chose, swore, lay, cast, sprang, awoke, grew, hid.*

9. Distinguish the forms of *-ing* in these sentences:—'I saw him *riding* yesterday.' 'This is my *riding*-horse.' '*Riding* is pleasanter than *walking*.' 'The *riding* of the cavalry was excellent.' 'He is *riding* his cob.' 'He keeps his health by *riding* regularly.' '*Riding* in the Row, I met the duke.' 'This curb is no good for *riding*.' 'He goes to the *riding* school.' 'I like *riding*.' 'I am very fond of *riding*.' 'He is gone *a-riding*.'

[In the last example, the *a* is a corruption of the preposition *on*.]

10. Distinguish by its appropriate name each of the following forms in *-ing*:
(a) '*Writing* yesterday he mentioned the matter to me.'
(b) 'The *writing* of impositions sometimes spoils a good hand.'
(c) '*Writing* impositions sometimes spoils a good hand.'
(d) 'Lend me your *writing*-desk.'

11. Parse the words in *-ing* in the sentence, 'Darkling we went singing on our way, with our walking-sticks in our hands, weary of toiling in town.'

[*Darkling* is an adverb signifying 'in the dark,' formed from the adjective by the suffix *-ling*. The suffix in *headlong* is of the same origin and is unconnected with the adjective *long*.]

12. Write three sentences, each of them containing the word *hunting*. Use *hunting* in (1) as a verbal noun, in (2) as a participle, in (3) as a gerund.

13. What is the origin of the form of expression, 'A house *to let* '?

14. Write short notes explaining the use of the words in italics:

    (1) 'The rose...would *smell* as *sweet*.'

    (2) 'Better *dwell* in the midst of alarms.'

[On (1) see § 148 and for *sweet* § 194 (*c*).

(2) *Dwell* is the infinitive *to dwell* used as a subject of *is* understood: 'To dwell in the midst of alarms is better than to reign in this horrible place.' Lady Macbeth says, 'Better *be* with the dead' (*Macbeth*, III. ii. 19), *i.e.* 'To be with the dead would be better.']

15. Draw up a scheme of tenses of the indicative mood of the verb *to go*.

16. Give illustrations of the use of the present indefinite tense to express (*a*) past action in graphic narrative, (*b*) habitual action, (*c*) future action.

17. In the expressions (1) 'I had to go,' (2) 'I had rather go,' by what mood is *had* followed, and why?

18. Give four verbs which have only one form for present tense, past tense, and past participle; also four which have two forms; and four in which all these three parts are different in form.

19. How do you distinguish between transitive and intransitive verbs? To which of these classes does the verb in the following sentence belong?—'Not a drum was heard.'

What are the transitive verbs corresponding to *fall, lie, sit, rise*?

20. Is any alteration necessary in the following sentence?—'Stand the gun in the corner.'

[If *stand* can be used transitively, signifying 'make or cause to stand,' the sentence is right. We do use it in this way in conversation, but in the more formal literary language, the transitive *set* or *place* would be employed.]

21. What class of verbs may be put into the passive voice? Change the verbs in the following sentence into the passive voice:

'The Persians attacked the Greeks again, but they did not make any impression on the little army.'

How have the subjects and objects been affected by the change?

22. Distinguish clearly between the meaning of 'It *is destroyed*,' 'He *is deceived*,' on the one hand, and that of 'It *is fallen*,' 'He *is risen*,' on the other. [See § 146.]

23. What does the *infinitive* mood express?
Parse fully the verbs in the following:—

'It is laughable to see beginners play.'

24. State the various ways in which the infinitive mood may be used. Give illustrative sentences.

25. Correct the mistakes in the following sentences:—

'The lion, having laid down, roared loud.'

'As he lay down the weight, it slipped and has broke his arm.'

'A look of immovable endurance underlaid his expression.'

'He lay himself down.'

'Thou dashest him to earth—there let him lay.'

'I would not like to say that the pistol laid yesterday as it lies now.'

'Will you lose that knot for me?'

'Will you allow my brother and I to finish what we have began?'

'I had wrote to him the day before.'

'It was sang at the Philharmonic last year.'

Comment on any grammatical peculiarity in the lines—

'And while his harp responsive rung,
'Twas thus the latest minstrel sung.'

'The sun had rose and gone to bed
Just as if Partridge were not dead.'

26. Name the several moods of a verb, and show, with examples, how each mood answers to its name.

27. Is any alteration required in the following sentence?—'He says he isn't going to go for it.'

[There is nothing formally wrong in saying 'going to go,' but the use of 'going,' in the sense of 'about,' to signify an action on the point of commencement, is avoided with the verb 'go' itself, though its employment might be defended more logically in this context than in such expressions as 'to be going to sit still,' 'to be going to stay here,' for if we continue to 'sit' and to 'stay,' we do not 'go' at all, and in saying that we do there is a contradiction in terms.]

28. Is it correct to say that the Infinitive Mood does not mark differences in the time of the action? Consider the forms *to write, to have written, to be going to write,* in answering the question.

[With regard to the expression *to be going to write,* we may remark that the combination of the verb *go* with *to write* does not constitute a tense. Other circumlocutions, or roundabout modes of expression, might be employed to convey the same meaning, and these circumlocutions would have as good a claim to recognition, as forms of the future infinitive, as the phrase *to be going to write: e.g. to be about to write, to be on the point of writing, to have the intention of writing.* See § 164, (2).

With regard to the form *to have written,* the case is different. This is a genuine tense of the infinitive mood. But according to some authorities, the difference of meaning between *to write* and *to have written* is a difference of completeness, not of time. If I say, ' He seems *to have written* the copy correctly,' ' He expects *to have written* the last chapter by to-morrow evening,' completed action, not past action, is expressed by the tense *to have written.* According to other authorities *to write* and *to have written* indicate, or at any rate may indicate, a difference of time. If I say, ' He seems *to write* his novels quickly,' *to write* expresses a habit, without any reference to time. If I say, ' He seems *to have written* his last novel quickly,' *to have written* marks the time as past.

29. What inflexions of nouns and verbs survive in modern English? How is it that there are so few?

Point out traces of some which have been lost.

30. Give examples from modern English of traces of inflexions which have fallen into disuse. How has the place of these lost inflexions been supplied?

31. Comment on the inflexion of each of the following words :— *geese, pence, brethren, vixen, whom, what, worse, eldest, could, did.*

CHAPTER XVII.

AUXILIARY AND DEFECTIVE VERBS.

174. The Auxiliary Verbs, which supply the deficiencies of inflexions and enable us to mark distinctions of Voice, Mood, and Tense, in the conjugation of a verb, are these :— *be, have, shall, will, may*, and *do.*

Be is used (1) as a Voice Auxiliary, forming with the Past Participle of transitive verbs the Passive : '*I am beaten*,' 'to *be beaten*' : and (2) as a Tense Auxiliary, forming the Imperfect Tenses in both voices : '*I am* beating,' '*I am* being beaten.'

Notice that, with the Past Participle of certain Intransitive verbs, *be* forms the Perfect Active : '*I am* come,' 'He *is* gone,' 'It *is* fallen.' See p. 146.

Have is a Tense Auxiliary and forms the Perfect Tenses both Active and Passive : '*I have* beaten,' '*I have* been beaten,' '*I had* beaten,' 'I shall *have* been beaten.'

Shall and **will** form the Future Tenses of the Indicative Mood, Active and Passive : '*I shall* beat,' 'He *will* be beaten,' 'They *will* be beating,' 'We *shall* have been beaten.'

May and **might, should** and **would**, are used as signs of the Subjunctive : 'Strive that you *may* succeed,' 'He strove that he *might* succeed,' 'I *should* be glad,' 'This *would* seem to be the case.'

Do is used as an auxiliary in negative and interrogative sentences: '**I** *do* not believe this,' '*Do* you believe this?'

We shall briefly discuss these verbs in turn.

175. **Be** is a defective verb, and its conjugation contains forms derived from three roots which we see in *am, was, be. Am* is the only form of a verb in English that retains the sign of the first person, *m,* which stands for *me.* The *t* in *art* is the sign of the second person, as in *shalt, wilt. Is* has dropped its ending *-t* : compare German *ist,* Latin *est. Are* is a Danish word which has taken the place of the Old English form of the third person plural. The simple tenses of the indicative and subjunctive moods have been given on p. 146.

Be is used as—

1. A Notional Verb, with a meaning of its own, signifying 'to exist,' when we say, 'God *is,*' 'There *was* a Palmerston.'

2. A Copula, connecting the terms of a proposition: 'The boy *is* lazy,' 'A griffin *is* an imaginary beast.' This account of *is* belongs to logic rather than to grammar however: in the language of grammar we should describe *is* here as a verb of Incomplete Predication.

3. An Auxiliary of Voice and Tense: 'He *is* beaten,' 'He *is* beating,' 'He *is* come.'

176. **Have** shows contraction in some of its forms,— *hast* for *havest, has* for *haves, had* for *haved.* It is used as—

1. A Notional Verb, meaning 'to possess,' and then admits of a passive use: 'This suggestion has long been *had* in mind.'

2. An Auxiliary of Tense to form the Perfects: 'He *has* written a letter,' 'He will *have* finished his work,' 'They *had* missed the train.' On this construction see § 160.

177. **Shall** was originally a past tense, meaning 'I have owed,' hence, 'I must pay,' 'I am under an obligation, or necessity.' The German word for 'debt,' *Schuld,* shows the same root. The idea of obligation is still conveyed in such expressions as 'You *should* do your duty,' 'He *should* not say so.' *Shall* acquired the sense of a present, and a weak past was then formed from it, but the absence of the ending *-s* from the third person singular *shall* is due to the fact that it was formerly a past tense. The same circumstance explains the forms *can, may, will, must,* in the third singular, instead of *cans, mays, wills, musts.* Compare these forms :

PRESENT.

Sing.	1.	shall	will	can	may
	2.	shal-t	wil-t	can-st	may-(e)st
	3.	shall	will	can	may
Pl. 1, 2, 3.		shall	will	can	may

PAST.

Sing. 1, 3, *Pl.* 1, 2, 3.	should	would	could	might
Sing. 2.	should(e)st	would(e)st	could(e)st	might(e)st

178. **Will** as an auxiliary contains only the tenses given above. As an independent, notional verb it can be conjugated regularly throughout : 'I did this because you *willed* it so,' 'It has been *willed* by the authorities.' Old English had a negative form *nill,* meaning 'will not,' as Latin has *volo* and *nolo. Nill* survives in the adverb *willy-nilly, i.e. will he, nill he,*—'whether he will or won't.'

179. **Shall** and **will** express the contrast between doing a thing under compulsion from outside and doing a thing from one's own inclination. When employed as Auxiliaries to form the future tense, *i.e.* to predict an action—to mark its futurity and nothing more—*shall* is used in the first person and *will* in the second and third. As a general rule, when *will* occurs with the first person it expresses intention, and when *shall* occurs with the second or third person it expresses a command, a promise, or a threat. Now the notion of intention, command, promise, or threat is something more than the notion of simple futurity, and when *shall* and *will* suggest more than simple futurity they are Notional verbs, not Auxiliaries.

Why was it absurd of the Irishman in the water to say, according to the venerable story, 'I will be drowned and nobody shall save me'? Because 'I will' and 'nobody shall' indicate the resolution, or determination, of the speaker, and not simple futurity.

180. **May** formerly ended in *g*, which is still written, though not sounded, in **might**. As a Notional Verb it expresses permission, 'You *may* go out for a walk,' or possibility, 'He *may* pass his examination': in the latter case, emphasis is usually laid upon the word. As an Auxiliary it occurs as a sign of the subjunctive mood: 'Give him a book that he *may* amuse himself,' 'They have locked the door so that he *may* not get out.'

181. **Must** was a past tense but is now used as a present indicative. It has no inflexions but can be used of all persons. It expresses the idea of necessity: 'You *must* work,' 'I *must* get that book,' 'This *must* be the case.'

182. **Can** was the past tense of a verb meaning 'to know:' compare the German, *können*, 'to know,' 'to be able,' and our *con*, 'to learn,' *cunning*, originally 'knowing.' What a man has learnt, he is able to do, so *can* came to signify 'to be able.' *Can* is always a Notional Verb, never an Auxiliary.

The *l* in *could* has been inserted owing to a mistaken notion of analogy with *should* and *would*, in which words the *l* is rightly present as part of the roots, *shall* and *will*. *Uncouth*, 'unknown,' and so 'odd,' or 'awkward,' shows the correct spelling without the *l*.

183. Dare was originally a past tense which came to be treated as a present, and a past tense *durst* was then formed from it. The *s* of *durst* is part of the stem, and not of the inflexion of the second person singular, which would be *durstest*. As *dare* was a past tense, the third singular of the present indicative properly takes no *-s*.

Dare has two meanings, (1) 'to venture,' (2) 'to challenge.' In the latter sense it is conjugated regularly throughout. The two sets of forms were confused in the Elizabethan period. At the present day, *dare* ('venture') is used for the third singular of the present tense with a negative, and *to* is not inserted before the infinitive which follows : thus, 'He *dare not* say so,' but 'He *dares to* say so.' For the past tense either *durst* or *dared* is employed : 'He *durst* not (or *dared* not) say so.'

184. Ought was originally the past tense of the verb *owe* which meant, first, 'to have,' and then 'to have as a duty,' 'to be under an obligation.' Shakespeare often uses *owe* in the sense of *own*, or 'possess.' It seems a little odd that 'I *owe* a thousand pounds' might signify in the Elizabethan age either 'I possess a thousand pounds,' or 'I am a thousand pounds in debt,' but our modern words *own* and *owe* express the same contrast, and the notion of possession is the older meaning of the two. As *ought* is now used with the sense of a present, we have to express past obligation by altering the tense of the dependent infinitive. Thus we render *non debet hoc facere*, 'he ought not to do this,' *non debuit hoc facere*, 'he oughtn't to have done this,' which is less defensible logically than the vulgar form of expression, 'he hadn't ought to do this.'

185. Need also drops the final *s* in the third singular present, when it means 'to be under the necessity' and is followed by a negative, or used interrogatively : *e.g.* 'He *need* not go, *need* he ? ' The reason for the omission is not clear, as *need* was not originally a past tense which has acquired a present force. Hence we cannot explain the absence of the *s* from *need* as we explain its absence from *can, may, shall, will, dare.*

186. **Do** has the following important uses :

1. As a Notional Verb, meaning 'perform': 'He did his work,' 'Do your duty.'

2. As an Auxiliary—

(*a*) in place of the present or past indefinite : 'I do repent' for 'I repent'; 'He did rejoice' for 'He rejoiced'; 'They did eat' for 'They ate.' The auxiliary *do* is here unemphatic.

(*b*) to emphasize our meaning : 'I *do* think so'; 'He *did* try hard'; 'They *did* eat'; '*Do* tell me.'

(*c*) in interrogative sentences : '*Do* you think so?' '*Did* he go?'

(*d*) in negative sentences : 'He *does* not think so'; 'I *did* not go'; '*Do* not move.'

The verb dependent on the auxiliary is in the infinitive mood.

3. As a substitute for other verbs, except 'be': 'He reads more than you *do* (read)'; 'I said I wouldn't take the money and I *did*n't (take it)'; 'You play well and so *does* (play) your brother.'

The forms *dost, doth* are mainly confined to the auxiliary use : *doest, doeth* are never auxiliary.

Do forms compounds, *don*, 'to do on,' 'to put on,' and *doff*, 'to take off,' of clothes : *dout*, 'to put out,' of a light or fire : *dup*, 'to do up,' *i.e.* lift the latch and so 'open,' of a door.

Do meaning 'to suffice,' 'to be suitable,' occurring in such expressions as 'Will that *do*?' 'This will never *do*,' was formerly supposed to have a different origin from *do* of common use. But this theory is now abandoned and *do*, in the sense 'to suffice,' 'to be suitable,' is held to be the same verb as *do*, 'to perform.'

187. The following verbs are practically obsolete:

Wit, 'to know,' has a Present *wot* and Past *wist*, (used to-day only in affectation of archaic style): 'I'll find Romeo to comfort you: I *wot* well where he is'; 'He *wist* not what to say.' The old gerund *to wit* now signifies 'namely.'

Worth is all that remains of an old verb signifying *to be* or *become*. 'Woe *worth* the chase, woe *worth* the day' means 'Woe be to the chase and the day.'

Quoth is a Past Tense, the Present of which appears in the compound *bequeath*. It occurs now only in the first and third persons singular and always precedes the pronoun: '*quoth* I,' '*quoth* he.'

QUESTIONS.

1. Explain the term *Copula*. Make the *copula* explicit in the sentence 'The fire burns.'

[The word *copula* belongs to Logic rather than to Grammar. In Logic, the proposition 'Man is mortal' would be described as consisting of two terms and a copula: the term *man* is the subject, the term *mortal* is the predicate, and the word *is*, which connects the two, is the copula. In Grammar, *mortal* is not the predicate, but together with *is* it forms the predicate. To bring the sentence 'The fire burns' into the form of the proposition in Logic we must say 'The fire *is* burning.' We have then made the copula explicit.]

2. Give in outline the history of the Auxiliary Verbs. Discuss the following constructions :—

    (1) 'I did come.'
    (2) 'I have come.'
    (3) 'I ought to come.'
    (4) 'I ought to have come.'

3. Make sentences in which the word *have* is used (*a*) as a transitive verb in the indicative mood, (*b*) as a transitive verb in the subjunctive, (*c*) as an auxiliary.

4. Conjugate the verbs *can, shall, will, ought, must,* and show how the places of the missing forms are supplied.

[Think, *e.g.*, how we express ourselves instead of saying, 'I shall not can go,' 'They will must stop.']

5. Write short notes on the following italicised words:—'He *must* go.'—'He *need* not go.'—'He *dare* not go.'—'*Methinks*.'—'*I wis*.'—'This will never *do*.'—'So *mote* it be.'

[*I wis* is not a verb at all, but an adverb *ywis*, 'truly,' where *y* represents an older form *ge*, as in *yclept*; compare German *gewiss*, 'certainly.'

Mote is the subjunctive of *mot*, 'I can, I may,' (but of different origin from the verb *may*,) from which *must* was formed as a past tense, though used also as a present.]

6. Write short notes on the following italicised verbal forms:—'How *do* you *do*?'—'I *do* you *to wit*.'—'Woe *worth* the day!'—'*Seeing* is *believing*.'—'He that hath ears *to hear*, let him hear.'

[In 'How *do* you *do*?' the first *do* is the auxiliary. The second is now considered to be *do*, Latin *facere*, not *do*, Latin *valere*, as was once supposed. The expression resembles the Old French equivalent, *Comment le faites vous?* literally, 'How do you make it?' and the German *Was machen Sie?* literally, 'What make you?'

I do you to wit means 'I cause you to know.']

7. As English verbs possess no inflexions to form the future tense, how are the ideas of simple futurity, of intention, and of compulsion respectively expressed?

8. Define *mood, tense, auxiliary verb*.

Write two sentences, each containing a verb in the subjunctive mood.

Explain the meaning of the word *perfect* as applied to tense.

Distinguish the various uses of *do* as an auxiliary verb.

9. Form sentences which illustrate the use of *will* and *shall* as Notional Verbs, and specify in each instance the notion which the verb conveys.

[*Intention:* 'I *will* be obeyed.' '*Will* you come out?' 'He said he *would* not pay.' *Command:* 'Thou *shalt* not steal.' 'You *should* speak respectfully.' 'The doctor said she *should* take more exercise.' *Promise:* 'You *shall* be told at once.' 'He *shall* apologise.' *Threat:* 'Idle boys *shall* be kept in.' 'The master told the idle boys that they *should* be kept in.']

CHAPTER XVIII.

ADVERBS.

188. An Adverb is a word which modifies the meaning of a verb, adjective, or other adverb.

Verbs usually indicate an action, and this action may be performed in various ways and in different circumstances. These variations in the conditions under which the action takes place are expressed by adverbs. Thus the action asserted in the sentence 'He bowled' is described as limited or modified, as regards the time when it occurred, if I say 'yesterday'; as regards the place, if I say 'here'; as regards the manner, if I say 'badly.' The vagueness of the statement 'He bowled' has been in large measure removed when I say 'Yesterday he bowled here badly.' Just as adjectives limit the application of nouns to things, so adverbs limit the application of verbs to actions. Just as the words 'clever boy' are applicable to fewer objects than the word 'boy,' so the words 'bowled yesterday' are applicable to fewer actions than the word 'bowled.'

Again, Adjectives denote attributes, and these attributes are such as, in many instances, but by no means in all, vary in degree. One way of indicating this variation is by comparison : another is by the use of adverbs which denote degree. If the reader will refer to the chapter on the Inflexion of Adjectives, he will see that the Demonstrative

Adjectives, *e.g. this, that, first, second*, do not admit of Comparison at all; that the same thing is true of the definite Quantitative Adjectives, like *none, both*, and the Cardinal Numerals; and that even of the Qualitative Adjectives there are several which cannot be compared. Hence it is only to *some* adjectives that adverbs can be applied. Moreover it is only *some* adverbs which are applicable to adjectives. Adverbs of time, place, manner, cannot be used to qualify adjectives, though they qualify verbs. The same remarks apply to the qualification of adverbs by other adverbs. We can say '*very* bad,' '*very* badly,' but there is no meaning in saying '*here* bad,' '*hither* badly,' '*anyhow* bad,' '*then* badly,' for though these words may possibly occur together in sentences, reflexion will show that in such cases it is the verb, and not the adjective or adverb, which is modified.

189. We may **classify Adverbs** on three different principles.

I. As **Simple and Conjunctive.**

Most adverbs are simple. They contain a meaning in themselves: · 'He thinks so *now*,' 'I live *here*,' 'We were *greatly* pleased.'

A few however have a meaning only when they are taken in connexion with another clause. 'He came *when*,' 'I waited *while*,' 'They are sitting *where*,' are meaningless assertions until the sentences are completed: 'He came *when* I called,' 'I waited *while* he wrote a letter,' 'They are sitting *where* we left them.' These adverbs have the force of conjunctions in joining clauses together. Hence they are called **Conjunctive Adverbs.** The reader will observe that in possessing this connecting force they resemble the so-called relative pronouns. In 'I know *who* it is,' the clauses 'I know,' 'it is,' are united by the relative pronoun *who*: in 'I know *where* it is,' they are united by the conjunctive adverb *where*.

190. II. According to their Meaning.

1.	Time	*when?* now, to-day, then, yesterday, soon, to-morrow	
		how long? always, ever	
		how often? twice, yearly, rarely	
2.	Place	*where?* here, near, below	
		whence? hence, thence	
		whither? hither, thither	
		in what order? secondly, lastly	

3.	**Degree,** or **Quantity** *how much?*	scarcely, quite, little, exactly
4.	**Manner,** or **Quality** *how?*	well, ill, and adverbs in *-ly*
5.	**Certainty**	certainly, not, perhaps
6.	**Reason** and **Consequence**	why, therefore, thus

191. Yes and No. What are we to call the words *Yes* and *No?*

They are usually classed as Adverbs of Affirmation and Negation, or, to use the term employed in our table, Adverbs of Certainty. Yet they are not exactly adverbs, for we cannot use them to modify verbs, adjectives, or other adverbs : we cannot say ' He *yes* did it,' ' He is *yes* good,' ' He acted *yes* wisely.' In some respects they resemble Interjections, but they are not, like them, the expression of a sudden feeling. They are really equivalent to sentences: 'Did he say so?' 'Yes,'—that is, ' He said so': 'No,'—that is, ' He did not say so.' As they are certainly words, we must either make them a new Part of Speech, which seems undesirable, or include them with Adverbs or with Interjections, though different from both. The student will of course understand that *no*, meaning *none*, is an adjective: ' *no* money,' ' *no* friends.'

192. III. According to their Origin or Mode of Formation.

The following are the principal modes in which Adverbs are formed :

1. Adverbs from Adjectives.

2. Adverbs from Nouns in their oblique cases.

3. Adverbs from Pronouns.

4. Compound Adverbs.

193. Illustrations of these Modes of Formation.

1 (*a*). The usual adverbial suffix is -*ly*, a corruption of *like*: so, 'godlike' became 'godly.'

(*b*). In Old English, adverbs were formed from adjectives by adding -*e*: *fast-e*, *hard-e*. This suffix disappeared along with many of our other inflexions, and adjective and adverb were no longer distinguishable in form. 'A *fast* rider': 'He rode *fast*.'

2. The comparative and superlative forms of such adverbs as are referred to above in 1 (*b*) are the same as those of the adjectives: 'A *faster* rider': 'He rode *faster*.'

The comparative and superlative forms of several adjectives which have irregular comparison are used adverbially also. See p. 115.

With these exceptions, *more* and *most* are generally employed in the comparison of adverbs.

3. Relics of case-inflexions appear in some adverbs:—

(*a*) genitive ending -*s* is present in *needs*, *unawares*, and disguised in *once*, *twice*.

(*b*) dative plural ending -*um* survives in *seldom* and in the archaic *whilom*, 'formerly.'

(*c*) instrumental case is seen in *why*, *the* (in 'the more the better,' originally *thi*), and *how*.

4. The survival of inflexions is illustrated by the adverbs which are derived from the pronouns *he*, *who*, and the demonstrative adjective *the*.

Stem	Suffix -*ther*	Locative case	Genitive case	Accusative case	Instrumental case
he	hither	here	hence	——	—— ——
who	whither	where	whence	when	why, how
the	thither	there	thence	then	the, thus

5. In a few cases a compound adverb is formed from two words written in one: *meanwhile*, *straightway*, *yesterday*, *thereupon*, *herein*, *hitherto*, *aboard* (where *a* is a corruption of *on*), *perchance*, *elsewhere*, *whensoever*.

194. The following points deserve attention:

(*a*) Words belonging to other parts of speech are sometimes used as adverbs:—

Nouns for adverbs: 'He went *home*,' 'I don't mind *a rap*,' 'The wound was *skin* deep.'

Pronouns for adverbs: '*somewhat* steep,' '*none* the worse.'

Verbs for adverbs: 'It went *crash* through the window,' '*Smack* went the whip.'

(*b*) Adverbs are sometimes used with nouns as if the adverbs were adjectives: 'The *then* prime-minister,' 'The *above* remarks,' 'My arrival *here*,' 'His journey *abroad*.'

(*c*) Is there any difference of meaning between 'He arrived *safe*' and 'He arrived *safely*'?

The adjective *safe* marks a quality of the agent *he*, the adverb *safely* marks the mode of the action *arrived*. If his horse ran away, and he narrowly escaped being upset, he might arrive 'safe,' but he certainly would not arrive 'safely,' that is, 'in a safe manner.'

QUESTIONS.

1. What difficulty would arise in conversation, if there were (*a*) no adjectives, (*b*) no adverbs?

[Illustrate the difficulty by an example of this sort. By the aid of adjectives we can distinguish different varieties of things, each of which distinctions would require a separate noun, if we had no adjectives. Thus, if we take *wine* as our noun, and *good*, *old*, and *red*, as its limiting adjectives, with these four words we can mark eight distinctions: viz., (putting initial letters to represent the words) W, GW, OW, RW, GOW, GRW, ORW, GORW, and for these eight distinctions we should need eight nouns. This gives a very inadequate idea however of the economy of words which adjectives enable us to effect. For if we take the same three adjectives *good*, *old*, and *red*, and change the noun from *wine* to *velvet*, we shall need another eight nouns to express the varieties of *velvet*; another eight would be required to express the varieties of *curtains*, and so on. The three nouns *wine*, *velvet*, and *curtains*, in combination with the adjectives *good*, *old* and *red*, would need twenty-four words instead of six.

The same point might be illustrated as regards verbs and adverbs. By combining *write*, *ride*, *walk*, with *gracefully*, *slowly*, *well*, we express by means of six words twenty-four distinctions. If we had no adverbs and wished to mark these distinctions, we should do so either (1) by using phrases composed of a preposition and a noun, *e.g.* 'with grace,' 'in a slow manner,' 'in a good style,' or (2) by adding twenty-one verbs to our vocabulary.]

2. Express by adverbs the adverbial phrases in the following sentence:—'To tell the truth I want the money in the course of the next few hours, and if you will let me have it at the present moment, without asking for what purpose it is required or in what manner I am going to spend it, I shall feel obliged to an extraordinary extent.'

3. Express by adverbial phrases the following adverbs:—*lastly, pleasantly, once, occasionally, there.*

4. Explain the use of *right* in—'Right against the stream they pulled.'

5. Apply your definition of *adverb* to the adverb in the phrase 'Quite within my recollection.'

[It appears at first sight as if the adverb *quite* qualified the preposition *within.* But this is not necessarily the case. It may be regarded as qualifying the whole phrase *within-my-recollection.* What sort of phrase is 'within-my-recollection'?]

6. Mention two adverbs of place, two of time, and two of degree; and form adverbs from the words *holy, whole, true, side, board, one, need, north, here, day, other, three.*

7. Refer to its class each of the following adverbs:—*weekly, weakly, possibly, enough, anyhow, hence, hardly, certainly, aloft, presently.*

8. Parse the word *above* in the following sentence:—'The above remarks, as we noticed above, apply above all to the third class.'

9. What parts of speech may an adverb modify?

Parse fully the words *alone, almost,* in each of the following sentences:—

(*a*) 'He almost succeeded alone.'

(*b*) 'He succeeded almost alone.'

(*c*) 'He, alone, almost succeeded.'

[As explained at the beginning of the chapter, adverbs limit, or modify, verbs and adjectives, words expressing actions and attributes: they also qualify other adverbs. As participles are verbal adjectives, participles admit of adverbial modification : '*much* disappointed,' '*twice* blessed.' The following uses of the adverb are only seemingly exceptional. In 'Yours *faithfully*' the possessive pronoun is really adjectival, expressing a quality. In 'He was *fully* master of the language' a noun appears to be modified, but the noun is used like a verb to express an attribute : 'He was *fully* master of the language' means 'He had *fully* mastered the language.' In 'I am *entirely* at your disposal,' 'He died *far* from his native land,' the adverb looks as if it modified a preposition, but it really modifies the whole adverbial phrase.]

10. Give examples of adverbs formed from nouns, pronouns, adjectives, and by combining various parts of speech.

11. What are the adverbs corresponding to the adjectives *shy, far, sly, fast, kindly, gay* ?

Explain the forms *betimes, whilom, piecemeal, ashore.*

[With *-meal* in *piecemeal* compare German *-mal* in *einmal.* The suffix represents an old English word signifying 'piece,' 'measure,' which was used in the dative plural to form adverbs.]

12.   Point out any difference in the adverbial use of *very* and *much.*

[*Very* qualifies adjectives in the positive and the superlative degree: *e.g.* 'a very steep hill,' 'the very steepest hill.' *Much* qualifies adjectives in the comparative degree: *e.g.* 'a much steeper hill.' Again, *very* should not be used to qualify participles when used as participles. Thus we cannot say 'He is very amusing the company,' and we ought not to say 'The company seemed very amused.' Participles used as adjectives may, however, be qualified by *very*: *e.g.* 'He is a very amusing fellow'; 'The company wore a very amused expression.']

CHAPTER XIX.

195. A Preposition is a word which is used with a noun or pronoun to show its relation to some other word in the sentence.

Case was defined as the form of a noun or pronoun by which we show its relation to some other word in the sentence. But the relations in which a noun may stand are far more numerous than those which the supply of cases, even in an inflexional language like Latin, will enable us to represent. And in a non-inflexional language like our own, we are almost entirely dependent on Prepositions for the means of expressing these relations. Thus the Romans, like ourselves, had recourse to prepositions when they said 'before the town,' 'against the town,' 'through the town,' 'across the town,' *ante urbem*, *contra urbem*, *per urbem*, *trans urbem*, although case-endings served their purpose in some instances in which we have to fall back on prepositions, and they could say *moenia urbis*, 'the walls *of* the town,' *dat agros urbi*, 'he gives lands *to* the town.'

196. A preposition and noun together form a phrase which is equivalent to either an adjective or an adverb. So, 'a statesman *of eminence*' is 'an *eminent* statesman'; 'a town *in Holland*' is 'a *Dutch* town'; 'a man *without education*' is 'an *uneducated* man.' The combination here is adjectival. In the following examples it is adverbial: *by force, in a* *curious fashion, with courage, at the present time, from this spot:* for these phrases we might substitute the adverbs *forcibly, curiously, courageously, now, hence.*

197. In the language of grammar we speak of the preposition as 'governing' the noun or pronoun to which it is attached. In Greek, or Latin, or German, the student finds it a serious business to learn the cases which follow the various prepositions, but in modern English, owing to the loss of inflexions, we are spared any trouble of this kind. The noun governed by the preposition is 'in the objective case,' and the form of the objective is identical with the form of the nominative. In the pronouns the differences of form are limited to the pronouns of the First, Second, and Third Persons, and to the Relative *who.*

Notice however that, though we speak of the noun as governed by the preposition, it is not necessary that the noun should come after the preposition. The preposition is often put at the end of the sentence. So, we may say 'This is the boy *whom* I gave it *to,*' '*What* are you talking *about?*' and the construction is the same as if we had said 'This is the boy *to whom* I gave it,' '*About what* are you talking?'

198. Prepositions might be classified, as Adverbs were classified in the preceding chapter, according to their meaning. But such a classification would be out of place in an elementary book. The relations in which things stand to other things are so various that the prepositions expressing these relations would require a large number of classes for their arrangement. Or, if the number of classes were small, the names of the classes would necessarily be so vague that the student would attach to them no clear and distinct meaning. Then again, the classification would be complicated by the fact that the same preposition is used in widely different senses and would therefore have its place in several groups. As an illustration of this, let us notice some of the relations indicated by the preposition *by*. We can use it to mark time, 'by day'; or instrument, 'stunned by a blow'; or agency, 'stabbed by Brutus'; or manner, 'hung by the neck'; or measure, 'sold by the pound'; or place, 'he lives by the river'; or as an appeal, 'I beg you by whatever you hold dear'; and these are not all of its meanings.

199. We may also classify Prepositions according to their **Origin.**

(1) Some are Simple : *at, by, to, up, on.*

(2) Others are Compound : *throughout, within, upon, into.*

(3) A few are Participles: *considering, regarding, concerning, during, pending.*

200. The use of *considering*, or *regarding*, as a true participle may be seen in such sentences as these: 'Considering the temptation, they let him off,' *i.e.* 'They, considering the temptation, let him off': 'Regarding your conduct, I am shocked,' *i.e.* 'I, regarding your conduct, am shocked.' But when we say, 'Considering the temptation, he was allowed to get off,' *considering* means 'in consideration of' and has become a preposition: when we say, 'Regarding your statement, you have been misinformed,' *regarding* means 'with regard to' and has become a preposition. The use of *concerning* as a preposition occurs in the A.V. in the passage, 'Now concerning the collection...even so do ye,' (1 Cor. xvi. 1): its participial origin is seen in such an expression as this ; 'Your remarks concerning me are unfounded.' Commercial men are quite needlessly pressing the participle 'referring to' into their service as a preposition, and their letters begin in this objectionable fashion: 'Referring to yours of yesterday lard has gone up.' Here *referring to* is used as a preposition signifying 'with reference to' and is no longer a participle: if it were, the construction would be 'lard referring to your letter,' which is absurd.

Some of these forms may be explained as originally Absolute constructions of the participle: '*during* the day' arose from 'the day during,' or 'lasting': '*pending* the verdict,' from 'the verdict pending,' or 'being in suspense': '*notwithstanding* the storm,' from 'the storm not withstanding,' or 'obstructing.' A similar explanation applies to *except*, which springs from the Latin past participle: 'all *except* John' was originally 'all, John having been excepted.' *Save*, as a preposition, exhibits the same absolute construction: the word is here an adjective equivalent to *safe*. So, 'all, *save* one' was 'all, one being safe.'

201. The beginner will find little difficulty in distinguishing between the functions of the same word as Preposition and as Adverb, if he remembers that a **Preposition is used with a noun or its substitute and governs it**: where there is no noun thus governed, the word in question is not a preposition. A few examples will make this clear: the following words are used as

Prepositions	Adverbs
He is *on* the roof.	Put it *on*.
Take it *off* the table.	Take it *off*.
He is gone *down* the town.	He is gone *down*.
It lies *beyond* the river.	It lies *beyond*.
We went *along* the bank.	Go *along*.

QUESTIONS.

1. Give the definition and derivation of (*a*) *pronoun*, (*b*) *preposition*. Shew how your answers apply to the words printed in italics in the following:—

> 'To be, or not to be,—*that* is the question.'
> 'They had nothing to amuse themselves *with*.'

['Pronoun' from Latin, *pro*, 'for,' *nomen*, 'name'. 'Preposition' from *prae*, 'in front', *positus*, 'placed', not because prepositions are usually placed before nouns, for they often come after them, but because in Greek and Latin they were prefixed to verbs to form compounds. The derivation of the name is only a source of embarrassment to beginners, as it suggests order in a sentence, with which it has nothing to do.

Remember that the infinitive is equivalent to a noun. What nouns can we substitute for 'to be,' 'not to be'?]

2. Specify the notions expressed by the preposition *on* in the following examples of its use:—'It rests *on* the earth'—'Weston is *on* the sea'—'He lectures *on* medicine'—'We returned *on* Saturday'—'The dew descended *on* the parched earth'—'He made an attack *on* the enemy'—'He started *on* receiving the telegram'—'He gave up business *on* account of his health.' [See Bain's *Higher English Grammar*, pp. 90—1.]

3. Construct sentences illustrating some of the principal uses of *for* and *of*.

4. In the following quotations from Shakespeare substitute prepositions in accordance with modern idiom[1]:—

'Have we eaten *on* the insane root?'
'Steal *forth* thy father's house.'
'From *out* the fiery portal of the East.'
'Sounds of music creep *in* our ears.'
'Our fears *in* Banquo stick deep.'
'We'll deliver you *of* your great danger.'
'A proper man *of* mine honour.'
'A plague *of* all cowards!'
'I stay here *on* my bond.'
'Prepare yourself *to* death.'
'The lady Beatrice hath a quarrel *to* you.'
'I live *with* bread like you.'

5. Express with the aid of a preposition the idea represented by the first part of these compound nouns :—*gravy-spoon, steam-ship, war-ship, land-breeze, sea-captain, Convalescent-Home, ground-swell, play-ground, life-preserver, wheel-barrow.*

6. What idea was originally represented by prepositions in English?
[Relations in space. These purely local meanings were then extended to express relations of time and of cause. So, *of* and *off* were once the same word; *by* meant 'close to'; *for* meant 'before.' See Mason's *English Grammar,* pp. 116—9.]

7. In the following phrases, is the use of the preposition inconsistent with its definition?—(*a*) *in short, after all, at last, for better, for worse:* (*b*) *till now, for ever, since then, from here.*
[In (*a*) the preposition is joined to adjectives which are used without the noun which they limit. In (*b*) the preposition is joined to adverbs employed as nouns: *now* is equivalent to 'the present time,' *ever,* to 'all time.' When these words are parsed, the adjectives should be described as adjectives used for nouns, or as adjectives with the ellipsis of nouns, and the adverbs as adverbs used for nouns.]

8. Write down the prepositions in the following lines and make short sentences to illustrate different uses of each:—

'As when upon a tranced summer night,
Those green-robed senators of mighty woods,
Tall oaks, branch-charmed by the earnest stars,
Dream, and so dream all night without a stir.'

[1] Selected from Abbott's *Shakespearian Grammar.*

9. Paraphrase the meanings of the prepositions in—

(*a*) ‘ Have it ready *by* to-morrow.’

(*b*) ‘ I shall do my duty *by* him.’

(*c*) ‘ It lies south *by* west.’

(*d*) ‘ He married *for* love.’

(*e*) ‘ *For* all his efforts, he remained poor.’

(*f*) ‘ The soldiers were *under* arms : *at* the word of command they stood *at* attention.’

10. Give four examples to show that the meaning of a verb may be differently modified by a preposition or an adverb according as the preposition or adverb is attached to the verb as a prefix or written after it.

[As, *e.g. understand* and *stand under.*]

11. Interpret the following pairs of sentences and comment on the idiomatic use of *but* which they exemplify :—

    1. (*a*) ‘ This specimen is all but perfect.’

       (*b*) ‘ This specimen is anything but perfect.’

    2. (*c*) ‘ I can but feel sorry.’

       (*d*) ‘ I cannot but feel sorry.’

[The idiomatic uses of *but* are full of difficulty. From its literal sense ‘ outside of ’ (*by-out*) the preposition *but* came to mean ‘ without,’ ‘ except.’ In the first pair of sentences substitute *except* for *but*. We can understand how the phrases *all but* and *anything but* arose, but it is curious that their meanings should be diametrically opposite. See Abbott’s *How to Parse*, p. 259.

In the second pair of sentences the presence or absence of the *not* leaves the meaning unaffected. In (*c*) we may substitute *only* for *but*, and in (*d*) we may supply an ellipsis : ‘ I cannot *do anything* but (*i.e.* except) feel sorry.’ See Mason’s *English Grammar*, § 538, where however it is maintained that in (*c*) a negative is improperly omitted.]

CHAPTER XX.

CONJUNCTIONS AND INTERJECTIONS.

202. A Conjunction is a word, other than a relative pronoun or conjunctive adverb, which joins words and sentences.

All conjunctions can join sentences together, but all words which join sentences are not conjunctions. 'This is the man who stole the money' contains two clauses, 'This is the man: (he) stole the money'; the two clauses are united by the relative pronoun *who* and form one complex sentence. The reader will remember that the distinguishing mark of a relative pronoun is this, that it has the force of a conjunction. But it is not itself a conjunction. Again, 'I know where he lives' contains two clauses, 'I know (the fact): he lives there'; the two clauses are united by the conjunctive adverb *where* and form one complex sentence.

203. What do Conjunctions join,—Sentences, or Words, or both ?

Conjunctions usually connect sentences even when they appear to connect only words. 'John *and* Mary are good players' is an elliptical or abbreviated way of saying 'John is a good player,' 'Mary is a good player.' But in some cases *and* connects words only, and there is no contraction or abridgement of two separate sentences. 'John and Mary are a handsome couple' cannot be resolved into 'John

is a handsome couple,' 'Mary is a handsome couple.'
'Two and two make four' is not a compact way of saying
'Two makes four,' 'Two makes four.' With the exception
however of the occasional use of *and* to join words, conjunctions join sentences. Thus 'He was poor but honest'
contains two statements ; 'He was poor: he was honest.'
'He is neither a knave nor a fool' means 'He is not a
knave : he is not a fool.' ' He is either a knave or a fool '
means ' He is either a knave, or he is a fool.'

204. Conjunctions are classified as (1) Co-
ordinating and (2) Subordinating.

(1) **Co-ordinating** Conjunctions join co-ordinate or
independent clauses : *e.g. and, but, either...or, neither...
nor.*

(2) **Subordinating** Conjunctions join a dependent
clause to the principal clause : *e.g. that, after, till, because,
though, if.*

205. The reader must now prepare himself to grapple
with a part of the subject which will present greater difficulties and call for the exercise of more intelligence than any
of the problems which he has hitherto encountered in the
study of grammar. Before going further, we must explain
the meaning of the terms *co-ordinate, dependent, clause,* which
have been introduced into the definitions of conjunctions
and classes of conjunctions. The discussion of these words
belongs indeed to syntax rather than to etymology. But
we have reached the threshold of syntax and may cross the
threshold without straying far beyond the strict limits of our
present subject ; for it is only by saying now some of the
things which would more properly be said in the concluding
chapters of the book, that we can hope to make the treatment of conjunctions intelligible.

A **Sentence** is a collection of words by which we say
something about a thing. The word which stands for the

thing about which we make the assertion is called the **Subject** of the sentence. The word by which we make the assertion about the thing is called the **Predicate**.

If a sentence contains only one subject and one finite verb, it is a **Simple** sentence: 'The general was knighted,' 'He told me this,' 'He gave me a contribution,' are simple sentences.

If a sentence contains two or more independent clauses joined by co-ordinating conjunctions, it is a **Compound** sentence: 'The general was knighted *and* presented with the freedom of the city,' 'He *neither* told me this, *nor* did he hint it,' 'He gave me a contribution *but* he grudged it,' are compound sentences, each of which contains two parts entirely independent. These two parts might form separate sentences without affecting the sense of the compound sentence.

But if a sentence contains two or more clauses, one of which is dependent on the other, it is a **Complex** sentence: 'The general *who won the victory* was knighted,' 'He told me *that the prisoner had escaped*,' 'He gave me a contribution *because he approved of the object*,' are complex sentences. The groups of words in italics contain, it is true, their own subjects and finite verbs. But they are not independent sentences: they occupy the place of an adjective, a noun, or an adverb, in relation to the rest of the sentence of which they form a part. Hence they are called **Subordinate Clauses.**

Thus in the sentence 'The general who won the victory was knighted,' the clause 'who won the victory' is equivalent to *victorious* and limits the application of the noun 'general.' It is an adjectival clause.

In the sentence 'He told me that the prisoner had escaped,' the clause 'that the prisoner had escaped' occupies the same position as might be occupied by such words as 'the fact,' or 'the rumour.' *The fact* or *the rumour* is a noun. Hence the clause, as it takes the place of a noun, is a noun clause.

In the sentence 'He gave me a contribution because he approved of the object,' the clause 'because he approved of the object' modifies the application of the verb *gave*, stating *why* he gave it. The words by which we limit the application of verbs are adverbs: 'He gave me a contribution approvingly, or cordially, or readily,' would express, approximately though not exactly, the same thing as 'He gave me a contribution because he approved of the object.' Such a clause as this, since it takes the place of an adverb, is an adverbial clause.

The sentences which form parts of an entire sentence we shall call **clauses.** 'The general won the victory and was knighted' is a Compound sentence consisting of the two co-ordinate or independent clauses: 'The general won the victory,' 'The general was knighted.' 'The general who won the victory was knighted' is a Complex sentence consisting of a principal clause, 'The general was knighted,' and a subordinate adjectival clause, 'who won the victory,' referring to 'general' in the principal clause. 'The general was knighted because he won the victory' is a Complex sentence consisting of a principal clause, 'The general was knighted,' and a subordinate adverbial clause, 'because he won the victory,' modifying 'was knighted.'

206. No rule of thumb can be supplied which shall enable the student to determine whether a subordinate clause is an adjective-clause, noun-clause, or adverb-clause, without the exercise of his wits. The same collection of words may be adjectival, substantival, or adverbial, in three different complex sentences. Take the words, 'where the battle was fought.' A beginner, recognising an adverb in the first word 'where,' might jump to the conclusion that a clause which begins with an adverb must be an adverbial clause. But the nature of the clause is not to be settled in this way: we must look at the clause in its relation to the principal clause and see what sort of work it does,—whether it does the work of an adjective, of a noun, or of an adverb. Observe its different functions in these three complex sentences:

    1. 'The spot where-the-battle-was-fought is unknown.'
    2. 'Where-the-battle-was-fought is unknown.'
    3. 'I live where-the-battle-was-fought.'

In (1), *where-the-battle-was-fought* is adjectival, limiting 'spot'; in like manner we might say 'the *exact* spot is unknown.'

In (2), it is a noun-clause, equivalent to 'The *spot* is unknown,' 'The *fact* is unknown,' '*It* is unknown.'

In (3), it is adverbial, modifying the verb 'live,' just as an adverb would modify it in the sentence 'I live *there*.'

When the reader has mastered the distinction between compound and complex sentences and between the three kinds of subordinate clauses, one or other of which every complex sentence contains, analysis will present very few difficulties to him. But his analysis of complex sentences will generally be wrong, if he attempts the task without an intelligent grasp of the principles which have been stated above. From this digression into syntax we must now return to the subject of conjunctions from which we may seem to have wandered far.

207. The reader should now be able readily to grasp our meaning when we say that **co-ordinating** conjunctions are those which **unite co-ordinate clauses**; and that **subordinating** conjunctions are those which **join subordinate clauses to the principal clause** of a complex sentence.

The subordinate clauses which a subordinating conjunction introduces are noun-clauses or adverbial clauses. Adjective-clauses are attached to the principal clause by a relative pronoun or by a relative adverb; as, 'The general *who* won the victory was knighted,' which is equivalent to 'The victorious general was knighted'; 'The house *where* nobody lives is to be pulled down,' which is equivalent to 'The empty house is to be pulled down.' Noun-clauses are generally introduced by *that*, and occur especially after verbs of saying, thinking, believing, asking, hoping, seeing, and others of similar import: 'I say that *he did it*,' 'I think that *this is so*.' But *that* is not essential to a noun-clause: thus the following clauses in italics are noun-clauses; 'I see *how you did it*,' '*When he did it* is not clear,' 'He asked *if I did it*,' 'We heard *you had gone*.'

208. The subordinating conjunctions by which adverbial clauses are introduced may be classified according to the various modes of dependence which they indicate, as—

1. Introductory or Appositional—*that.*

2. Conditional—*if, unless.*

3. Concessive—*though.*

4. Temporal—*after, till, while, as.*

5. Consecutive, marking Result—*that* ('so that').

6. Final, marking Purpose—*that* ('in order that'), *lest.*

7. Causal—*because, since, as.*

8. Comparative—*than, as.*

209. Conjunctions have grown out of other parts of speech.

The conjunction *that* was originally the neuter demonstrative pronoun. ' I know *that* you did it' represents 'You did it : I know *that*,' the order of the clauses being reversed. *Both,* used with *and,* is the same word as the adjective ; *either,* used with *or,* is the same word as the distributive pronoun. *Than, though, while,* were once adverbs. *Before, after, since,* were once prepositions and were followed by 'that.' To distinguish Conjunctions from Prepositions is easy : Conjunctions never govern a case. To distinguish Conjunctions from Adverbs is often difficult, and our remarks on the distinction shall be reserved till we are dealing with the Syntax of Adverbs and Conjunctions. (See p. 255.)

210. Conjunctions which occur in pairs are called **Correlatives** : *both...and, either...or, so...as, so...that, as...so, whether...or,* are examples of Correlative Conjunctions.

211. Interjections.

An Interjection is a sound which expresses an emotion but does not enter into the construction of the sentence.

As Interjections have no connexion with the grammatical structure of the sentence, their claim to recognition among the Parts of Speech is a small one. *O ! ah ! pooh ! psha !* like the barking of a dog or the lowing of a calf, are noises, not words. If there were any advantage in classifying these sounds, we might group them according to the feelings which they express, as Interjections denoting joy, disgust, surprise, vexation, and so forth.

Interjections which are corruptions or contractions of words, or elliptical forms of expression, may be referred to the parts of speech to which they originally belong. So, *adieu* is 'to God (I commend you),' *goodbye* is 'God be with you,' *hail !* is 'be thou hale' or 'healthy,' *law !* or *lawks !* is a corruption of 'Lord !' and *marry !* of ' Mary !'

QUESTIONS.

1. What are Correlative Conjunctions? Give the correlatives of *either, though, both*, and of *such* and *so* with different senses.

2. *What, since, well.* Illustrate by short sentences the various grammatical uses of each of these words, and mention in every instance its part of speech in your sentence.

3. Construct three Complex sentences, each containing as its subordinate clause the words *when the accident happened*. In the first sentence the subordinate clause is to be a noun clause, in the second an adjective clause, and in the third an adverbial clause.

CHAPTER XXI.

Compounds and Derivatives.

212. If we were to read down a column of words on a page of an English dictionary, we should find that the great majority of these words have been formed from other words, either by joining two words together, or by adding to a word a sound which by itself is without meaning. Thus from *man* in combination with other words there have been made *freeman, mankind, midshipman, footman,* while, by the addition of an element which has no significance alone, *manly, unman, mannikin,* have come into existence. The former process is called **Composition,** the latter **Derivation**: words made by the former process are called **Compounds,** by the latter, **Derivatives.** The terms 'Derivation' and 'Derivative' are not well chosen, as their meaning is here narrowed down from the sense in which they are generally used. When we speak of the *derivation* of a word we usually signify the source from which it comes: thus we say that *phenomenon* is of Greek 'derivation' and *vertex* of Latin 'derivation,' though as these words have been transferred ready-made from foreign languages they are not, in this special sense, English derivatives at all. But the employment of the terms *derivation* and *derivative,* in contrast with the terms *composition* and *compound,* is too well established to allow of our making a change, and the student must therefore bear in mind that when used in this connexion they indicate an important distinction in the mode of the formation of words.

Composition is the formation of a word by joining words together.

Derivation is the formation of a word—

(1) by adding a part not significant by itself,

or, **(2) by modifying an existing sound.**

The part not significant by itself when attached at the beginning of a word is called a **Prefix**; when attached at the end, a **Suffix**.

A Hybrid is a compound or derivative containing elements which come from different languages.

213. Unlike Greek and German, modern English does not lend itself readily to the formation of long compounds. If the reader cares to turn to his Greek lexicon and to look up the word beginning ὀρθροφοιτο- or the still more formidable λεπαδοτεμαχο-, he will see this facility for making compounds burlesqued by Aristophanes. A humourist of our own day, Mark Twain, deals with German compounds in a like playful fashion.

In compound words, the first word usually modifies the meaning of the second. A *ring-finger* is a particular kind of finger; a *finger-ring* a particular kind of ring. In true grammatical compounds there is usually a change of form or of accent. So *spoonful* is a true grammatical compound of *spoon full*. *Poorhouse* and *Newport* carry an accent on the first syllable as compounds: as separate words each of the two is accented equally. Compare 'a poor house by the new port' with 'the poórhouse at Néwport.' Words joined by a hyphen with no change of form or of accent are merely printers' compounds.

214. Words disguised in form.

The appearance of some words is deceptive, suggesting as it does that they are compounds when they are not, or that they contain elements which do not really belong to them. Examples of this are seen in *cray-fish*, really from *écrevisse*, 'a crab,' and quite unconnected with 'fish': *causeway*, the same word as *chaussée*, and nothing to do with 'way': *kickshaws* from *quelques-choses*, *goodbye* from *God be with you !* *shame-faced* for *shamefast*, 'fast' or 'firm in shame,' *i.e.* in modesty, formed like *steadfast*.

215. Derivatives are generally formed **by means of prefixes or suffixes**: a few however are formed without the addition of a new sound **by the change of an existing sound**. Thus from *glass* we get *glaze*; from *sit*, *set*; from *fall*, *fell*; from *drink*, *drench*; from *gold*, *gild*; from *tale*, *tell*. In these cases we have modification but not addition.

Prefixes and Suffixes once possessed a meaning and existed as separate words. Thus the ending *ly* represents the word *like*: *godlike* and *godly* contain elements originally the same, but *godlike* is now described as a compound, and *godly* as a derivative.

216. A few of the more important Suffixes are given here for the purpose of illustration. They are distinguished according to (1) their *force*, (2) their *origin*. In the following list, Suffixes derived from the Romance languages are described as of Classical origin.

Noun Suffixes.
Diminutives :

(*a*) of English origin: maid-*en*, cock-e-*rel*, kern-*el* (from *corn*), lass-*ie* or bab-*y*, farth-*ing* (small *fourth* part), duck-*l·ing*, lamb-*kin*, bund-*le* (from *bind*), hill-*ock*.

(*b*) Of Classical origin: glob-*ule*, animal-*cule*, parti-*cle*, mors-*el*, violon-*cello*, vermi-*celli*, rivu-*let*, lanc-*et*, cigar-*ette*.

Notice that some of the latter group are not English formations: the words are diminutives in the foreign language from which we borrowed them, but they are not English diminutives any more than *testatrix* is an English feminine.

Diminutives sometimes express not smallness but (1) endearment, *darling*, *Charlie*, or (2) contempt, *mannikin*, *worldling*, *wastrel*.

Augmentatives express the opposite idea to that expressed by Diminutives:

Classical: drunk-*ard*, wiz-*ard*. The suffix -*ard*, though ultimately of Teutonic origin, comes to us from Old French -*ard*. *Sweetheart* is a compound of *sweet heart*, and not, as has been thought, an augmentative, sweet-*ard*. Other augmentative endings appear in ball-*oon*, tromb-*one* (a big trumpet), milli-*on* (a big thousand).

Denoting agent:

(*a*) English: law-*yer*, garden-*er*, sail-*or*, li-*ar*.

(*b*) Classical: act-*or*, preach-*er*, bombard-*ier*, engin-*eer*, secret-*ary*; (Greek) crit-*ic*, anarch-*ist*, enthusi-*ast*, patri-*ot*.

Marking feminine gender:

(*a*) English: spin-*ster*, vix-*en*.

(*b*) Classical: govern-*ess*, testatr-*ix*, (Greek) hero-*ine*.

Act, state, quality, are denoted by many suffixes:

(*a*) English: free-*dom*, brother-*hood*, god-*head*, dark-*ness*, friend-*ship*, tru-*th*, gif-*t*, hat-*red*, slaugh-*ter*.

(*b*) Classical: bond-*age*, infam-*y*, matri-*mony*, just-*ice*, opin-*ion*, forti-*tude*, cruel-*ty*, cult-*ure*, prud-*ence*, brilli-*ance*.

ADJECTIVE SUFFIXES.

Denoting the possession of a quality:

(*a*) English: quarrel-*some*, god-*ly*, wood-*en*, north-*ern*, thirst-*y*, wretch-*ed*.

(*b*) Classical: leg-*al*, mund-*ane*, instant-*aneous*, lun-*ar*, div-*ine*, tim-*id*, sens-*ible*, frag-*ile*, nat-*ive*, test-*y*, brilli-*ant*.

The -*ed* in 'wretched' is the ending of the past participle, but it is attached to nouns as well as to verbs to form adjectives, as in 'horn-*ed*,' 'feather-*ed*,' 'kind-heart-*ed*.' A great outcry was raised some years ago against the words *gifted, talented, moneyed,* and a few similar adjectives, on the ground that they are formed like participles, but that there are no verbs from which they come. If however we can talk of a 'wretch-*ed* beggar,' there seems no reason why we should not talk of a 'gift-*ed* poet.' The further objection was brought against *talented* and *moneyed* that they are hybrids, since *talent* comes from the Greek and *money* from the Latin. But the same objection might be urged against the past participle of every weak verb of foreign origin in the language, from *preached* down to *telegraphed*.

Possession of a quality in a high degree is indicated by (English) care-*ful*, (Classical) verb-*ose*, glori-*ous*: in a low degree by (English) black-*ish*; and the absence of a quality by (English) fear-*less*, hope-*less*, where -*less* stands for *loose*, meaning 'free from,' and is not connected with the comparative adjective *less*.

Verb Suffixes.

Causative:

(*a*) English: sweet-*en*; (*b*) Classical: magni-*fy* (Latin *facio*).

Other verbal suffixes, of English origin, are seen in clean-*se*, start-*le*; and of Latin origin in flour-*ish* (*floresco*), facilit-*ate*. The common ending -*ize*, or -*ise*, is of Greek origin: critic-*ize*, theor-*ise*.

Frequentative:

(*a*) English: flut-t-*er* (from *float*), sput-t-*er* (from *spout*), scut-t-*le* (from *scud*).

Hybrids. As our vocabulary is composed of words from Latin, Greek, and native sources, hybrids are naturally numerous. Indeed, as the grammatical forms of our language are almost entirely of English origin, any word from a Latin or Greek source which takes our English inflexions might in strictness be called a hybrid.

The term is usually reserved however for words which obtrusively present a combination of different elements: such are *bi-gamy* and *bi-cycle*, because *bi(s)* is Latin and the remainder is Greek. *Journal-ist* combines Latin and Greek, *mon-ocular* Greek and Latin; *shepherd-ess* English and French, *grand-father*, French and English; *false-hood*, Latin and English; *un-fortunate*, English and Latin.

217. The following are a few of the principal Prefixes, classified as English, Latin, or Greek, according to their origin[1].

English:

a-, usual meaning 'on': *a*-foot, *a*-bed.

be-, from preposition 'by': (i) changes the meaning of a transitive verb, *be*-hold, *be*-set: (ii) converts an intransitive to a transitive, *be*-moan, *be*-wail: (iii) has an intensive force, *be*-daub, *be*-praise.

for-, not the preposition 'for': (i) intensive force, *for*-bear: (ii) privative, *for*-get, *for*-swear. Notice that *fore*-go ('to go without'), *fore*-do, should be *for*-go, *for*-do: the verb *fore*-go means 'to go before.'

fore-, as in 'be-*fore*': *fore*-tell, *fore*-see.

mis-, with sense of 'a-*miss*': *mis*-deed, *mis*-take.

un-, (i) meaning 'not': *un*-wise, *un*-belief: (ii) marking the reversal of an action; *un*-fasten, *un*-wind, *un*-lock.

with-, meaning 'against': *with*-stand, *with*-draw.

Latin:

a-, ab-, abs-, 'from': *a*-vert, *ab*-rupt, *abs*-tain.

ad-, 'to': *ad*-jective; variously modified, *e.g. ab*-breviate, *ac*-cuse, *af*-fable, *ag*-gravate, *al*-ly, *an*-nex, *ap*-pear, *ar*-rears, *as*-size, *at*-tain, *a*-vow.

---

[1] For complete list see Skeat's *Concise Etymological Dictionary*, pp. 624—630, or Nesfield's *English Grammar Past and Present*, pp. 378—417.

ante-, 'before,' *ante*-chamber.

bi-, bis-, 'twice,' *bi*-ped, *bis*-cuit.

contra-, 'against,' *contra*-dict, *counter*-march.

in-, (i) 'in': *in*-fuse, *im*-pel, *en*-rol: (ii) 'not': *in*-sensible, *im*-possible, *ir*-responsible.

minus-, '*mis*-chief,' with meaning of English prefix *mis*-, but of different origin.

non-, 'not': *non*-conformity.

per-, 'through': *per*-secute, *pur*-sue, *per*-jure, (compare '*for*-swear').

re-, 'again,' 'back': *re*-cur, *re*-turn.

super-, 'over': *super*-fine, *sur*-vive, *sir*-loin.

vice-, 'instead of': *vice*-roy, *vis*-count.

GREEK:

an-, a-, 'not': *an*-archy, *a*-theist.

ana-, 'again,' 'back': *ana*-logy, *ana*-lyse.

anti-, 'against': *anti*-pathy, *ant*-agonist. In *anti*-cipate however we have Latin *ante*.

archi-, 'chief': *archi*-tect, *arche*-type, *arch*-bishop.

auto-, 'self': *auto*-biography, *auto*-maton.

ek-, ex-, 'out of': *ec*-logue, *ex*-odus.

eu-, 'well': *eu*-logy, *ev*-angelical.

hyper-, 'beyond': *hyper*-bolical.

meta-, 'change': *meta*-phor.

mono-, 'single': *mono*-poly, *mon*-arch.

pan-, panto-, 'all': *pan*-acea, *panto*-mime.

para-, 'beside': *para*-graph.

syn-, 'with': *syn*-od, *syl*-lable, *sym*-bol.

218. Division of Words into Syllables.

A **Syllable** consists of a single vowel sound with or without accompanying consonants. It is pronounced by a single effort of the voice. *Through* is a single syllable, though it contains seven letters: *ideality* with eight letters has five syllables. In *through* there is one vowel sound, the long *o* of *cool*, here represented by *ou*: in *ideality* there are five distinct vowel sounds, with three consonants dispersed amongst them.

There are no hard and fast rules for the division of words into syllables, when a division is necessary in writing. In this matter, as also in the matter of punctuation, writers are very much at the mercy of the printers. From the nature of the case, no division can be made in words of one syllable however long. *Straight, scratch, drought,* contain only one vowel-sound and must be written and printed entire. Two principles should regulate the separation of words of more than one syllable into parts : as far as possible we ought to follow (1) the etymology, (2) the pronunciation.

Hence the hyphen is placed between the prefix or suffix and the root of derivatives, and between the constituent parts of compounds : *en-large, duch-ess, free-man.* But sometimes the division according to pronunciation is at variance with the division according to etymology. For example, *orthography, geology,* would be divided thus, if we follow the pronunciation as our guide,—*orthog-raphy, geol-ogy,* whereas their etymology would direct us to divide them thus,— *ortho-graphy, geo-logy.* In cases of conflict of this kind it is generally best to place the hyphen consistently with the etymology [1].

QUESTIONS.

1. Add to each of the following words the prefix which reverses the meaning :—*contented, proper, visible, pleasant, ingenuous, natural.*

2. Define the terms *prefix* and *suffix.* Illustrate your answer by analysing the following words into their component parts :—*believing, darling, forlorn, islet, nethermost, requital, spinster, uncouth.*

3. Does the phrase ' Ærated bread' require correction?

[' Ærated bread' would be bread made of bronze (Latin *aes, aeris*). What sort of bread is sold at the ABC shops, and whence does it get its name?]

4. Break up the words *mistrustfully, unwholesomeness,* into syllables, and explain how each syllable contributes to the meaning of the words.

5. Why are the following words hybrids ?—*forbear-ance, duke-dom, somnambul-ist, un-just, social-ism, master-ship.*

[1] In practice the division is usually made so as to begin a new syllable with a consonant, if possible, and when two consonants come together, to put the former into one syllable and the latter into another. Accordingly we find such divisions as *solilo-quy, peru-sal, fes-tive, par-ticle.* See Skeat's *Student's Pastime,* p. 119.

6. Give the derivation and history of the following words; and mention any case of double meaning, or of change of meaning:— *alderman, defeat, drake, idiot, invalid, involve, kaleidoscope, middle, megrim, monk, orchard, pilgrim, scholar, uncouth.*

7. What are the chief constituent elements of the English language?

Give the derivation of the following words, pointing out any change of meaning:—*ally, agony, dyspeptic, girl, journal, lord, person, ornithologist, poison, rival, sherry, silly, somersault, telegraph, villain, volume.*

8. Give the derivation of the following words, showing from what languages they were taken:—*caitiff, cardinal, frenzy, seraph, nightingale, welkin.*

9. Give the etymology of the following words:—*gazette, tinsel, blame, loyal, archbishop, sheriff.*

10. Which is the right place for the hyphen in the following words? Why?—*sui-cide* or *suic-ide*; *locom-otive* or *loco-motive*; *viad-uct* or *via-duct*; *apo-stle* or *apos-tle*; *epig-ram* or *epi-gram*; *dec-line* or *de-cline*; *sus-pect* or *susp-ect*; *kin-dred* or *kind-red*; *lanc-et* or *lan-cet*; *mor-ning* or *morn-ing*; *hil-lock* or *hill-ock*; *univers-ity* or *univer-sity*; *semin-ary* or *semi-nary*; *catas-trophe* or *cata-strophe.*

11. What is the force of each of the following prefixes, and from what language does it come? Give a word in illustration:—*with-, contra-, dia-, sub-, per-, sym-, arch-, un-, ab-.*

12. Point out the prefixes in the following words and give their force:—*extract, misuse, retrograde, antecedent, antipathy, outdo, besmear, accede, ignoble, immense.*

13. What is the force of the *-en* in each of the following words?— gold-*en*, sweet-*en*, vix-*en*, childr-*en*, maid-*en*.

14. Give the force of the suffixes in these words:—black-*ish*, yeoman-*ry*, spin-*ster*, malt-*ster*, young-*ster*, doct-*or*, dar-*ling*, man-*hood*, god-*head*, free-*dom*, lanc-*et*, ring-*let*, shad-*ow*.

15. Give the Primary Derivatives from the following words :—*hale, sit, weave, deep, lie, bath, love.*

[By a Primary Derivative is here meant a word formed from another word as its root, by the addition of a sound not significant alone, or by the modification of an existing sound. Thus from *strong* is formed *strength*, where we have both addition and modification; from *glass* is formed *glaze*, where we have modification only. Now if, from the Primary Derivatives, fresh words are formed by similar processes, these words are called Secondary Derivatives. So, from the Primary Derivative *strength* we form *strengthen*; from *glaze, glazier. Strengthen* and *glazier* are Secondary Derivatives.]

16. Distinguish derivatives and compounds.

Comment on the following formations:—*witticism, oddity, wondrous, honeyed.*

[Some of the words are hybrids. For *honeyed* read p. 202.]

17. Reverse the meaning of each of the following words by adding a prefix: *happy, possible, rational, contented, valid, noble, sense.*

Give four examples of *diminutive* forms in English nouns.

What is meant by saying that the word *bicycle* is a hybrid?

18. Write three derivatives with English suffixes, three with Latin, three with Greek, and three with French.

19. What suffixes are used in English to express diminutiveness (*a*) in nouns, (*b*) in adjectives, (*c*) in verbs?

Mention suffixes which indicate (1) agency, (2) state.

[With reference to (*c*) observe that the frequentative endings have also in some instances a diminutive force: glim-m-*er* (from *gleam*), gam-b-*le* (from *game*), dazz-*le* (from *daze*), wadd-*le* (from *wade*) are examples.]

20. In the following words what is the force of the parts printed in italics?—*a*round, numer*ous*, govern*esses*, *re*cite, Engl*ish*.

21. Why is it important which part of a compound word is placed first?

22. State the meaning of the following prefixes and suffixes:— *for*lorn, *mis*use, *abs*tract, *be*speak, liveli*hood*, whit*en*, swin*ish*, satch*el*.

23. Mention the force of the following suffixes and the language from which each is derived: *-fy, -ness, -ion, -ible, -en, -isk, -ly, -tude.*

24. What is the force of the following prefixes and suffixes?—*fore-, in-, meta-, -en, -le, -er.*

Explain and derive the words *umpire, icicle, jovial, tawdry, sirloin, squirrel, trivial, utopian, solecism, boycott.*

25. By the addition of prefixes or suffixes convert the following adjectives into verbs:—*large, just, strong, wide, dim, clean, dear.*

26. Mention some suffixes by the addition of which we form (1) adjectives from nouns, (2) nouns from adjectives, (3) verbs from nouns or adjectives, (4) adverbs from pronouns.

27. With what familiar English root-words can you connect the following derivatives?—*ditch, wander, gift, month, husband, length, woof, seed, burden, forlorn, vixen, shadow.*

28. Give the meaning and account for the form of each of the following words:—*kine, riches, rather, naught, hillock, surname.*

29. Comment on the forms of the words *empress, alms, nearer, none, atheism, surface.*

30. By the use of a suffix change each of the following nouns into an adjective:—*sister, fame, quarrel, slave, silver.*

31. Distinguish the meanings of *older* and *elder*; *latest* and *last*; *masterly* and *masterful*; *virtuous* and *virtual*; *stationary* and *stationery*; *idiotic* and *idiomatic*; *idol* and *idyll*; *politic* and *political*; *confident* and *confidant*; *expedient* and *expeditious*; *credible* and *creditable*.

32. Write short notes on the etymology of the following words:— *cambric, dandelion, drawing-room, laconic, nostril, posthumous, tantalise, profusely, bicycle, surgeon.*

33. What is the force of the suffix in *darkness, hillock, friendship, drunkard, farthing*? Can you explain the vowel in the first syllable of *elder, thimble, vixen*? [See § 54, (3).]

34. Explain the force of the adjectival endings *-ish, -ine, -en, -y, -al, -ic, -ous, -less, -some*, adding an example of each.

35. Comment on the structure of the following words and state whether any of them are anomalous in form:— *kine, shepherdess, spinster, unjust, mineralogy, deodorize, children, sovereign, talkative, laughable.*

36. What ideas are indicated by the following suffixes and prefixes?— Jew-*ry*, duck-*ling*, wit-*ness*, trump-*et*, tromb-*one*, *a*-board, *Arch*-duke.

37. Mention English words containing prefixes and suffixes of Latin and Greek origin corresponding in their force to the following of native origin:— *al*-mighty, *ill*-starred, *thorough*-fare, *with*-stand, wood-*en*, black-*en*, learn-*ed*.

38. 'In word-building, Prefixes alter the meanings of words and Suffixes alter their functions.' Illustrate this statement.

[The term 'functions' is explained in § 64. The antithesis in the passage quoted above is scarcely accurate, for a word which changes its function must change to some extent its meaning. The writer wishes to call attention however to a distinction which is sometimes real and important. Take, for instance, *kind*. *Unkind* reverses its meaning: *kindly* and *kindness* change its functions. Treat the roots *man, trust, dress, truth*, in a similar way.]

39. Mention some of the chief ways in which the vocabulary of a language may be increased. Give illustrations.

[See the note to Q. 11, p. 20, and think what processes there are, besides importation from foreign sources, by which fresh words may be added to an existing stock.]

40. Mention other English words cognate with *hospital, vision, tenant, victor, sequel.*

[As an example of what is required, let us take the word *frail* and give some of its cognates. *Frail* is a derivative from Latin *frango, fractum*, and from the same ultimate source we obtain *fragile, fracture, fragment, fraction, refraction*, &c. These are called 'cognates.']

CHAPTER XXII.

ANALYSIS OF SENTENCES AND PARSING.

219. Syntax deals with the combination of words in sentences, their government, agreement, and order.

In the course of our treatment of Etymology, many points belonging strictly to the province of Syntax have been already touched upon. The remaining chapters will contain a brief recapitulation of these points, with the addition of such details as are required to complete the information, on the subject of Syntax, which may fairly be looked for in an elementary text-book.

When, in dealing with Conjunctions, we explained the difference between a Compound and a Complex Sentence, our transition from Etymology to Syntax was complete. The student is recommended to read again the remarks on this difference which were made in Chapter xx., as they form a suitable introduction to the concluding section of this book. Syntax has to do with the relations of words to each other in sentences. To enable us intelligently to discuss these relations, it is essential that we should clearly understand the nature of a sentence, the elements of which it is composed, and the varieties of form which it assumes.

220. We described a Sentence as a collection of words by which we say something about a thing.

This account of the nature of a sentence served our purpose at the time when we made use of it, but as a definition applicable to sentences generally it is clearly incomplete. A Sentence may express—

(*a*) A Judgment; 'Birds fly,' 'The Bill will not pass,' 'Brutus killed Caesar.' In such cases we do 'say something about a thing,' or 'make assertions,' and sentences of this kind we took as the type of sentences in general. But in other sentences we give utterance to—

(*b*) A Command; 'Come,' 'Give it me.'

(*c*) A Question; 'Will he come?' 'Did you go?'

(*d*) A Wish; 'Would he were here!' 'May you grow wiser!' 'God save the Queen!'

These four varieties of sentences may be called (1) Declaratory, (2) Imperative, (3) Interrogative, (4) Optative.

Shall we say then that a Sentence is a collection of words expressing a statement, command, question, or wish? This would be an enumeration of different kinds of sentences rather than a definition of a Sentence itself; just as it would be no definition of a triangle, if one were to say that a triangle is an equilateral, isosceles, or scalene figure. Perhaps a better as well as a shorter definition is this:

A Sentence is the complete expression of a thought in words.

In defining the Subject and the Predicate of a Sentence, for the sake of simplicity and conciseness we shall take cognisance only of sentences in which statements are expressed:

The Subject of the sentence is the word which stands for the thing about which the assertion is made.

The Predicate is the word by which the assertion is made.

221. The following points require careful notice:

(1) The Subject of a Sentence is a word, but the assertion is made about the thing. When we say 'The sun shines,' the word *sun* is the subject of the sentence, but we do not assert that the word shines.

(2) Our definition of the Subject of a Sentence, as the word which stands for the thing about which the assertion is made, has been attacked on the ground that, when we say 'Brutus killed Caesar,' we make an assertion about Caesar as much as about Brutus: yet 'Caesar' is not the Subject. To this criticism we may reply that, in the sentence 'Brutus killed Caesar,' our assertion is made directly, or explicitly, about Brutus, but only indirectly, or by implication, about Caesar. The assertion implied about Caesar is given in a direct form when we say 'Caesar was killed by Brutus.'

(3) Cannot a sentence be formed by a single word? Is not 'Go' a sentence?

Here the subject is understood, though not expressed. 'Go' is equivalent to 'Go (you),' and in analysing a sentence in the Imperative mood, we must supply the subject which is omitted in modern English.

(4) The Predicate is a verb or contains a verb. The sentence 'Birds fly' contains a complete predicate 'fly.' But in 'They are,' 'I shall be,' 'You became,' 'Walpole was created,' something is wanting to make sense; the verbs are incomplete predicates and require a **complement** to produce a meaning: 'They are happy,' 'I shall be there,' 'You became secretary,' 'Walpole was created Earl of Orford.'

Again, some verbs need another verb in the Infinitive mood to carry on, or complete, their construction. Thus, 'I wish,' 'You must,' are meaningless unless we supply, in thought or expression, some complement; 'I wish *to go*,'

14—2

'You must *remain*,' 'We are able *to pay*,' 'They ought *to leave*.' These infinitives are called **Prolative**, because they 'carry on' (Latin *profero*, *prolatum*) the meaning of the preceding verb.

222. Different kinds of subjects. As the subject of a sentence is the name of the thing about which we make an assertion, the subject of a sentence must be a noun or the equivalent of a noun. The following sentences illustrate different kinds of subjects :

   1. **Noun** :—'*Birds* fly.'

   2. **Pronoun** :—'*They* were defeated.'

   3. **Infinitive** :—'*To read* good books improves the mind.'

   4. **Adjective** with noun understood :—'*Rich* and *poor* live together.'

   5. **Noun-clause** :—'*That he did it* is certain.'

223. When we join an adjective to a noun, we increase the meaning of the name and consequently limit its application. *White horse* suggests to our minds more attributes than *horse*, but is applicable as a name to only a smaller number of objects. As the adjective thus joined on to the noun attributes to the thing represented by the noun the possession of some quality, we call the adjective an attributive adjunct to the noun, and the noun which stands as the subject of a sentence is said to be **enlarged** or **expanded** by the **attributive adjunct.** So, in the sentence 'White horses are never driven in hearses,' the subject *horses* is *enlarged* or *expanded* by the attributive adjunct *white;* for though the number of things to which we could apply the name *horse* has been limited, or restricted, by the addition of the word *white*, the significance of *white horse* is greater than the significance of horse : *horse* denotes more things, but *white horse* implies more qualities.

The **enlargement or expansion of the Subject is effected by adjectives** and their equivalents :—

1. **Adjective** :—' *Good* wine needs no bush.'

2. **Noun in Apposition** :—' Brunel, *the engineer*, designed the bridge.'

3. **Noun in the Possessive case** :—' *Lucy's* love restrained him,' or its equivalent with *of*, 'The love *of Lucy* restrained him.'

4. **Adjective-clause** :—'The man *who stole the money* was arrested.'

5. **Adjective-phrase** :—'The man, *unsuspicious of any charge against him*, left the town.'

6. **Participle** :—'The candidate, *fuming* and *beaten*, addressed the crowd.'

224. The student must notice the word **Phrase** which is introduced here for the first time. Our vocabulary provides us with three words, *Sentence, Clause,* and *Phrase,* of which we shall avail ourselves in this book in the following manner. A **Sentence** we have already defined and have distinguished three varieties,—Simple, Compound, and Complex. A **Clause** is a part of a sentence containing a finite verb : thus a Compound sentence must contain at least two co-ordinate clauses : ' We stayed, but he left.' A Complex sentence must also contain at least two clauses, one principal, the other subordinate : ' We stayed, after he left.' A collection of words without a finite verb we shall call a **Phrase**. In the sentence 'The boy got the prize,' we may enlarge the subject ' boy ' by an adjective, ' the *industrious* boy'; by an adjective-clause, 'the boy *who was industrious*'; or by an adjective-phrase, ' the boy, *possessed of industrious habits.*' Similarly we may enlarge the predicate by an adverb and say ' The boy got the prize *easily* '; by an adverbial-clause, '*because nobody else went in for it* '; or by an adverbial-phrase, ' *in a very easy fashion.*'

225. The Object of a verb is the word which
stands for the thing towards which the action
indicated by the verb is directed.

There are the same possible substitutes for a noun as
Object as there are for a noun as Subject in a sentence, and
the Object can be enlarged in the same ways as those in
which the Subject was shown to admit of enlargement.
With a little reflexion the reader should be able to make
his own sentences illustrating five different kinds of Object,
and to enlarge the Object in six different ways.

Many verbs take two Objects, one the **Direct,**
the other the **Indirect** or **Dative-like Object.** The
verbs *teach, tell, give, lend, show, provide, refuse, get,* are
examples. The noun which represents the Indirect Object
might be construed with a preposition : thus, 'Give (to) me
the book,' 'Show (to) us the way,' 'Provide (for) him
accommodation,' 'Get (for) me a cab.' See pp. 100, 144.

226. By attaching an adjective to a noun, we increase
the meaning of the noun and limit its application. In like
manner by attaching an adverb to a verb, we increase the
meaning of the verb and limit its application. 'Sings
sweetly' cannot be affirmed of as many individuals as
simply 'sings,' but it signifies more. When we say of
a prima donna 'She sings sweetly,' our statement goes
further in the way of conveying information than the statement that 'she sings.' We may therefore describe the
adverb *sweetly* as an **enlargement** or **extension of the
Predicate** *sings,* because it adds to the meaning of the
Predicate, though it narrows or restricts its application.

The Object of a Transitive Verb has really the force of
an Adverbial Adjunct. If we say 'He loves' and then add
'music,' 'Mary,' 'his country,' 'virtue,' and so on, we limit
in each case the application of the Predicate, but we increase,
or enlarge, or extend, the information which it contains.
The relation of the Object to the Transitive Verb is one of

such importance, however, that our analysis of sentences recognises it as distinct from the other adverbial adjuncts by which the Predicate is enlarged.

The **principal Adverbial Adjuncts** by which the **Predicate is extended or expanded** are these :—

1. **Adverb** :—'She dances *beautifully.*'

2. **Adverbial clause** :—' He left *when I arrived.*'

3. **Adverbial phrase** :—'She dances *in a beautiful style.*'

4. **Nominative Absolute** :—'*The door being open,* the steed was stolen.'

This last is a particular kind of Adverbial Phrase.

227. Elliptical Sentences. In our ordinary use of language we save ourselves the trouble of making two sentences when one will express our meaning, and effect this economy by the use of conjunctions. Thus 'John and James preached in Jerusalem and Judaea' contains four sentences in one : 'John preached in Jerusalem,' 'John preached in Judaea,' 'James preached in Jerusalem,' 'James preached in Judaea.' ' He is either a knave or a fool' is equivalent to 'Either he is a knave, or he is a fool.' 'He writes fast and well' means 'He writes fast, and he writes well.'

Again, we frequently contract our sentences, not by leaving out precisely the part which has been expressed already, but by leaving out a part which is naturally suggested by what has gone before, though different from it. So, we say ' I like you better than he,' which means 'I like you better than he *likes you,*' whereas 'I like you better than him' would mean 'I like you better than *I like* him.' ' He is sharper than you' is an abbreviated form of 'He is sharper than you *are sharp.*' 'I would rather incur death than dishonour' is an abbreviated form of 'I would rather incur death than *I would incur* dishonour.'

In all such instances there is **an omission of a word or words necessary to the complete grammatical structure of the sentence.** This omission is called **Ellipsis,** and in analysing sentences of this elliptical character it is necessary to make them complete by supplying the missing words.

228. The student is now in possession of all the information which is requisite to enable him to attack a sentence and break it up into its component parts. Analysis is a capital exercise for the wits, as it cannot be effected by the use of a set of rules mechanically applied. Nor is it to be learnt by merely reading a book on the subject, any more than by reading a treatise on swimming or cricket one could become proficient in the side-stroke or the cut. Books may furnish useful directions, but practice is the only way of acquiring these arts. And so, after giving a few suggestions to the reader as to how he should set to work, and supplying examples of analysis to guide him on points of form, we shall pass on to the treatment of other questions of Syntax.

229. Hints for the Analysis of a Sentence.

1. Take a large sheet of paper and divide it into columns by ruling vertical lines. At the head of these columns write 'Sentence, Kind of Sentence, Subject, Adjuncts of Subject, Predicate, Adjuncts of Predicate, Object, Adjuncts of Object.' Instead of using the term Adjuncts, you can use the term Extension, Expansion, or Limitation, for, as we saw, the effect of an Adjunct is to produce an extension or enlargement of the information which we obtain from the word to which the Adjunct is attached, and a limitation or restriction in the number of things to which the word is applicable. Again, instead of making one column for Predicate, you may, if you like, make two, in case you have to distinguish between an Incomplete Predicate and its Complement. Similarly you may have separate columns for Direct and Indirect objects. But this excessive subdivision makes the sheet present a very complicated appearance and has few compensating advantages. These distinctions may be indicated equally well after the words which require them in the columns headed 'Predicate' and 'Object'.

There are other forms in which the analysis may be worked out, but the **tabular form** is certainly the neatest, and it possesses this clear superiority over the rest, that the person who corrects the exercise can see at a glance whether the essential points have been correctly grasped.

2. Read the passage over and consider carefully whether it is a Simple, a Compound, or a Complex Sentence, with which you are dealing. Describe it accordingly at the top of the page. Remember that wherever you find a finite verb you have got a separate clause. Supposing that the Sentence is Complex, make sure that you pick out the Principal Clause correctly: a mistake here will turn the whole into nonsense. Then determine what is the relation of the different Subordinate Clauses to the parts of the Principal Clause. This general outline is the element of real value in the entire product. An elaborate analysis, brimful of details, crowded with subdivisions, and elegantly executed, is absolutely worthless, if it starts wrong and represents subordinate clauses as principal clauses.

3. Write down the Principal Clause at the head of your analysis. Find its Subject; then find its Predicate; then, if the verb is transitive, set down the Object.

4. Next look for the Adjuncts of each. The Adjuncts of the Predicate will be adverbial. The Adjuncts of the Subject or Object will generally be adjectival, but not necessarily so: they may be nouns or noun-clauses in apposition. Thus in each of these sentences, 'The statement *that he has resigned* is not true,' 'I don't believe the statement *that he has resigned*,' the subordinate clause is a noun-clause in apposition with the subject and object respectively.

Subordinate clauses must be dealt with in the same fashion as the Principal clause,—subject, predicate, and object, with the adjuncts of each, being placed in their proper columns.

5. Complete the structure of sentences in which there is an ellipsis before you analyse them. Supply the subject to sentences containing a verb in the Imperative mood. 'Come' must be treated as if it were 'Thou come' or 'You come.' Bear in mind that elliptical sentences expressing a comparison by means of *than* or *as* are complex: the clause in which the ellipsis occurs is a subordinate clause. Thus 'I am stronger than you' in full is 'I am stronger *than you are strong*'; 'I am as strong as you' in full is 'I am as strong *as you are strong.*' The clauses in italics are adverbial adjuncts.

6. The interrogative pronouns may be treated like demonstratives and may form the subject or object of a sentence. In '*Who* struck him?' *who* is the subject: in '*Whom* did he strike?' *whom* is the object. The analysis is similar to that of the sentences '*He* struck him,' '*Him* did he strike,' *i.e.* 'He did strike *him*.'

7. Observe that a clause introduced by relative pronouns or conjunctive adverbs is usually, though not necessarily, adjectival. In the

sentence 'The man *who stole the money* was arrested' the subordinate clause is adjectival, describing the man; but in 'I know *who stole the money*' it is a noun-clause: it takes the place of the noun or pronoun, 'the man' or 'him,' and refers to no other noun or pronoun as an antecedent. Compare 'I know the place *where he is living*' (adjective-clause), and 'I know *where he is living*' (noun-clause).

8. Observe also that these relative words sometimes introduce what is really not a subordinate but a co-ordinate clause. 'I met John *who gave me your message*' is equivalent to 'I met John and he gave me your message': 'I saw him in London *where he was living*' is equivalent to 'I saw him in London: he was living there.' The clauses in italics make fresh statements and are not limitations of *John* and of *London*. They must therefore be analysed as principal sentences.

9. A relative pronoun is often omitted when it represents the Object: it must be inserted in the analysis. So, 'Here is the book ∧ I want' requires *which* as the object of *want*: 'The man ∧ I saw yesterday' requires *whom* as the object of *saw*.

10. Pure Conjunctions have no place in the analysis, because they serve merely to join sentences or clauses. Interjections are excluded, because they do not enter into the construction of the sentence. The same remark applies usually, but not invariably, to Vocatives, *i.e.* Nominatives of Address. Thus in 'O Solitude! where are thy charms?' the subject is *charms*, and *O Solitude* must be left out from the analysis: but in 'O Solitude, thou hast no charms' the subject is *thou*, and *Solitude* may be described as an enlargement of the subject.

11. An Absolute phrase is an adverbial adjunct of the Predicate. Do not mistake its noun or pronoun for the Subject of the sentence. In '*The door being open*, the steed was stolen,' the words in italics give the reason why the stealing was possible: the subject of the sentence is *steed*, not *door*.

12. Notice that, when the verb comes before the real subject, the word *It* or *There* often stands at the beginning of the sentence: thus, 'It is hard to earn a living,' 'It is true that he did this.' These assertions are equivalent to saying 'To earn a living is hard,' 'That he did this is true.' The *it* comes first as an indication that the real subject is to follow. In analysing such a sentence, however, 'It' may be called the subject, and the real subject may be regarded as an enlargement or adjunct. *There* is only the adverb without its full force as marking place. 'There are many pickpockets about' is grammatically the same as 'Many pickpockets are about there': *there* is an adverbial adjunct of the predicate.

13. When a Complex Sentence contains as its Subject or Object a noun-clause, this noun-clause forms an essential part of the whole sentence and must be inserted as the Subject or Object of the principal verb. Thus, in the Complex Sentence '*How he did it* is not certain,'

the words *How he did it* are the subject of the predicate ' is not certain.'
In the Complex Sentence 'I know *how he did it*,' the words *how he
did it* are the object of the principal verb 'I know.'   To indicate the
relation of the Principal and the Subordinate clause in sentences of this
kind, write the entire sentence at the head of your analysis, underline
the subordinate clause, and add the information ' Noun Clause' at its
close.   The sentence ' How he did it is not certain' should be written
thus:—'*How he did it* (Noun Cl.) is not certain.'   To describe as a
Principal clause the words 'is not certain,' without supplying their
subject, would be absurd.   Similarly, the sentence ' I know how he did
it ' should be written in this form :—'I know *how he did it*' (Noun Cl.).

230.   Examples of analysis in tabular form.

A.   Go, lovely Rose !
        Tell her, that wastes her time and me,
          That now she knows,
        When I resemble her to thee,
        How sweet and fair she seems to be.

B.   When a horseman, who had been sent to reconnoitre,
reported that the Greeks were amusing themselves outside
the walls, Xerxes asked what this madness might mean.

C.   As thro' the land at eve we went
          And pluck'd the ripened ears,
        We fell out, my wife and I,
          And kiss'd again with tears.
        And blessings on the falling out
          That all the more endears
        When we fall out with those we love
          And kiss again with tears !

Observe that the two clauses, *When we fall out with those we love
And kiss again with tears*, may be regarded as adjectival adjuncts of
falling out, instead of being taken as adverbial adjuncts of *endears*.

A. Contains two Sentences : (I) Simple, (II) Complex.
Prin. Clause of (II), Tell her *that now she knows &c.* (Noun Cl.).

	Sentence or Clause	Kind of Sentence	Subject	Adjuncts of Subject	
A.	(I.) Go, lovely Rose	Simple	(Thou)	lovely Rose	
	(II.) Tell her ... seems to be	Complex	(Thou)		
	that wastes her time	Adj. Cl. limiting *her*	that		
	that wastes me	Adj. Cl. limiting *her*	that		
	that now she knows ...seems to be	Noun Cl.	she		
	how sweet and fair she seems to be	Noun Cl.	she		
	when I resemble her to thee	Adv. Cl. lim. *knows*	I		
B.	When a horseman... might mean	Complex	Xerxes		
	when a horseman... outside the walls	Adv. Cl. lim. *asked*	horse-man	1. a 2. who had been ...to reconnoitre	
	who had been sent to reconnoitre	Adj. Cl. limiting *horseman*	who		
	that the Greeks... outside the walls	Noun Cl.	Greeks	the	
	what this madness might mean	Noun Cl.	madness	this	

B. A Complex Sentence.

Prin. Cl., Xerxes asked *what this madness might mean* (Noun Cl.)

Predicate	Adjuncts of Predicate	Object	Adjuncts of Object
go			
tell	her that... time and me	That now... seems to be	
wastes		time	her
wastes		me	
knows	1. now 2. when I... her to thee	how sweet and fair she seems to be	
seems *Incomplete* to be how (1) sweet (2) fair *Compl.*			
resemble	1. when 2. to thee	her	
asked	when a horseman... walls	what this... mean	
reported	when	that the... the walls	
had been sent	to reconnoitre		
were amusing	outside the walls	themselves	
might mean		what	

C. Contains two Sentences, (I) Compound and Complex.
(II) Complex.

Sentence or Clause	Kind of Sentence	Subject	Adjuncts of Subject	
(I.) 1. As through the land...my wife and I	Complex	we	my wife and I	
As through the land at eve we went	Adv. Cl. limiting *fell out*	we		
(As we) plucked the ripened ears	Adv. Cl. limiting *fell out*	we		
2. As through the land...(we) kissed a-gain with tears	Complex	we		
(II.) Blessings (be) on...with tears	Complex	Blessings		
That all the...with tears	Adj. Cl. limiting *falling out*	that		
When we fall out with those we love	Adv. Cl. limiting *endears*	we		
(Whom) we love	Adj. Cl. limiting *those*	we		
(When) we kiss again with tears	Adv. Cl. limiting *endears*	we		

Principal Clauses of (I), 1. We fell out.
2. We kissed again with tears.
Principal Clause of (II), Blessings on the falling out.

Predicate	Adjuncts of Predicate	Object	Adjuncts of Object
fell out	1. as through the land... we went 2. as we plucked ... ears		
went	through the land, at eve		
plucked		ears	ripened
kissed	again with tears also adjuncts 1 & 2 as above		
be *Incompl.* on *Compl.*		falling out	that all ... with tears
endears	1. all the more 2. when we... with tears		
fall out	with those we love		
love		whom	
kiss	1. again 2. with tears		

231. Directions for Parsing.

In analysing a sentence, we break it up in such a manner as to show how it contains the essential constituents of every sentence, Subject and Predicate, and round these elements we group the remaining words, phrases, or clauses, as adjuncts: to one of these adjuncts of the predicate we assign a place apart from the other adverbial adjuncts and call it the Object.

In parsing, we deal with every word in a sentence separately, stating its Part of Speech, its inflexion, if it has any, and its syntactical relations with other words in the sentence. Thus parsing is concerned with both the etymology and syntax of words, whilst analysis takes no cognisance of etymology.

Unless the student is directed to give a history of the forms of the words, in addition to stating their parts of speech and particulars connected with their accidence and syntax, he may feel satisfied that he is carrying out his instructions to " parse fully " when he furnishes the following information :—

1. **Noun** and **Pronoun.** State the kind of noun or pronoun, its gender, number, case, and give the reason why the word is in that case. The gender of a pronoun cannot always be determined.

2. **Adjective.** State the kind of adjective and its degree, and what word it limits. As adjectives (except *this* and *that*) undergo no inflexions of number, gender, or case, it is better to speak of them as 'limiting' nouns than as 'agreeing' with nouns. 'Agreement' suggests inflexion.

3. **Verb.** State the kind of verb, its voice, mood, tense, number, person ; the subject with which it agrees, and its object, if it has one.
Participle. State the kind of verb of which it is a participle, its voice and tense, and show which word it limits; also mention its object, if it has one. The participle used in combination with auxiliaries to form a compound tense need not be parsed separately, though it may be parsed in this way. So, *shall have been beaten, were beating, may have been beating*, are adequately parsed as compound tenses, but the student should understand the construction of the separate words.

4. **Adverb.** State the kind of adverb; its degree, if it is an adverb of quality admitting of this modification : name the word which it limits, or 'qualifies.' The latter is the term generally used of adverbs.

5. **Preposition.** Name the noun which it ' governs,' that is to say, the noun whose relation to other words it shows.

6. **Conjunction.** Say whether it is co-ordinate or subordinate, and point out what it joins.

Abbreviations may be used with advantage, but not in such a way as to cause ambiguity. The particulars should be given in uniform order and as concisely as possible. The following examples of parsing illustrate these directions.

I.

Can I forget the dismal night *that* gave
My *soul's* best part for *ever* to the grave !
How silent did his old companions tread,
By *midnight* lamps, the *mansions* of the dead.

Can verb defect. trs. of incompl. predication,—act. indic. pres. sing. 1st.—agreeing with *I* : has for object infin. *forget*.

I pers. pron. of 1st pers.—sing. nom.—subj. of *can*.

forget verb, strong, trans.—act. infin. pres.—prolative infin. depending on *can* : has for object *night*.

that pronoun relat.—referring to anteced. *night*, subj. of *gave*.

soul's noun com.—neut. sing. possess.—dependent on *part*.

ever adv. of time, used here as substitute for noun : 'for ever' = 'for all time.'

how adv. of degree—qualif. *silent*.

silent adj. of quality, posit.—used as adv. of manner qualif. *tread*, or as adj. limiting *companions*.

midnight noun sing.—neut. sing.—used as adj. limiting *lamps*.

mansions noun com.—neut. plur.,—object of *tread*.

II.

For who, to dumb *forgetfulness a prey,*
    This pleasing anxious *being e'er* resigned,
Left the warm *precincts* of the cheerful day,
    Nor cast *one longing,* lingering *look behind*?

For conj. subord. (Some writers take it as co-ord.)

who pron. interrog.—masc. or fem., sing.—subj. of *resigned.*

forgetfulness noun abstr.—neut. sing. objective,—gov. by *to.*

a demonst. adj. (or indef. art.)—limiting *prey.*

prey noun com.—neut. sing. nom.—in appos. with *who.*

this pronom. adj. demonst.—sing.—limiting *being.*

being noun abstr.—neut. sing.—object of *resigned.*

e'er adv. of time—qualif. *resigned.*

left verb, weak, trans.—act. indic. past indef. sing. 3rd,—agreeing with *who*; has for object *precincts.*

precincts noun com.—neut. plur.—object of *left.*

one adj. quant. card. num.—limiting *look.*

longing pres. part. act. of verb *long*,—used as adj. limiting *look.*

look noun com.—neut. sing.—object of *cast.*

behind adv. of place—qual. *cast.*

III.

He had *laid* him *low.*

It *were best let alone.*

Choose whom you will, we will pay *him* respect.

laid participle past, passive, of trans. verb 'lay,' limiting *him.* (If *had laid* were parsed in combination, it would be described as verb, weak, trans.—act. indic. past perf. sing. 3rd,—agreeing with *he.*)

low adj. of qual. used as adv.—qualif. *laid.*

were verb defect. of incompl. predication,—act. subj. past. indef. sing. 3rd,—agreeing with *it.*

best adj. of qual.—superl.—complement of predic. *were* and limiting *it.*

let participle past passive, of trans. verb *let*,—limiting *it.*

alone adj. of qual.—limiting *it.*

choose verb, strong, trans.—act. imperat. plur. 2nd,—agreeing with *you* understood : has for obj. *him* understood.

whom pronoun relat.—referring to suppressed anteced. *him*, masc. sing. object of *will (choose)*, the full constr. being *choose you him whom you will choose.*

him pronoun demonstr. of 3rd pers.—masc. sing. objective,—indir. obj. of *pay.*

QUESTIONS.

1. What is a sentence? What are the necessary parts of every sentence? Write down the shortest sentence you can compose, and show that these necessary parts are comprised therein. Give examples showing how each part may be expanded.

2. What is the subject in the following sentence?—'It makes no part of my present subject, to detail how the success of a few ballads had the effect of changing all the purpose and tenour of my life.'

3. Are the following exclamations sentences?—'Go.'—'Hence.'— 'Yes.'

[How much may be left out of a sentence without its ceasing to be a sentence? Make use of your answer to this question as a principle to determine your answers about 'Go' and 'Hence.' As regards 'Yes,' the matter is different. Here we get beyond mere ellipsis. 'Yes' is a substitute for a sentence rather than a sentence from which part has been omitted.]

4. Explain the meaning of *subject, predicate*, and *copula*, and point out each of them and their expansions in the following sentence :—

'Is this a dagger that I see before me?'

[For *copula* see p. 177, Question 1.]

5. What is the subject in each of the following sentences?

'Who is this?'

'Give me your hand.'

'There is said to have been a battle.'

'His horse being killed, he was taken prisoner.'

6. Define the subject of a sentence, and give one example of each of five different kinds of subjects.

7. In what cases may the subject be omitted in English?

Explain the construction of *methought* in the sentence—' Methought the billows spoke and told me of it.'

[The subject may be omitted (1) With verbs expressing a command: 'Go' (you); or (2) a wish, '(I) Would it were so!' (3) The antecedent to the relative is sometimes omitted: '(He) Who breaks, pays.' (4) Impersonal verbs of course have no subject.]

8. Point out the subject, predicate, and object, with their extensions, in the following :—

'At once his trusty sword the warlike chieftain drew.'

9. Make use of the words *horse, kick, man*, as subject, predicate, object, respectively, to form one sentence in which (*a*) the subject is enlarged by an *adjective clause*, (*b*) the predicate is enlarged by an *adverbial clause* relating to *cause*.

10. Distinguish between a *phrase* and a *sentence*.

'The Saxons invaded England.' Write out this sentence (*a*) with the predicate extended by a *prepositional phrase*, (*b*) with the predicate extended by an *adverbial* clause relating to *time*.

[A 'prepositional phrase' is a phrase composed of a preposition and a noun. As the prepositional phrase here is to extend the predicate, it must have an adverbial force, describing how, why, when, or where, the

15—2

Saxons invaded England: *e.g.* 'in pirate-boats,' 'with a fair wind,' 'from a desire for pillage,' 'after the departure of the Romans,' 'on the coast of Sussex.']

11. Write a sentence containing two extensions of the predicate, and let one of these contain an object with two enlargements of different kinds.

12. Name the three kinds of subordinate clauses. Explain why an *adjective clause* is so called. State to which kind each of the subordinate clauses in the three following sentences belongs, and give your reason :—

'I asked where he lived.'

'I have often seen the house where he was born.'

'I shall sit where you wish.'

13. State and explain the various terms used in the Analysis of Sentences.

14. Write three sentences, introducing in the first a clause equivalent to a noun, in the second a clause equivalent to an adjective, in the third a clause equivalent to an adverb.

15. Construct a complex sentence with two subordinate clauses of different kinds, and state the relation of each to the principal clause.

16. 'The thief avoided the policeman.'

Rewrite the above sentence—

(1) enlarging the subject with a noun in apposition,

(2) enlarging the object with an adjectival clause,

(3) extending the predicate with an absolute phrase.

17. Rewrite the subjoined sentences, supplying in full the words required to make the construction of the subordinate clauses complete, and describe each such clause :—

(a) 'She sings worse than ever.'

(b)   'Better late,

Our proverb says, than never to do well.'

(c) 'Things happened precisely as you guessed.'

18. To what Parts of Speech do the following words belong ?—*fifty, few, kill, cavalry, their, those, sheer, pell-mell, as, why, bravo.*

19. Parse the following italicised words :

(i) '*When* you are established in the house *where* you intend to reside, I will call on you, *if* I may.'

(ii) 'I had *but* one house, *as* you know: *since then* I have bought another.'

20. Parse the italicised words in the following sentences:—'Have you *any*?' 'No, I have *none*.' '*When* did you come?' '*Why* is he here?' 'He went away *rejoicing*.' 'This is *talking* at *random*.' 'It is not true *that* he said *that*.' 'I saw the *same as* he did.'

21. Parse the italicised words:—'*Which* is *which*?' 'He was *forgiven* the *fault*.' 'The lady protests *too much, methinks*.' '*Perish* the thought!' 'The ship is *building*.' 'Sit *thee* down.' 'I saw him *taken*.' 'So *be* it.'

22. Parse these sentences:—'In the front of the eye is a clear transparent window, exactly like the glass of a watch.'

'When a man falls from his horse, he is often seriously hurt.'

'He rushed into the field, and foremost fighting fell.'

'Life has passed
'With me but roughly since I heard thee last.'

23. To what parts of speech would you refer the following words?— *next, no, the, together, past, else, but, ere.*

[*Else* is an adverb signifying 'besides.' In the compound phrases *anybody else* or *somebody else* it takes the possessive inflexion, *anybody else's, somebody else's.*]

24. Parse the italicised words in the following sentences:—'*Please write* clearly.' '*Thank* you.' '*Thanks*.' 'You can if you *like*.' 'Get *you* gone.' 'He was accused of *cheating*.' 'He was accused of *having cheated*.'

[The construction of *please* was formerly impersonal, but 'It pleases me' has become 'I please,' as 'It likes me' has become 'I like.' We may regard *write* as infinitive dependent on *Please*,—'May you please (*i.e.* May it please you) to write clearly,'—or we may regard it as an imperative,—'Write clearly, if you please, (*i.e.* if it please you').

The construction in the last sentence, though in common use, has been condemned by some writers as grammatically indefensible, on the ground that *of* should be followed by the gerund, whilst *having cheated* is the past participle. The objection would be valid if *having cheated* were indeed a past participle here, but it is not: it is a compound gerund form. (See § 162, 6.) Just as we say 'He was supposed *to have* (Infinitive) cheated,' so we may say 'He was accused *of having* (Gerund) cheated,' 'He was rejected *for having* cheated.']

CHAPTER XXIII.

SYNTAX OF NOUNS.

232. SYNTAX deals with the relations of words when they are arranged so as to form sentences. Most of these relations come under the heads of **Concord** and **Government.** By Concord we mean the agreement of two or more connected words, as regards their gender, number, case, or person. By Government we mean the influence exercised upon the case of a noun or pronoun by another word: thus a transitive verb or a preposition is said to 'govern' a noun. Owing to the scanty supply of inflexions in modern English, the relation of a word to other words in the sentence is often indicated by its position. Hence we may say that syntax has to do with the **Order** or **Arrangement** of words, as well as with their **Concord** and **Government.**

The principles of Syntax might be enumerated under these three heads, but the student will obtain a clearer view of the subject, if we deal with the Syntax of the different parts of speech in succession, as we have already dealt with their Etymology. In our treatment of the meaning and use of words, we discussed many points which belong strictly to Syntax. What remains to be done in this section of the book is to give a short summary of these and to supply others which have been omitted.

Syntax of Nouns. Our remarks on the Syntax of Nouns may be grouped most conveniently under the different cases.

Nominative Case.

233   The Nominative case is used—

(1)   When a noun stands as the **Subject** of a sentence, whether the verb of which it is the subject be active or passive : ' He works,' 'I have been wounded.' The concord of the verb with its subject is discussed under the Syntax of Verbs.

(2)   As a **Vocative,** or **Nominative of Address :** 'Milton ! thou shouldst be living at this hour.'

(3)   To **complete the predicate** after certain intransitive verbs of incomplete predication : such verbs as *to be, become, continue, seem, feel,* often require a complement : ' He became prime minister,' **'** I continued secretary,' ' He seemed and felt a hero.'

(4)   With certain **transitive verbs in the passive to complete the meaning:** ' He was made secretary,' ' I was appointed treasurer,' ' You were called John.' Such transitive verbs are called **factitive** or 'making' verbs, because the verb 'to make' (Lat. *facio*) is a type of the class.

(5)   When a noun is in **apposition** with another noun in the nominative.

(6)   When the noun or pronoun, combined with a participle, is in the **absolute construction.** Thus, ' *The door being open,* the steed was stolen,' ' *My partner having returned,* I shall go for my holiday.'

(*Absolutus* means in Latin ' set free ' or ' untied ' : an *absolute* phrase can be detached without affecting the construction of the sentence.)

It is disputed whether the case of the noun in the absolute construction is really the nominative in modern

English. In old English it was the dative. As the dative ending has disappeared from our nouns, it is only when one of the personal pronouns is used that we can still see what the case actually is. Should we say '*He* excepted' or '*Him* excepted'? '*I* returning' or '*Me* returning'? It scarcely admits of doubt that the nominative would be preferred to the objective as the absolute case at the present day.

234. The following sentences illustrate a very common blunder in connexion with the use of the participle in a construction which is meant to be absolute but is not.

'Walking across the common, my hat was knocked off by a cricket-ball.'

As the sentence stands, *walking* is a participial adjunct of *hat*, and the construction is therefore 'My hat walking across the common was knocked off by a cricket-ball,' which is absurd. The required correction may be made in various ways: (1) By completing the absolute phrase. Add the missing pronoun and say 'I walking across the common, my hat was knocked off.' This makes the syntax regular, but the expression would be unusual. (2) By substituting 'I had my hat knocked off' for 'my hat was knocked off.' *I* is then the subject, and *walking across the common* is quite rightly the adjunct of *I*, instead of being the adjunct of *my hat* as before. (3) By converting the participle into a past imperfect tense indicative. Say 'As I was walking across the common, my hat was knocked off.'

'Going into the garden, the grass wetted my feet.' We may correct this by substituting (1) 'I going into the garden (absolute phrase), the grass wetted my feet,' or (2) 'Going into the garden, I wetted my feet in the grass,' or (3) 'On my going (gerund) into the garden, the grass wetted my feet.' The first expression is one which nobody would ever employ, but it is grammatically correct. A captious critic may raise the further objection that, as my feet were wetted, probably after I had reached the garden and not on my way thither, *having gone* is more likely to suit the facts than *going*.

235. Apposition. This is a suitable point at which we may bring together remarks on Apposition that would otherwise be scattered in various parts of the book.

When one noun is used to explain the meaning of another, it is put in the same case, usually in the **same number,** if possible in the **same gender,** and is said to be in **Apposition.** The following sentences contain nouns in apposition:

'Turner, the baker, lives here': *Turner* is the subject, *the baker* is in the nominative case in apposition.

'I saw Turner, the baker': both nouns are in the objective case.

'This is Turner's, the baker's, shop': both nouns are in the possessive case.

In practice we rarely employ the last form of expression. Instead of saying 'This is Turner's, the baker's, shop,' we should say 'This is Turner the baker's shop.' Here there is no apposition, but *Turner-the-baker* is treated as a compound noun. **Identity of case is essential to apposition.**

The noun in apposition usually agrees in number, but not necessarily: a collective noun in the singular may be used in apposition with a noun in the plural, and *vice versâ*: 'Four hundred *boys*, the whole *school*, turned out to receive him': 'This year's *team*, eleven well-tried *men*, will give a good account of themselves.'

Owing to the absence of any appropriate feminine form, it is often impossible to mark a concord of gender between the noun in apposition and the noun to which it refers. Thus we have to say 'Scott the novelist,' or 'writer,' and

'Miss Evans the novelist,' or 'writer,' as no feminine of *novelist* or *writer* exists. But we should say 'Scott the poet,' or 'author,' and 'Miss Evans the poetess,' or 'authoress,' making the noun in apposition agree as regards gender when it is practicable to do so.

236. Order of the Noun in the Nominative Case. The subject precedes the verb, as a general rule, but comes after it—

i. in questions: 'Did you say so?'

ii. in commands: 'See thou to that.'

iii. in certain uses of the subjunctive mood: 'Were he here, you would not say this,' 'Would I could find him!' 'May you prosper!'

iv. when *nor* precedes the verb: 'I said I would not do it, nor will I,' 'He wanted only a pretext, nor was he long in finding one.'

v. in the phrases 'said I,' 'quoth he,' 'answered he,' etc.

vi. when the sentence is introduced by *there*, as 'There are some who deny this.'

vii. for emphasis: 'Great is Diana,' 'Indeed will I, quoth Findlay.'

Possessive Case.

237. Possession is only one of the relations indicated by nouns in the possessive case: 'John's hat' means 'the hat possessed by John'; 'the master's cane' means 'the cane possessed by the master.' But 'Byron's poems' does not mean 'the poems possessed by Byron'; 'Peel's Act' does not mean 'the Act possessed by Peel'; 'Cade's insurrection' does not mean 'the insurrection possessed by Cade'; 'an hour's detention' does not mean 'the detention possessed by an hour.' The term *possessive* is therefore inadequate as a description of the functions performed by this case.

What feature is common to all these uses of the so-called possessive case? The common feature is this: **the noun in the possessive has the limiting force of an adjective.** Just as 'John's hat' is a particular kind of hat, so 'Byron's poems' are a particular kind of poems,

'Cade's insurrection' is a particular kind of insurrection, and 'an hour's detention' a particular kind of detention.

The Latin word for 'kind' is *genus*, and we might therefore call the case which marks the kind the *generic* case. Perhaps this is what the Roman grammarians thought they were doing when they called it the *genitive* case. But 'genitive' in its proper sense has a much narrower meaning and signifies 'belonging to birth or origin.' It is appropriate to describe the case of *father's* when we speak of 'the father's son,' because the son derives his birth or origin from the father; but it is not appropriate to describe the case of *son's* when we speak of 'the son's father,' because the father did not derive his birth or origin from the son[1]. Now the term 'generic' would describe the case equally well in both instances : 'the father's son' is a particular kind of son, 'the son's father' is a particular kind of father. We cannot however displace either the term 'possessive' or the term 'genitive,' though each is insufficient as a description of the relations often marked by words in the possessive or genitive case. With these criticisms on the terms we will go on to consider the syntax of the so-called possessive case.

238. The Substitute for the Inflected Possessive Case.

The preposition *of*, with the objective case of the noun which follows it, takes the place of the inflected possessive and is used in many instances in which the inflected form would be inadmissible. Thus instead of saying 'the master's cane' we can say 'the cane of the master'; for 'Byron's poems,' 'Cade's insurrection,' 'an hour's detention,' we can say 'the poems of Byron,' 'the insurrection of Cade,' 'a detention of an hour.' It is only the inflected form however that is to be called a possessive *case* : 'of Byron' must not be parsed as the possessive, but 'Byron' must be parsed as the objective governed by the preposition *of*. For if 'of Byron' is entitled to the name 'possessive case,' 'to Byron' has an equally good claim to the name 'dative,' and 'from Byron' to the name 'ablative.' But if 'to Byron' and 'from Byron' are cases, on what ground are we to

[1] See Max Müller's *Lectures on the Science of Language*, 1st series, p. 105.

refuse to describe as cases the combinations 'about Byron,' 'through Byron,' 'in Byron,' 'on Byron,' and so forth?

239. Subjective and Objective Genitive. The **genitive case** is described as **subjective** or **objective** according as the noun in the genitive stands for the subject or for the object of the action denoted by the word on which it depends. Thus 'Carlyle's praises' may signify either (1) 'Carlyle praised somebody': here *Carlyle* is the subject of the proposition, and the genitive is subjective: or (2) 'Somebody praised Carlyle': here *Carlyle* is the object of the proposition, and the genitive is objective. The expression is used in the former way when we say 'Carlyle's praises were rarely bestowed': it is used in the latter way when we say 'Carlyle's praises were loudly sung.' 'Ravaillac's murder' is subjective, 'Henry IV.'s murder' is objective. Not that we can combine the two inflected forms in the same sentence and say 'Ravaillac's Henry IV.'s murder.' We should have to employ the preposition *of* to denote the objective relation and say 'Ravaillac's murder of Henry IV.,' 'Ruskin's praises of Carlyle.' Speaking generally, we may say that the inflected form is subjective in modern English. The form made by combination with the preposition *of* admits of the same double use: 'the persecution of the Puritans' is objective when we say 'The persecution of the Puritans drove them to Massachusetts': it is subjective when we say 'The Quakers of New England suffered from the persecution of the Puritans.'

240. How are we to explain such expressions as 'a novel of Scott's,' 'a play of Shakespeare's'?

They are not pleonastic, that is to say, they do not contain any redundancy or excess of expression. On the contrary they are elliptical, a noun being left out on which the noun in the possessive case depends. The complete expression would be 'a novel of Scott's novels,' 'a play of Shakespeare's plays.' Hence we cannot properly say 'a father of John's,' though we can say 'a brother of John's,' for 'a father of John's fathers' would be absurd. As a fact however we do employ this elliptical construction for purposes of disparagement, real or pretended, in cases where it is logically indefensible. Thus we say 'that disreputable old father of John's,' 'this sweet wee wife of mine.'

There are other ellipses, or omissions, of the noun which ought to follow the noun in the possessive case, and these we have to supply according to the sense required by the context. 'He goes to St Paul's' may signify in different connexions 'St Paul's cathedral,' 'St Paul's school,' or 'St Paul's station.' 'A picture of Agnew's' and 'a picture of Gainsborough's' alike require the word 'pictures' to supply the ellipsis, but in the former case the meaning is 'belonging to Agnew,' in the latter 'painted by Gainsborough.'

241. How are we to explain such expressions as 'the city of Rome,' 'the month of June'?

When we bear in mind that the function of the noun in the genitive case is to limit the application of the noun on which it depends, the explanation of such phrases as 'the city of Rome,' 'the month of June,' seems fairly simple. 'The city of Rome' is a particular city, 'the month of June' a particular month, just as 'the top of the mountain' is a particular top. We do not say 'the river of Rhone' but we might have done so : we use *river* and *Rhone* in apposition. It is merely a matter of idiom, or form of expression peculiar to our language. The Latin idiom was to say 'city Rome,' *Urbs Roma;* our idiom is to say 'city of Rome.'

The construction of two nouns in apposition in the possessive case has been already discussed.

242. Order. The inflected possessive always stands before the noun on which it depends; 'Carlyle's praise,' 'the master's cane.' The preposition *of* and its noun in the objective usually come after the governing noun : 'the praise of Carlyle,' 'the cane of the master.' But for emphasis this order may be inverted : 'Of the spoil each man received a share,' 'Of virtue a great part consists in this.'

Objective Case.

243. The **objective case** in modern English marks relations which are expressed in Latin by the accusative and by the dative. It is the case both of the direct and of the indirect object. The following are its chief uses.

The objective is the case—

(1) of the direct object of a transitive verb: 'Brutus killed *him*.'

(2) of the factitive object : 'They made him *consul*,' 'He called her *Mary*,' 'We thought him a *lunatic*.'

(3) of the noun of kindred meaning which sometimes follows intransitive verbs: 'I dreamt a *dream*,' 'He slept a sound *sleep*.' This is called the cognate objective. See p. 137.

(4) of the noun in apposition to another in the objective : 'They slew him, their *archbishop*.'

(5) of the adverbial adjunct of the predicate, marking limitations as regards time, space, or manner : 'We stayed a *year*,' 'The ditch is three *yards* wide,' 'This is worth *half-a-crown*.'

(6) of nouns governed by prepositions : 'He plays for *money*.'

(7) of the indirect object: the noun in this case stands for the thing to or on behalf of which the thing is done. The verb 'to give' may be taken as the type of verbs which are followed by an indirect object : 'Give *me* (indir. obj.) the book' (dir. obj.).

(8) of the pronoun in the two surviving impersonals, *methinks, meseems*.

(9) after the adjectives *like, worth,* and *near* : 'like *me*,' 'worth *us* two together,' 'near *him*.'

(10) of the person for whose advantage a thing is done, or by whom it is regarded with interest : these uses correspond with the *Dativus Commodi* and *Dativus Ethicus* of the Latin Grammar. ' Do *me* this favour' is an example of the Dativus Commodi, or Dative of Advantage ; *me* signifies *for me.* 'Just as I was approaching, he whips *me* out his dagger': here *me* marks merely the fact that the speaker had an interest in the action : it gives a lively touch to the narrative. *Me* is called the Ethical Dative.

The Retained or Adverbial Object.

The reader will remember that many transitive verbs which take two objects in the active voice, may retain either of these as its object in the passive. Thus 'He taught me music' converted into the passive becomes either 'I was taught music by him,' or 'Music was taught me by him.' In the first form, *music*, in the second, *me*, may be described as the Retained Object after the passive verb. Or we may describe *music* and *me* as adjuncts of the predicate, or adverbial objectives. Just as we call 'three miles,' 'three hours,' adverbial objectives when we say 'He walked three miles,' 'He walked three hours,'—*objectives* because they are in the objective case (though there is no inflexion of the nouns from which we can see this) and *adverbial* because they limit or qualify the statement that 'he walked,'—so we may call *music* an adverbial objective limiting the statement that he 'taught me,' or *me* an adverbial objective limiting the statement that he 'taught music.'

244. Order. The noun in the objective case usually follows the verb or the preposition by which it is governed. But—

(1) When the word in the objective case is a relative or interrogative pronoun, it comes before the verb : 'The book *which* you gave me,' '*Which book* did you give me?'

(2) When *that* is used as a relative and governed by a preposition, the preposition comes at the end of the sentence : 'This is the book *that* you told me *of.*' When *who* or *which* are used as relatives and governed by prepositions, they may stand before or after the prepositions : 'This is the man of whom and that is the book of which you told me,' or 'This is the man whom you told me of, and that is the book which you told me of.'

(3) For emphasis the noun in the objective case is sometimes placed before the verb : 'Jesus I know, and Paul I know, but who are ye?' 'Silver and gold have I none.'

------

245. Correction of Sentences. In his school exercises the student is sometimes required to alter the construction of faulty sentences. His aim should be to make them formally correct by the introduction of the smallest changes which are necessary for the removal of obscurity or error. A free paraphrase of an ungrammatical passage suggests an evasion of the difficulty. Thus 'I went into the garden and wetted my feet in the grass' expresses grammatically the meaning which the sentence 'Going into the garden, the grass wetted my feet' was intended to convey. But this new version raises a doubt whether the nature of the mistake has been grasped by the pupil. To take another illustration ; the sentence 'Shakespeare is greater than any dramatist' is corrected, if we say 'Shakespeare is the greatest dramatist,' but this correction might be made by one who had failed to see anything amiss with the sentence in its original form.

If, on the other hand, we insert the word *other* and write 'Shakespeare is greater than any other dramatist,' we introduce the minimum of alteration and put our finger on the faulty spot.

246. Examples of wrong construction with the participle are furnished in the following sentences. Rewrite them correctly.

'Being a fine day, I went out for a walk.'

[To correct this sentence we may either—

(1) Complete the absolute phrase and say 'It being,' or—

(2) Substitute an adverbial clause for *being* and say 'As it was.']

'Sailing in a yacht, the coast seems to move faster than we.'

'Courting the favour of neither rich nor poor, success attended his career.'

'Foiled and disgraced, his candidature was abandoned.'

'Louis was in some respects a good man, but being a bad ruler his subjects rebelled.'

'Being early killed, I sent a party in search of his mangled body.'

'Having failed in this attempt, no further trial was made.'

'Travelling along the line, the tower of the castle came in sight.'

'Judging from the time taken, the race was rowed quicker than in all previous years.'

'Having perceived the weakness of his poems, they now reappear to us under new titles.'

'Vainly endeavouring to suppress his emotion, the service was abruptly brought to an end.'

'Left for dead upon the ground, his companions rushed to his assistance.'

'Arrived at the spot, a scene of horror presented itself to their eyes.'

'Hastily discussing the position of affairs, prompt measures were adopted and a telegram was sent to the police station.'

'Not having had the accounts of the company properly audited for some years, it was resolved by the directors that the services of an accountant should be secured.'

CHAPTER XXIV.

I. Adjectives.

247. ADJECTIVES limit nouns **attributively** and **predicatively.** When we say 'a clever boy,' the use of the adjective is attributive: when we say 'The boy is clever,' it is predicative. With certain transitive verbs of incomplete predication, such as *make, think, call, consider*, an adjective is used **factitively** to complete the statement: 'They made, or thought, or called, or considered, him clever.'

Some adjectives can be used only predicatively. We can say 'The man is afraid, or awake, or well, or ill,' but not 'the afraid man,' 'the awake man,' 'the well or ill man.' Sometimes an adjective changes its meaning when it is used attributively: 'He is a sorry fool' does not signify the same thing as 'The fool is sorry.' 'Glad' can be used attributively in only a few connexions : 'glad tidings,' 'glad heart.'

248. Concord. To speak of the **agreement** of the Adjective with its Noun in modern English is to use a term which seems scarcely appropriate, for the inflexions marking gender and case have disappeared entirely from English adjectives; and the demonstratives *this* and *that* are the only adjectives which admit of the inflexion of number.

Collective nouns in the singular are often followed by verbs in the plural, but they must not be preceded by *these* or *those*. It is a common error to say 'those sort,' 'these kind.' Thus:

'Those sort of things do not affect me at all.' The best way of correcting this is to say 'Things of that sort do not.' There is a harshness which should be avoided whether we say 'That sort of things do not,' or 'That sort of things does not,' though either expression admits of defence as grammatical, if *sort* is taken as a collective noun signifying 'class.'

249. The uses of *many* and *few*.

We may say (1) 'many roses,' using *many* as an indefinite numeral adjective; or (2) 'many a rose,' using *many* as a multiplicative numeral adjective, so that the expression is equivalent to 'a rose manifold,' or 'many times one rose'; or (3) 'a many roses,' a construction which survives in poetry, but occurs in ordinary use only with *great* prefixed to *many*, 'a great many roses.' Here we may regard *many* as a collective noun and suppose that there is an ellipsis of a following *of*: 'a great many of roses.'

Notice the difference of meaning between 'few,' 'a few,' and 'the few.' *Few* means 'not many': *a few* means 'some': *the few* means 'not many, but all there are.' Thus, 'I gave him the few shillings I had' signifies (1) 'I had not many shillings,' (2) 'I gave him all.' Similar distinctions are expressed by *little, a little, the little. Less* is often wrongly used where *fewer* would be the right word. *Less* denotes quantity, *fewer* denotes number. Hence we ought not to say 'No less than twenty persons were present.'

250. *Each, every, either, neither,* are distributives, and their construction is therefore singular. Hence the following are wrong:

'Each of the boys read in their turn.' We may alter *each of* to *all*, making *turn* plural, or we may alter *their* to *his*.

'They followed each in their turn.'

This sentence is not on precisely the same footing as the last, for if we substitute *his* for *their*, we may be making a mistake, as *they* may mean women, or both men and women. Supposing that 'they' refers to both men and women, are we to say 'his or her turn respectively'? This phraseology is suggestive of a legal document rather than of ordinary diction. In such a case two courses are open to us,—to say simply 'in turn,' or to dispense with the *each* and say *all*.

The use of **adjectives as adverbs** has been dealt with on p. 175, and of **adjectives as nouns** on p. 106.

251. Errors in connexion with the **use of the comparative and the superlative degree** are illustrated in the following passages:

1. Use of the superlative when fewer than three things are compared—

'Of London and Paris the former is the wealthiest.'
'Which is the most learned of the two scholars?'

and of the comparative when more than two things are compared—

'The town consists of three distinct quarters, of which the western one is by far the larger.'

To object to speaking of the division of a town into three *quarters* would be hypercritical: when used of a town, 'quarter' means 'a part,' not necessarily 'a fourth part.' In like manner we may speak of 'a weekly journal,' though originally a journal must have been a publication issued every *jour* or 'day.'

2. Confusion of the comparative and superlative forms of expression—

'Of all other nations England is the greatest.'

Unless we have already specified one nation as the greatest and are making a comparison between all the remaining nations, this sentence is faulty. To say 'America is the greatest nation, and of all other nations England is the greatest' is correct. But if this is not our meaning, we must say either (1) 'England is the greatest of all nations,' or (2) 'England is greater than all other nations.' To blend the two expressions produces an illogical result, for England is not one *of* the other nations and therefore cannot be the greatest of the other nations. 'All other nations' signifies all the nations *except* England.

Milton, imitating a Greek construction, speaks of—

'Adam the goodliest man of men since born
'His sons; the fairest of her daughters Eve.'

But how could Adam be one '*of* men since born,' or Eve one *of* her own daughters?

An analogous mistake is illustrated in this sentence:

'Tennyson was greater than all the poets of his age.' 'All the poets' includes Tennyson. He could not be greater than himself. Say therefore 'all the other poets.'

3. Pleonasm or excess of expression. Double comparatives and superlatives were common in Shakespeare's time: 'more better,' 'most unkindest,' 'most straitest.' We avoid such obvious redundancies of form now-a-days, but sometimes employ expressions which really are pleonastic: 'more perfect,' 'most universal.'

'He advised me to choose the smallest of the two, and which certainly appears to be the most preferable.' Note here (1) 'smallest and most preferable of two'; (2) 'preferable' is already comparative in meaning; 'most preferable' is therefore pleonastic; (3) *and* is redundant. Say, 'Of the two he advised me to choose the smaller, which certainly appears to be preferable.'

Observe however that although 'most preferable,' or even 'more preferable,' is pleonastic in this context, since only two things are compared, a case might occur in which the use of 'more preferable' and 'most preferable' would be legitimate. Suppose that four things, A, B, C, and D, are set before us, and a choice is allowed. Then, if we like B better than A, C better than B, and D better than C, we may say that in our opinion B is preferable to A, but C is more preferable, and D the most preferable of all.

252. Should we say, 'The two first' or 'The first two'?

Strictly speaking there can be only one first, but 'first' and 'last' are often used to signify 'in front' and 'towards the end' respectively: so we say 'the first remarks I have to make,' 'the first days of the year,' 'the last lines of the play.' Now if we talk of 'the first' or 'the last days of the year,' we may talk of 'the two first' or 'the two last days of the year.' 'The first two' is free from this objection, but it is open to another. It suggests a 'second two,' whereas there may be only three in the entire series.

253. The uses of the so-called **Definite** and **Indefinite Articles** are given on p. 109.

Some care is necessary in the use of the Articles to avoid ambiguity in those cases in which ambiguity is possible. 'A black and a white horse' means two horses, one black, the other white; 'a black and white horse' means one piebald horse. 'The secretary and the treasurer' means two officials; 'the secretary and treasurer' means one man who holds both offices. But when no misunderstanding is possible, the article is frequently repeated for the purpose of emphasis: 'A dark and a distant unknown,' 'This machine is the cheapest and the best.'

The following are clearly wrong:
'I saw the secretary and treasurer, and they examined my accounts.'
'He could not distinguish between the red and green signal.'
'A statesman and politician are two very different persons.'

When there is no chance of ambiguity, because the adjectives cannot be taken as descriptive of a single thing, English idiom allows us either to repeat the article with the noun in the singular, or to use it only once with the noun in the plural. So we may say 'The Old and the New Testament,' or 'The Old and New Testaments;' 'the singular and the plural number,' or 'the singular and plural numbers;' 'the primary and the secondary meaning,' or 'the primary and secondary meanings.' But 'the black and white horses' might signify either the piebald horses, or those horses which are all black and those which are all white. When the latter meaning is intended, there are two forms of expression free from all risk of misinterpretation, namely, 'the black and the white horses,' or 'the black horses and the white ones.'

Correct:—'It is sometimes said that the Nile is longer than all the rivers of the eastern and of the western hemispheres. During the past week it has overflown its right and left banks.'

The following points require consideration: (1) As the Nile is one of the rivers of the eastern hemisphere, can it be longer than '*all* the rivers of the eastern hemisphere?' (2) 'The eastern and the western hemispheres,'—'the eastern and the western hemisphere,'—'the eastern and western hemispheres:' which of these forms may we use? why? Apply the same principle to 'right and left banks.' (3) From what verb does *overflown* come?

254. Government. The adjectives *like* and *near* govern an objective case: 'I met a man like *him*,' 'The

boy near *me* made a disturbance.' *Like* is used also as an
adverb; 'like as a father pitieth his children,' meaning 'in
like manner as.' But it should never be used as a conjunction, followed by a nominative case and a finite verb.
Such solecisms[1] as 'like you said,' 'like I told you,' though
in common use, are peculiarly grating and offensive.

'These sort of men are sure not to speak true like we do.'

Here we have (1) 'these sort,' already commented on: (2) 'speak
true' instead of 'truly' (or 'the truth'): 'true' can be defended however
on the ground that the adjective is used as an adverb, p. 183. (3) 'like'
used as a conjunction instead of 'as.' *Like* would require *us* after it,
but we cannot make *us* the subject of *do*, therefore *like* must be
discarded, unless we say 'like as we do,' employing *like* as an adverb.
But such an expression is out of date.

255. Order. A single adjective used attributively
generally stands before the noun, but in poetry sometimes
comes after it, *e.g.* 'tempests fierce,' 'shadows dark,' and in
certain phrases it always occupies this position owing to
Norman French influence: *e.g.* 'knight errant,' 'heir
apparent,' 'malice prepense,' 'sign manual.' When several
adjectives are attached to one noun they are sometimes
placed after it for emphasis: 'We reached the town, dull,
dismal, and deserted.'

II. Pronouns.

256. Concord. In so far as Pronouns possess inflexions, they may be said to agree with the Nouns for which
they stand in Gender, Number, and Person: their Case is
regulated by their relation to their own clause. Thus we
say 'Your sister borrowed my dictionary yesterday: I met
her this morning, and *she* gave *it* back to me:' 'Let us
divide the books: you take *these* and I will keep *those*.'

[1] By a solecism is signified a violation of syntax or of idiom. The
people of the Athenian colony of Soli in Asia Minor spoke Greek with
many blunders. Hence an error in grammar or pronunciation was
called σολοικισμός, from which we borrowed the word *solecism*.

The anticipatory *It* is used however of masculine and of feminine nouns, and of nouns both singular and plural: 'It is the prince and princess.' *You*, the pronoun of ordinary address, though applied to single individuals, is followed by a verb in the plural: 'You are old, father William.'

257. Great care is needed in the employment of pronouns: the promiscuous use of them is frequently a source of obscurity[1]. The historian Clarendon is a notorious transgressor against clearness in the use of the pronouns. In the following extract from Goldsmith's *History of Greece*, the numbers 1, 2, 3, inserted after the pronouns of the Third Person, refer respectively to Philip, Aristotle, and Alexander:

'*He* [1] wrote to that distinguished philosopher...begging of *him* [2] to undertake *his* [3] education, and to bestow upon *him* [3] those useful lessons which *his* [1] numerous avocations would not allow *him* [1] to bestow.'

In Indirect Narrative the dangers of ambiguity from this cause are naturally great. Thus—

'A father who brought his boy to the police court complained that *he* got up and ran away before *he* was out of bed.'

'He told his friend that, if *he* did not feel better in half-an-hour, *he* thought that *he* had better go home.'

258. Construction of the Relative Pronoun. How far is it correct to say that there is agreement of the relative with its antecedent in gender in English? *Who* is used only of persons, *which* (in modern English) of other animals and inanimate things. *That* is used in reference to antecedents of all kinds. The concord of the relative with the antecedent in number and person can be seen only in the inflexion of the verb which agrees with the relative. Thus, in the following sentences—

---

[1] See Angus' *Handbook of the English Tongue*, p. 289, and Salmon's *School Composition*, pp. 181—3.

> ' I, who *am* here, see this,'
>
> ' Thou, who *art* here, seest this,'
>
> ' He, who *is* here, sees this,'
>
> 'We, you, they, who *are* here, see this,'

the change in the person or number of the relative *who* is seen in the change in the verb which agrees with it. *Am, art, is*, are not in agreement with *I, thou, he;* they are in agreement with *who. I, thou, he*, are nominatives to *see, seest, sees*, respectively: *who* is the nominative to *am, art, is*, and the person of *who* is determined according as it refers to *I, thou, he.*

The following sentence is wrong. Probably most students would correct it, but only a few would give the right reason.

'Thou **art** he who hast commanded us.' *Hast* should be *has.* Why? Not, as five people out of six would say, "Because it must agree with its subject *he*," for *he* is not its subject; but because it must agree with its subject *who*, and *who* is here of the 3rd person, since it refers to an antecedent *he*, which is the pronoun of the 3rd person.

Ought we to say 'It is I, your master, who command you,' or 'It is I, your master, who commands you'?

Either construction admits of defence. In the former case *who* refers to *I* as its antecedent; in the latter to *master*, the noun in apposition with *I.*

The following **examples** are wrong because the relative does not agree with its antecedent in number: the **mistake** is due to **attraction** of *one.*

'It is one of the most valuable books **that** has appeared in any language.'

Has should be *have*, because its subject *that* refers to a plural antecedent, *books.*

'Johnson's *Lives of the Poets* are now published in six octavo volumes, forming one of the most elegant editions that was ever offered to the public.'

Here (1) *are* should be *is:* (2) *was* should be plural, as *that*, its nominative, refers to a plural antecedent, *editions;* (3) *was* should be *have been*, as the statement covers all editions up to the time of writing the notice.

The **case** of the relative is determined by its **construction in its own clause.** Thus in the sentences 'This is the man *who* lost his money,' 'This is the man *whose* money was lost,' 'This is the man *whom* they robbed,' the antecedent *man* is in the nominative case, but the case of the relative varies according to the requirements of the clause in which it occurs.

Errors in the case of the relative occur in the following sentences :

'He picked up the man who he had knocked down.' *Who* should be *whom*, object of *knocked down*.

'I offer a prize of six pairs of gloves to whomsoever will tell me what thought is passing through my mind.' *Whomsoever* cannot stand as subject of *will tell*. The error arises from the suppression of the antecedent, which would be in the objective case, governed by *to*. The full expression is 'to *him whosoever* will tell.' *Whosoever* is wrongly attracted to agree in case with the antecedent, which is omitted.

259. Government. Errors of case sometimes occur in the use of the personal and relative pronouns. Such expressions as the following are often to be heard : 'Ask him to let you and *I* go,' 'Between you and *I* it stands in this way,' 'You are taller than *me*,' '*Whom* do men say that I am ?' Two common forms of faulty construction of the interrogative pronoun are commented on in the following paragraphs.

'Who did you ask to come ?'

What are we to say about the grammar of this sentence? Clearly the *who* is indefensible on formal grounds, as we see by throwing the sentence into the shape of an assertion, 'You asked *him* (not *he*) to come.' And in deliberate or dignified speech or writing, *whom* is the word which we should employ. But in ordinary conversation *who* is often used in sentences of this sort by people who are quite aware that *whom* is grammatically the correct form. Expressions of this type have indeed been defended on the assumption that there is an ellipsis of the words *is it that* after *Who*:—'Who *is it that* you did ask to come?' in which expanded sentence the relative pronoun *that* is the object required. But this ingenious assumption rests on no valid foundation, and the slovenly constructions in question must be avoided by those who wish to speak correct English.

'Who do you believe he is ?'

To test this construction, let us once more change the form from that of a question to that of a statement. We may say (1) 'I believe *(that) it is he,*' or (2) 'I believe it *to be him.*' Both are right. In (1) we have a subordinate noun clause, ' It is he ': in (2) we have a construction which corresponds to the Latin accusative and infinitive. Restoring the parallel interrogative forms, we get (1) 'Do you believe (that) he is who?' *i.e.* 'Who do you believe (that) he is?' and (2) ' Do you believe it to be whom?' *i.e.* 'Whom do you believe it to be?'

But the two constructions must not be confused in the same sentence. To say, 'Whom did you suppose was going?' is as wrong as it would be to say, ' Did you suppose him was going?' We may correct the error by saying (1) 'Who did you suppose was going?' or (2) ' Whom did you suppose tò be going?'

QUESTIONS.

1.   Distinguish between the meaning of ' He had few followers,' and ' He had a few followers '; ' I got little credit for it,' and 'I got a little credit for it '; ' She has a black and white pony,' and ' She has a black and a white pony.'

2.   Correct and give reasons for your corrections:

' He pays no regard to those kind of things.'

' He is good-looking and good-mannered, but one of those impulsive men that says just what he thinks.'

' The son walks exactly like the father did.'

' I had more rather he be neither a soldier or lawyer.'

' Neither of these persons consider themselves competent.'

' The master told every boy to do their work and said he would punish whoever he saw idle.'

3.   Write short notes explaining the use of the words in italics:

   (1)   I could a tale unfold *whose* lightest word...
   (2)   As *who* should say...
   (3)   Smite *me* him quickly.

[These sentences contain no grammatical error.

   (1)   *Whose* was originally of all genders and served as the possessive case of both *who* and its neuter *what.* Its use as a neuter possessive is now confined to the diction of poetry: this is rather a drawback, as *of which* is a more cumbrous expression.

   (2)   *Who* is here an indefinite pronoun meaning ' any one,' 'some one,' not the relative *who* with antecedent *one* suppressed. The neuter *what* survives as an indefinite pronoun in the expression ' I can tell you *what*,' that is, ' I can tell you something.' 'As who should say ' is archaic, but Dickens frequently employs it, *e.g.* in *Our Mutual Friend.*

   (3)   The *me* is the Indirect object, and the construction corresponds with the Latin *Dativus Commodi*: see p. 238. *Me* signifies ' for me.']

4. What is to be noticed in this passage from *Coriolanus*?

'Him I accuse
The city ports by this hath entered.'

[Complete the construction by supplying the suppressed antecedent. The sentence then reads '*He whom* I accuse...hath entered.' Now we may omit the antecedent and say 'Whom I accuse,' or omit the relative and say 'He I accuse'; but Shakespeare omits the relative and allows the antecedent to be attracted to the objective case of the relative.]

5. State the laws which determine the use of the words 'who' and 'that' in a relative sentence. Give a sentence showing how the sense is affected according as the one or the other of these two words is used.

[Respecting the first part of the question, see p. 128. If *who* and *which* were used purely as co-ordinating relatives, and *that* as the restrictive or limiting relative, ambiguity would sometimes be avoided. Thus 'His friends who lived in London missed him greatly,' in the mouth of the ordinary speaker, may signify either (1) His friends missed him greatly and his friends lived in London, or (2) Those particular friends living in London missed him though his friends in other towns may not have done so. In this latter sense the use of the restrictive *that* instead of *who* is recommended, but the distinction is not carried out in modern practice. Similarly, 'I will give you my books which are at my lodgings' may signify either 'all my books, and my books are at my lodgings,' or 'those particular books at my lodgings out of my entire stock.' If *that* were reserved for the latter meaning, the expression would be free from risk of a wrong interpretation.]

6. Explain the term *Attribute*, and give instances of five different ways of enlarging or qualifying the subject of a sentence.

[An attribute is a quality *attributed* to a thing: when we say 'The horse is white,' we explicitly assert the presence of the attribute or quality *whiteness*. When we speak of 'the white horse,' we implicitly affirm the presence of the attribute. See p. 104. As the adjective marks the presence of the attribute or quality in a thing, the adjective attached to a noun is sometimes called the attribute of the noun, but this misuse of terms should be avoided.

For the enlargement of the subject, see p. 213.]

7. State the rule for the agreement of the relative with its antecedent. When may the relative be omitted? Give an example.

Correct:—'Let him and I settle who we will invite.'

8. When the words *either, such, one, as*, are used as pronouns, to what classes do they severally belong?

Write down one example of the pronominal use of *as*.

Parse the italicised words in:—'Go, get *you* to your house;' 'He did it *himself*;' '*Such* a lovely day!'

9. Correct the following sentences. Each sentence contains more than one error; some contain several.

'Somebody called, I could not firstly tell whom, but, after, I found it was her.'

'Three courses suggest themselves to me; but neither of these, or indeed any other seem acceptable to the President, whom people think is one of the most incompetent men that has ever occupied the Chair.'

'My niece, whom it was supposed had been murdered, is a girl of ten years old.'

'Do you remember my cousin whom we thought had settled in Australia? There is some talk of him returning.'

10. Is any correction required in the following sentence?—'I, he, and you can go.'

[In this sentence there is nothing formally wrong, but usage enjoins a different arrangement of the pronouns. From motives of politeness the first place is given to the person addressed : from feelings of modesty the speaker mentions himself last. Hence we should say 'You, he, and I can go.' When a speaker joins others with himself and uses the plural number, considerations of courtesy and modesty are no longer applicable, and the pronouns occupy their natural positions, *we* standing first, *you* second, and *they* third : 'We, you and they can go.']

11. Correct the following sentences, and give a reason for every change :

'For ever in this humble cell
Let thee and I, my fair one, dwell.'

'Who did you see at the regatta?'

'The latter of the three solutions is more preferable.'

'If this be him we mean, let him beware.'

'I saw the pickpocket and policeman on opposite sides of the street.'

'These kinds of birds are found in Africa.'

'It is unfair to argue like you do.'

'This principle is of all others the most important.'

'The logical and historical analysis of a language often coincides.'

'Who can it be for.'

'Government sells arms to whomsoever wishes to buy.'

'They show marks who they come from.'

'I am one of those who cannot describe what I do not see.'

'It was the most amiable, although the least dignified, of all the party squabbles by which it had been preceded.'

CHAPTER XXV.

Syntax of Verbs.

260. Concord. The Verb agrees with its Subject in Number and Person.

Thus we say 'He is,' 'They are,' 'Men work,' not 'He are,' 'They is,' 'Men works.' Observe, however, that—

1. Collective nouns in the singular may be followed by a verb in the singular or plural, according as we are thinking of the aggregate, or of the individuals composing it. We may say 'The Committee *were* divided in opinion,' or 'The Committee *was* unanimous.'

2. Several nouns which are plural in form are usually construed as singular, since their meaning is singular or collective: thus, 'The news *is* true.' Other examples are given on p. 89, (3).

The same explanation applies to our employment of a singular verb with a plural noun which forms the title of a book: the book is singular though the title is plural. We say therefore 'Johnson's *Lives of the Poets has* been edited afresh'; 'Macaulay's *Biographies is* a reprint from the Encyclopædia Britannica.'

Two or more nouns in the singular joined by *and* require a verb in the plural: 'He and I *were* astonished.' But if the nouns are names of the same thing, the verb is singular : so we say 'The secretary and treasurer *has* absconded,' when one man holds the two offices. And on similar grounds, when the different nouns together express one idea, the verb is frequently in the singular : 'Two and two *is* four' :

> 'Early to bed and early to rise
> '*Makes* a man healthy, wealthy, and wise.'

But if we employ 'with' or 'as well as' in the place of 'and,' the verb is not plural, unless indeed it would be plural without the addition of these words and the noun which follows them. Thus, 'The minister, with his private secretaries, *was* present'; as *with* is a preposition, it is impossible that *secretaries* should be a nominative to the verb, for *secretaries* is in the objective case governed by *with*. Again, 'Veracity, as well as justice, *is* to be our rule,' not *are*, for the elliptical clause 'as well as justice' is introduced as a parenthesis.

Nouns in the singular joined by *or* or *nor* require a verb in the singular : the force of these conjunctions is to present the subjects as **alternatives,** not jointly.

Hence the following are wrong :
'Nor want nor cold his course delay.'
'Death or banishment were the alternatives placed before him.'

If *or* or *nor* connects two **Pronouns of different persons,** it is doubtful what the construction of the verb should be. Perhaps the safest rule would be to make the verb agree with the pronoun which immediately precedes it, but even this arrangement produces very harsh effects. Should we say—

> 'Either he or I *are* going,'
> 'Either he or I *am* going,'
> 'Either he or I *is* going'?

The usage of different people may vary. A good many would say *are*, although as *or* is an alternative conjunction and indicates that the subjects are to be taken separately, the verb must at any rate be singular. If we say *am*, the verb agrees with the subject *I* but not with the subject *he* : if we say *is*, it agrees with *he* but not with *I*. In practice it is easy, and also desirable, to avoid this difficulty by modifying the sentence thus : ' Either he is going or I am.'

Grammatical blunders often arise through mistaking for the subject a dependent noun of a different number from that of the subject, owing to its position immediately before the verb. The following are illustrations of this error :

' To Marat, and Danton, and Robespierre, *are* due the honour of having made it universal.' The subject of the verb is *honour*, and the verb should be singular.

' His knowledge of French and English literature *were* far beyond the common.' The writer is misled by the words ' French and English literature' which come next the verb, and forgets that the noun ' knowledge ' in the singular is subject of the verb.

When words take irregular constructions owing to the influence of other words, they are said to be *attracted*.

261. Government. The *Direct Object* and the *Indirect Object* are dealt with on p. 100, the *Cognate Object* on p. 137, the *Retained Object* in the Passive construction with verbs which take a Direct and an Indirect Object on pp. 143, 238. Note that, when both Objects follow the verb, the Indirect Object precedes the Direct Object. For if this order is reversed, a preposition is required before the Indirect Object, and the noun or pronoun is then the object of the preposition and no longer the Indirect Object of the verb. So, ' Get me a cab ' becomes ' Get a cab *for* me': ' I gave him a book ' becomes ' I gave a book *to* him.'

262. Moods. The uses of the Subjunctive are set out on p. 147. The constructions of the different parts of the Verb Infinite, Noun and Adjective, are given on pp. 149—154. The student is advised to read these passages again and then to consider carefully Questions 6 to 20 at the end of this Chapter.

263. Uses of Shall and Will.

In the Chapter on Auxiliary Verbs, it was pointed out that *Shall* and *Will*, when employed as auxiliaries, express futurity. A more detailed statement of their different uses is given in a convenient form in the following table [1]:

To express	1st pers.	2nd & 3rd pers.	Examples.
1. Futurity	shall	will	I *shall* come to-morrow. You *will* get back late. He *will* arrive first.
2. Question	shall	shall, will	*Shall* I pass? *Shall* you pass? *Will* he pass?
3. Determination	will	will	I *will* have my own way. You *will* have your own way. He *will* have his own way.
4. Promise	will	shall	I *will* pay you to-morrow. You *shall* be paid to-morrow. He *shall* be paid to-morrow.
5. Compulsion	shall	shall	He says I *shall* do it. You *shall* obey me. He *shall* surely die.

[1] Adapted from Sir E. B. Head's *Shall and Will*, p. 119.

The student should learn the first column of this table containing the list of different notions under which our uses of *shall* and *will* are classified. Then, if he grasps the meaning of the terms employed, he can easily make his own examples and, by the exercise of his intelligence, write down either *shall* or *will* as appropriate to the different persons. This will be a much better course for him than burdening his mind with a table of details mechanically got by heart.

264. In a similar manner we can make a table of the **Uses of Should and Would.**

To express	1st pers.	2nd & 3rd pers.	Examples.
1. Contingent Futurity	should	would	(I *should* be surprised, if it rains. You *would* be surprised, if it rains. He *would* be surprised, if it rains.
2. Hypothesis	should	should	(If I *should* see him, I will tell him. If you *should* see him, tell him. If he *should* see you, tell him.
3. Determination	would	would	(I *would* go, if I could. You *would* go, if you could. He *would* go, if he could.

265. Sequence of Tenses. The Tense of a verb in a Subordinate clause is usually in accordance with the following rules:

In the Principal Clause		*In the Subordinate Clause*
I. { Present Future }	may be followed by	Any Tense.
II. Past	must be followed by	Past.

Illustrations of Rule I.

He says that he works hard.
He says that he will work hard.
He says that he was working hard.
He says that he had worked hard.
He will tell you that he had been working hard.
He is working hard so that he may pass.
He has worked hard so that he may pass.
He will pass if he work hard.
He will see that he was wrong.
He acts as if he were mad.
He has promised that you shall be paid.

Illustrations of Rule II.

He said that he would come.
He hoped that he might pass.
He thought that he had passed.
He acted as if he were mad.
He could do it if he liked.
He would do it if he were able.

If however the dependent clause affirms a proposition which is true for all time, the present tense is generally used, though the principal clause contain a past tense : so, 'Shakespeare affirmed that cowards *die* many times,' ' Carlyle asked if virtue *is* a gas.' But the past also would be quite admissible.

What is the difference of meaning between 'I intended to write' and 'I intended to have written,' ' He hoped to get the prize' and 'He hoped to have got the prize'?

By our English idiom a peculiar meaning is attached to the Perfect Infinitive when it follows the Past tense of verbs of future import, such as *intend, hope, expect, wish.* If I say, 'I intended to write,' there is nothing in the use of the Indefinite Infinitive, *to write,* to show whether or not my intention was carried out. Thus, in reply to the thanks of a friend for an unexpected letter from me, I may say, 'I always intended to write,' or in reply to his complaint that he has not heard from me, I may say, 'I quite intended to write.' If, on the other hand, I say, 'I intended to have written,' the use of the Perfect Infinitive implies that my intention was never executed. Perhaps something prevented, or I forgot. In like manner, if a person says of a boy, 'He hoped to have got the prize,' we should conclude that the prize had gone to somebody else, whilst the statement, 'He hoped to get the prize,' is consistent with the possibility that he succeeded or failed.

A similar distinction is made when the idea of duty is expressed. If we say, ' It was his duty to do it,' we do not imply either that he did his duty or that he failed to do it. If we say, 'It was his duty to have done it,' or ' He ought to have done it,' we imply that his duty was left undone.

266. Reported Speech. In reproducing the precise words used by a speaker we quote his speech *directly.* But if we introduce his remarks with 'He said that,' or an equivalent expression, it is necessary to alter the pronouns and tenses, and the speech is then reported *indirectly,* or in 'oblique narrative.' This distinction was denoted in Latin by the terms *Oratio Recta* and *Oratio Obliqua.* As an illustration, take the following passage :

"I wish you would play up," said the captain : "why are you all so slack? Do keep the ball low. They will get another goal directly, if you don't look out."

Here we have the speaker's own words given in direct narrative. They may be indirectly reported in three ways:

    (1) by the speaker himself;

    (2) by one of the team;

    (3) by an outsider.

Captain's original speech.	Captain reports himself.
I wish you would play up. Why *are you* all so slack? *Do* keep the ball low. They *will* get another goal directly, if *you don't* look out.	(I said) *I wished they* would play up. Why *were they* all so slack? *They must* keep the ball low. The other fellows *would* get another goal directly, if *they didn't* look out.
One of the team reports Captain.	Outsider reports Captain.
(He said) *He wished we* would play up. Why *were we* all so slack? *We were* to keep the ball low. They *would* get another goal directly, if *we didn't* look out.	(He said) *He wished they* would play up. Why *were they* all so slack? *They must* keep the ball low. The other fellows *would* get another goal directly, if *they didn't* look out.

After a present tense of the principal verb, (*He says*), the tenses of the reported speech will be different from those given above. In the absence of directions to the contrary, a passage for conversion to indirect narrative is supposed to be introduced by a verb in the past tense, (*He said*), and the reporter is supposed not to form one of the persons addressed.

As a further exercise let us write in the third person the following speech of King Richard, avoiding ambiguity, and beginning *King Richard said that*—

'I wish I may forget my brother John's injuries as soon as he will forget my pardon of them.'

This becomes—'He wished he might forget his brother John's injuries as soon as John would forget the King's pardon of them.'

Copious examples for practice in the conversion from the direct to the indirect form, and from the indirect to the direct form of narrative, are furnished by the daily newspapers in their parliamentary reports.

QUESTIONS.

1. What rules about Concord are still observed in English?

[Concord occurs in the following instances:

(1) The verb and its subject in number and person.

(2) The adjectives *this* and *that* in number.

(3) The noun in apposition in case.

(4) The pronouns in gender, number, and person.]

2. Give rules respecting the concord of verbs with their subjects, when subjects differing in number, or person, or both, are connected by a conjunctive or alternative conjunction.

3. Comment on the following constructions from Milton and Shakespeare:

> 'Bitter complaint and sad occasion dear
> '*Compels* me to disturb your season due.'

> 'No ceremony that to great ones 'longs,
> 'Not the King's crown, nor the deputed sword,
> 'The marshal's truncheon, nor the judge's robe
> '*Become* them with one half so good a grace
> 'As mercy does.'

4. Correct the following sentences:—

'This and that man was born there.'

'Honour as well as profit are to be gained by this.'

'Homer as well as Virgil were studied by him.'

'But the temper as well as knowledge of a modern historian require a more sober and accurate language.'

'The happiness or misery of men's lives depend very much on his early training.'

'Neither Thomas nor John were there.'

'I, whom nor avarice nor pleasure move.'

'Neither you or me are invited.'

'The diligent study of classics and mathematics prepare the mind for any pursuit in which it may engage.'

'Nothing but misfortunes have been the result.'

'Bacon's *Essays* are the most important of these two works.'

'Three spoonsfull of water to one of wine is not near sufficient.'

[Notice here, (1) the compound noun in the plural is *spoonfuls*: in *spoons full* we have two words, *spoons*, a noun, and *full*, an adjective limiting the noun. We may say either 'three spoonfuls' or 'three spoons full.' Here the former is more suitable, as it is a quantity of liquid that is spoken of, not a number of spoons. (2) The singular *is* may be defended, as the subject, though plural in form, represents a whole. Similarly we say 'Twice two *is* four,' 'Twenty years *is* a long time,' 'Two-thirds *has* been lost.' (3) *Near*? Can this be justified?]

5. Explain the term *Indirect Object*. Write two short sentences in illustration of its use after verbs, and one of its use after an adjective.

Give instances, one of each kind, of words (1) governed by, (2) agreeing with, (3) qualifying, other words.

[*Like, unlike, near,* will furnish the construction of the Indirect Object required after adjectives.]

6. Explain with full examples the uses of the different *moods* of the verb.

Notice especially the cases when *if* can be followed by the indicative, and when it must have a subjunctive.

[For an answer to the former part of the question see p. 145. The latter part is dealt with below, Q. 8.]

7. Give a definition of the Subjunctive Mood, distinguishing it from the Indicative.

State the Mood of the word *may* in—

(*a*) You may go.

(*b*) I give that you may give.

(*c*) May good digestion wait on appetite.

Give reasons for your answer in each case.

[In (*a*) *may* has its own meaning as a notional verb: 'You may go' signifies 'You are at liberty to go.' In (*b*) it has parted with its own meaning and become a mere auxiliary of *give*, marking the subjunctive mood. The same is true of its use in (*c*) where, as an auxiliary of *wait*, it serves to express a wish.]

8. What is the general rule for the use of the indicative or the subjunctive mood in dependent sentences? Illustrate this rule by an example.

[If the condition expressed by the verb in the dependent sentence is assumed as a fact, but without our wishing to imply that we think it likely or unlikely to be fulfilled, the indicative should be used: but if the condition is stated as something conceived by the speaker either as unlikely or as actually impossible, the subjunctive should be used. As we remarked before however (p. 147), the indicative has very largely taken the place of the subjunctive where the use of the latter would be more appropriate.

This distinction may be illustrated thus:

'If he *is* in the garden, I will find him,' (He may be or he may not for anything that I know; but assuming that he is, I will find him.)

'If he *be* in the garden, I will find him,' (I am doubtful: it is unlikely that he is.)

'If he *were* in the garden, I would find him,' (I deny that he is.) Hence the subjunctive is the right mood in which to express a wish, 'I wish he *were* less idle,' which he is not; and a purpose, 'Mind that you *be* ready by one o'clock,' for as the event is future, it must be regarded only as conjectured, not realised.]

9. Give examples of the different ways in which *is* can be altered into the subjunctive mood in English. Give a classification of the various uses of the subjunctive mood.

[Take the sentence 'He *is* idle.' We may convert this from indicative to subjunctive in these ways: (1) Though he *be* idle, he will pass his examination : (2) Though he *may be* idle, he will pass: (3) Though he *should be* idle, he would pass : (4) Though he *were* idle, he would pass.

The answer to the latter part of the question is given on p. 147.]

10. Write out the past tense of the subjunctive mood of the verb *to be,* and give an example of the use of the 3rd person singular of this tense after the conjunctions *if, that, though,* respectively.

[For the conjugation see p. 146.

'If he were here, you would not say so.'

'I wish that he were here.'

'Though he were here, I should say just the same.']

11. How is future time indicated in the subjunctive mood?

[As the subjunctive has no future tenses, the present tense is used. 'We shall be sailing up the Channel to-morrow'
'We shall have passed Dover to-morrow' if the wind *keep* favourable.']
'We shall reach the Nore to-morrow'

12. Correct:—'If he don't know, I am sure I don't.'

[Consider what *don't* is a contraction of. *Don't* is 'do not,' so the sentence is 'If he do not know, I am sure I do not.' On a suitable occasion 'If he do not' is correct English, the verb being in the subjunctive mood. But this is not a suitable occasion on which to employ the subjunctive. 'If' is not used in this sentence with its ordinary conditional sense. On the contrary it signifies rather 'assuming as a fact.' Hence the indicative should be used both in the antecedent and in the consequent clause, and we ought to say 'If he doesn't know, I am sure I don't,' our meaning being this,—' Seeing that he is certainly ignorant, I am certainly ignorant too.']

13. What parts of the Verb may be used as (*a*) nouns, (*b*) adjectives? Apply your answer to the verb *speak*, by making short sentences in which this verb is used in the different ways you have mentioned.

14. What is the subject in the following: *To perform is better than to promise*? Write this with a verbal noun for subject.

Give not more than three examples of noun sentences as objects to *I remember*, and show how to express the same ideas with verbal nouns instead of verbs, using as far as possible the same words.

Comment on any peculiarity of grammar in—'He cannot choose but hear.'

[What part of speech is *but*? Think what word would be substituted for it. What mood is *hear*? What might we expect to find with it?]

15. Parse the infinitives in the following sentences :—

'To tell the truth I think you are to blame for going to sleep to kill time.'

'To think that any one, who can help it, should be content to live with nothing to do!'

[Consider carefully the uses of the gerundial infinitive specified on p. 150 and the examples in illustration of them.]

16. Give the derivation and definition of the term *Participle*.

Shew how your answer applies to the participles in the following sentence :—

'In playing tennis he was always forgetting that a ball returned by his opponent, if it touched the top of the net dividing the courts, was likely to twist.'

['Participle,' from the Latin *pars*, 'part,' *capio*, 'take'; Participles are so called because they participate in the character of both adjective and verb. Like adjectives they limit the application of nouns; like verbs (when formed from transitive verbs) they are followed by an object.]

17. Carefully parse the words ending in *ing* in the following sentence—'*Fearing* that the load was *injuring* the horses I felt no more pleasure in *travelling* through that *entrancing* scenery.'

[Notice that *entrancing*, though originally a participle describing an act, has here become an adjective describing a quality. Like an adjective, therefore, it precedes the noun which it limits : as a participle, its position would naturally be after the noun, as in the phrase 'the scenery *entrancing* our eyes.' As an adjective it can be qualified by *very*, but our English idiom does not allow us to qualify participles by *very*. We can say 'very entrancing scenery,' but not 'the scenery entrancing our eyes very.' There are indeed a few past participles which usage permits us to qualify by the use of *very*,—participles of such common occurrence that they are treated as adjectives; 'very pleased,' 'very tired.' But *much* is used with past participles regarded as past participles:

we say ' much hurt,' ' much applauded,' ' much abused,' not ' very hurt,'
' very applauded,' ' very abused.']

18. What is a Gerund? and how is it different from the Imperfect
Participle? Give examples.

Write down three sentences, in which the word 'walking' is used as
a participle, an adjective, and a verbal noun, respectively.

19. i. 'Seeing is believing.'
What different opinions have been held by grammarians as to the
origin and nature of this idiom?

ii. 'I heard of him running away.'
Is there any error in this sentence? If so, correct it, stating your
reasons for the change you make.

[i. These forms in *ing* have been called nouns, gerunds, and infinitives.
The Old English termination of the verbal noun was -*ung*; the infinitive
ended in -*an*, and its dative case, which served as a gerund, ended in
-*anne.*

ii. This sentence is not necessarily ungrammatical, but it conveys a
meaning which is different from what was probably intended. As it
stands, *running* is a participial adjunct of *him*, and the meaning is 'I
heard of *him*, when he was running away.' But the speaker's intention
was doubtless to state that he heard, not of *him*, but of the *running
away*. In that case the sentence ought to be 'I heard of *his* running
away,' where *running* is not a participle but a gerund.]

20. In how many different ways may the word *judging* be parsed?
Illustrate each of them by a sentence.

21. Correct the following sentences:

'I heard of him saying as you were ill.'

'I soon expect to hear of it being done.'
[Notice the position of the adverb *soon*. Which word should it
qualify? Put it next to that word.]

'The forgiving injuries is a Christian duty.'
[Alter in two ways, making *forgiving* (1) a Verbal Noun, (2) a
Gerund.]

'His friends were very alarmed to find that he had weakened instead
of strengthened his position.'
[Can we say '*very* alarmed'? A finite part of the verb cannot
follow a preposition: *of* requires the gerund. Or we can correct the
sentence without altering *strengthened*, if we substitute for *instead of*,
either *and not* or *rather than.*]

'If I had only ran the last few yards instead of walked, I should
have caught the train easy enough.'

'If I had not broke your stick instead of hit you with it, you would
never have ran home nor begun to tell those kind of lies which nobody
but foolish men believe.'

22. Give a short rule for the proper use of *shall* and *will*. Why are the phrases, ' I *will* be under the necessity,' ' We *will* be compelled,' incorrect ?

23. Distinguish between the use of *would* and *should*, giving examples original or quoted.

Correct :—' If I was to run quick, I would fall.'

' How will we know whether is the greatest of the two ? '

' Directly we fight we will be beaten, unless you support us.'

24. Errors of sequence of tenses occur in some of the following sentences : correct them.

' He said he won't give me any.'

' I said that I will try again.'

' She told you and me that she will come.'

' As soon as he has gone away, he wrote and told you and me to come directly.'

' I intended to have bought a moderate-sized microscope, but was told that these minute organisms can be seen only under the best instruments.'

' I was going to have written him a letter.'

' They all hoped to have succeeded.'

' Swift, but a few months before, was willing to have hazarded all the horrors of a civil war.'

[In what circumstances would *to hazard* and *to have hazarded* be respectively appropriate ?]

' Each of the three last were expected to have stopped and voted.'

' I had hoped never to have seen the statues again.'

25. State what changes in the mode of expression are made when a speech is reported in the indirect form.

Deduce from the following report the words used originally by the speaker :—' He urged them to tell him of a single enterprise in which they had succeeded, and, if they could not, to give him some better reason than their own word for believing that they were blameless. He would inquire into the facts and judge for himself.'

26. Convert the following speech into Indirect Narrative, introducing your report with the words *He said that* :

' You cannot conquer America. If I were an American, as I am an Englishman, while a foreign troop was landed in my country, I never would lay down my arms,—never, never, never ! '

27. Rewrite the following passage in Indirect Narrative, introducing the report with the words *He said that* :

' People have not been, I am told, quite as calm as sensible men should be. Bear in mind the advice of Lord Stanley. Do not let your newspapers bring you into that frame of mind under which your Government, if it desires war, may be driven to engage in it.'

28. Point out the ambiguities in the following sentence:—' Ethel told Mary that it would not be her fault if she did not succeed.'

[This report in oblique narrative may represent four different statements of Ethel's in the direct form. Give them.]

29. Correct the following sentences:

' Snapping at whomsoever laid in its way, the police siezed the dog, on account of it not only being dangerous, but also unmuzled according to law.'

[This sentence teems with errors of various kinds. First, there are two words misspelt. Secondly, there are grammatical blunders, *whomsoever, laid*, and *it*. Thirdly, there are mistakes of arrangement, whereby nonsense is made. Put the participial phrase ' snapping at whomsoever laid in its way ' next to the word of which it is the adjunct : at present it appears as if the police were snapping. The order of the words *not only being* must be changed. And was it ' according to law ' that the dog had its mouth open, or that the police captured it?]

' Bicycling down a hill, a stone tripped him up and his leg was broke. He laid there insensible some time, and when they had awakened him with some spoons full of brandy, he couldn't hardly recognise whom his friend was.'

' I hope to thoroughly master the subject in a week.'

[The separation of *to* from the verb,—a solecism called ' the split infinitive,'—should be avoided. Alter the position of the adverb in more ways than one.]

' Whom do you think I met to-day? Your two cousins ! The eldest had on a new and a most fashionable pair of boots, just like you saw Henry wearing yesterday, and the other was nearly dressed the same.'

30. A confusion of two constructions is called *Anacoluthon*, from a Greek word which means ' not following along,' ' not in sequence with ' something else. Show that the following sentences furnish illustrations of this error.

' They had awoke him, he learned, to be told that the river had overflown its banks.'

[Two constructions are blended here : ' They had awoke him to tell him,' and ' He had awoke (or been awaked) to be told.']

' He had two sisters, the one a wealthy spinister, the other a married sister is the wife of a farmer.'

' I cannot write any more now and believe me, yours sincerely.'

[To join a verb in the indicative mood to a verb in the imperative makes nonsense. Put both coordinate clauses in the indicative, changing 'believe me' for some other expression, or cancel the former clause and substitute one which contains a verb in the imperative mood.]

'My lawyer is a man whom I know is trustworthy.'

'When Nelson was ill he complained of "the servants letting me lay as if a log, and take no notice."'

'Should any one not receive the goods ordered in ten days, kindly write to the advertiser.'

'This is the man whom I perceived was in fault.'

'I think it may assist the reader by placing them before him in chronological order.'

'Mrs Jones presents her compliments to Miss Robinson and will be much obliged if she will prevent her dog from coming into my garden.'

'More than one swimming-prize is to be given for boys of thirteen years old.'

31. Criticise the following expressions :—
(1) 'Our mutual friend.'
(2) 'A reliable statement.'
(3) 'A phenomenal success.'
(4) 'I sha'n't do more than I can help.'
(5) 'If I am not mistaken.'
(6) 'Send a written message, not a verbal one.'
(7) 'Important events have transpired.'

[In (1) *common* should be substituted for *mutual*, which implies reciprocal relationship. If *A* likes *B* and *B* likes *A* their friendship is mutual. In (2) 'trustworthy' might take the place of 'reliable.' Just as *penetrable* means 'what can be penetrated' and *eatable* 'what can be eaten,' so strictly *reliable* must mean 'what can be relied,' which is nonsense. 'What can be relied *on*' would be *rely-on-able*, as 'what can be got *at*' is colloquially said to be *get-at-able*. The words *laughable*, *available* and *indispensable* are open to a similar somewhat pedantic criticism. (3) *Phenomenal* is a word misapplied by journalists in the sense 'remarkable.' Give the true meaning. (4) *Help* means 'avoid' in this context. One who wishes to do as little as possible does no more than he *cannot* avoid. (5) Why passive? The expression is always used to signify 'If I do not misunderstand,' not 'If I am not misunderstood.' (6) *Verbal* means 'in words,' so 'a written message' is 'a verbal one.' What adjective signifies 'by word of mouth'? (7) What does *transpire* mean? Events do not transpire except in journalese.]

32. Quote four examples of common errors of speech, and show wherein the faultiness consists.

33. Show that the number of rules of concord and government in any language depends on the variety and extent of its inflexions.

34. Illustrate the different kinds of grammatical concord, and show that the following sentences are faulty :

(a) 'Neither of these men are patriots at heart.'
(b) 'This is one of those things that is managed better abroad.'
(c). 'The number of failures were very great.'
(d) 'Thou great First Cause, least understood,
        Who all my sense confined.'

35. Comment on the construction of the verb in each of the following sentences :—

'Is the news true?'

'The people are divided.'

'Every limb and every feature appears with its appropriate grace.'

'Justice as well as benevolence is our rule.'

36. How can you distinguish the objective case from the nominative in English?

State the case and government (if any) of each of the italicised words in the following sentences.

(a) 'Prize *me* no prizes, for my prize is *death.*'
(b) 'She let *concealment*, like a *worm* i' the bud,
        Feed on her damask *cheek.*'
(c) 'For my *brethren* and companions' sakes.'
(d) 'That is not for such as *you.*'

37. Correct the following sentences where necessary:

'Thou lovest, but never knew love's sad satiety.'

'Nothing but grave and serious studies delight him.'

'The ship with all the passengers were lost.'

'He knows not what spleen, langour, or listlessness are.'

'The king with the lords and commons form the legislature.'

'The posture of your blows are yet unknown.'

'There is sometimes more than one auxiliary to a verb.'

'He objects to me having the book.'

'If I were old enough to be married, I am old enough to manage my father's house.'

[See the note to Q. 12, p. 262.]

'And so was also James and John, the sons of Zebedee, which were partners with Simon.'

'The steam-engine as well as the telegraph were at that time undiscovered.'

[Is *undiscovered* the right word?]

'I have not wept this forty years.'

'It must be confessed that a lampoon or a satire do not carry in them robbery and murder.'

'He must decide between you and I going to him or him coming to us.'

CHAPTER XXVI.

SYNTAX OF ADVERBS, CONJUNCTIONS, AND PREPOSITIONS.

267. THERE are some words which are variously used as Prepositions, as Adverbs, and as Conjunctions. The following sentences illustrate this threefold use of *but*, *before*, *since*.

PREPOSITIONS.	ADVERBS.	CONJUNCTIONS.
I saw nobody *but* him.	I have *but* one.	I saw him *but* not you.
Songs *before* sun-rise.	He went *before*.	He went *before* I arrived.
Since Easter.	I have not seen him *since*.	I will do so *since* you wish it.

How are such words to be distinguished?

If the word in question governs a noun or pronoun, it is a Preposition. Bear in mind the fact that the preposition frequently comes after the relative pronoun which it governs : 'I gave the book *that* he asked *for* to the man *whom* I spoke *to*'; 'This is the place *which* you told me *of*.' And this relative pronoun is often dropped out altogether : the words *that*, *whom*, and *which*, would probably be omitted from these sentences in conversation. Nevertheless, *for*, *to*, and *of* are still prepositions, for they govern these pronouns understood.

But to distinguish Adverbs from Conjunctions is often a difficult matter, for there are many adverbs which join sentences and therefore do the work of conjunctions. For identifying an adverb there is a rule-of-thumb which directs us to move the word about and observe whether the grammatical structure of the passage in which it occurs is destroyed by the process : if it is not destroyed, we are to conclude, according to this rule, that the word is an adverb. Thus the sentence '*Meanwhile* the mob continued shouting' would retain its grammatical structure unimpaired, if the word *meanwhile* were placed after *mob,* or after *continued,* or after *shouting.* But though this freedom of movement on the part of adverbs is a feature which deserves notice, it is quite useless as a practical test in precisely those instances in which the student might find a difficulty in deciding whether the word in question is to be called an adverb or a conjunction, for in those instances the word cannot be moved about, and yet it. would frequently be rightly described as an adverb. Take the sentences 'I know *where* he lives,' I saw him *when* he called,' 'I ascertained *how* he escaped.' The words *where, when, how,* cannot be shifted to other places in the sentence without making nonsense of the whole. Hence a student applying this test in his uncertainty would say they were not adverbs. Yet they are adverbs : *where* qualifies *lives, when* qualifies *called, how* qualifies *escaped,* just as much as the adverbs *there, then,* and *so* qualify these verbs when we say ' He lives *there,*' ' He called *then,*' ' He escaped *so.*' It is true that *where, when,* and *how* also join the clauses 'I know...he lives,' 'I saw him...he called,' 'I ascertained...he escaped.' But though they join clauses, they do not therefore cease to be adverbs, any more than the relative pronouns cease to be pronouns because they also join clauses. The co-ordinate clauses 'I know the man...he did it,' are united in one complex sentence by *who,* when we say 'I know the man *who* did it'; still we do not call *who* a conjunction. 'Conjunctive' or 'connective' pronouns we might indeed call them, and the name would be more appropriate than 'relative' pronouns; and 'conjunctive' or 'connective' adverbs is the proper name for words which, while acting as adverbs, also join clauses.

Ask the question therefore,—Does the word about which I am in doubt not only join two clauses but also qualify some verb or adjective in the clause which it introduces? If it does, it is a conjunctive adverb: if it does not, it is a conjunction. Thus in the sentences 'I will go *if* you wish,' 'I know *that* he died,' the words *if* and *that* connect two clauses without modifying any word which follows them; but in the sentences 'I will go *when* you wish,' 'I know *where* he died,' *when* and *where* connect two clauses and also modify the verbs *wish* and *died* respectively.

However, the student, who finds this distinction too subtle to serve him as a practical criterion, will commit no serious error if he describes a conjunctive-adverb as an adverbial-conjunction, and writers on grammar can be quoted in his support, whichever term he adopts[1].

268. The meaning affected by the position of the Adverb.

Though the grammatical structure of the sentence may be unimpaired by the shifting of the adverb from one place to another, the meaning will often be affected by the change of position. Consider the difference in the information conveyed when we say '*Only* John passed in Latin,' 'John *only* passed in Latin' and 'John passed *only* in Latin.' Errors in the position of *only* are of constant occurrence. At one of the large London Clubs, members are informed

---

[1] Cf. Mason's *English Grammar*, § 263, and Bain's *Higher English Grammar*, p. 101.

that 'Smoking is only allowed in this room after 8 o'clock.' This notice, strictly interpreted, implies that the authorities go so far as to allow, but would by no means encourage, smoking after 8 o'clock.

269. Construction with 'Than.' In an earlier stage of the language *than* was an adverb, but it may now be treated as a conjunction simply. As a conjunction it should be followed by the same case as the case of the word denoting the thing with which the comparison is made. Thus, 'I like you better than he,' and 'I like you better than him' are both correct, but with different meanings. Supplying the ellipses, we get in the former sentence, 'I like you better than he likes you'; in the latter, 'I like you better than I like him.'

'**Than whom.**' When the relative pronoun *who* is used with *than*— a form of expression which occurs but seldom—*who* is invariably put in the objective case. Thus Milton writes of Satan, 'than *whom* none higher sat.' Sometimes the objective is the right case: *e.g.* 'than *whom* I like no one better,' *i.e.* 'I like no one better than *him*.' But sometimes the nominative would be the right case: *e.g.* 'than *who* none sat higher,' *i.e.* 'no one sat higher than *he*.' Some writers argue that *than* is a preposition, but if so we ought to say, 'no one sat higher than *him*.' It is whimsical to call *than* a conjunction before *he* and a preposition before *whom* in sentences otherwise identical. Perhaps the safest thing to say is that *than whom* is an idiom, and 'Idioms are rebels against Grammar, with which the powers of literature have made peace and agreed to waive their claim to conformity.' *It's me* is another idiom, sanctioned by usage, but grammatically indefensible and (unlike *than whom*) avoided in literary English.

270. Construction of 'As.' *As* is a conjunctive adverb: it not only joins clauses but qualifies a word in the clause which it introduces. Thus, 'He whistled *as* (*i.e.* while) he went for want of thought': 'They died *as* (*i.e.* in what manner) soldiers should.' *As* is used also as a demonstrative adverb antecedent to this conjunctive *as*: 'He is *as* good as (he is) clever.' Another antecedent to *as* is *so*: 'You are not *so* silly *as* you seem.' *So* is only a demonstrative adverb, not a conjunctive adverb like *as*.

The nouns or pronouns connected by *as* must be in the same case. 'Is she as tall as *me*?' is therefore wrong : it should be 'Is she as tall as *I* (am tall)?' 'You could have done it as well as *him*' should be 'You could have done it as well as he (could have done it).'

271. 'As follows' or 'As follow'? Ought we to say 'The words are *as follows*' or 'The words are *as follow*'?

If *as* is here a relative pronoun, the relative should agree with its antecedent in number. Now the antecedent to *as* is *words*, therefore *as* requires a verb in the plural, *follow*, not *follows*. Yet we always say *as follows*, regardless of the number of the antecedent. Perhaps however *as* is here a conjunctive adverb, and there is an ellipsis of the subject *it* before *follows* : 'The words are as *it follows*.' At any rate, the phrase *as follows* has now become an adverbial expression. In like manner we say 'Your remarks so far *as concerns* me,' where *concern* would be the right form if the ellipsis after the conjunctive adverb *as* is to be supplied by *they*, 'Your remarks so far as *they concern* me.' In this instance again, we may maintain that the construction is really impersonal, and that *it*, not *they*, is the word omitted : 'Your remarks so far as *it concerns* me.' Similarly *as regards* is used in the singular whatever the number of the noun to which reference is made : 'Your intentions *as regards* me.'

272. Construction of 'No.' *No* is both an adjective and an adverb. As an adjective it is the equivalent of *none*, as an adverb, of *not*. Now it is contrary to English idiom to qualify verbs with the adverb *no*. We say 'I will *not* go,' 'Do *not* say so,' not 'I will *no* go,' 'Do *no* say so.' Hence the expression 'whether or *no*' admits of defence only when there is an ellipsis of a noun : 'Whether he is a knave or no I cannot say' may be explained as an abridgment of 'Whether he is a knave or *no knave*,' whereas 'Whether he is a knave or *not*' is an abridgment of 'Whether he is a knave or *is not* a knave.' When a verb is suppressed, 'whether or *not*' is the only admissible expression. That it is wrong to say 'Whether or *no* he did it,' we may see by

resolving the sentence into its component parts : 'Whether he did it, or he did it *not.*'

273. Ellipsis arising from the desire to be brief **is a frequent cause of error.** We say 'You are as good or better than he,' where *as* is required after *good* to make the sentence formally correct. So again in the sentence 'You work harder but not so successfully as he,' *harder* requires *than.* To supply these missing words and to say 'You are as good as or better than he,' 'You work harder than but not so successfully as he,' would be to employ modes of speech too elaborately precise for everyday purposes. We can steer clear of an error of syntax on the one hand and of pedantry on the other by saying 'You are as good as he, or better,' 'You work harder than he does, but not so successfully.'

Ellipsis is seen in the following sentence :—'He did it without intending to.'

Sentences of this type are usually condemned as ungrammatical, on the ground that the missing words, required after *to* for the completion of the sentence, are not *did it* but *do it.* It seems pedantic however to object to such a form of expression. If it is allowable to say 'He is taller than you,' where we supply 'are tall' to make the construction complete, it ought to be allowable to supply in thought 'do it' as suggested by 'did it.' Such expressions may be justified as constructions κατὰ σύνεσιν, that is, 'according to the understanding,' which supplies what is needed, by appropriately modifying what is already given.

The following example is too slip-shod to pass muster :—'Tense shows whether something is, has, or will happen.'

274. Redundant use of 'And.' *And* is often used pleonastically, that is to say, where it is superfluous, before *who* and *which:* 'He is a man of a thousand *and in whom*

I place entire confidence,' 'These are some of the errors in his books *and which* it would be tedious to enumerate.' The presence of the *and* seems to be due to a desire to avoid misunderstanding in the reference of the relative to its antecedent. If we said 'a thousand in whom,' *whom* might be taken as referring to 'thousand' instead of to 'man,' and if we said 'in his books which,' *which* might be taken as referring to 'books' instead of to 'errors.' The *and* however is clearly redundant, and ambiguity should be avoided by casting the sentence differently. When one relative clause has occurred already, a second relative clause is rightly introduced by *and*: 'This is the book *which* you lent me *and which* I have read with interest.' There is no reason in grammar or in logic why *and which* should not be used, even if no relative clause has occurred already, provided that the antecedent of *which* has already been limited by adjectival adjuncts: 'He has painted a picture striking, suggestive, refined, *and which* no other artist has equalled.' The clause introduced by *and* is equivalent to 'excellent.' We should say 'striking, suggestive, refined, and excellent,' so there is no reason why we should not say 'striking, suggestive, refined, and which no other artist has equalled.' At the same time one must admit that the construction has an unpleasant sound, though Thackeray, who is a master of style, often makes use of it.

Repetition or Omission of the Conjunction. The student should notice that, although we ordinarily insert *and* before only the last of several nouns or adjectives which occupy the same relation to the rest of the sentence, for rhetorical purposes the conjunction may be either repeated or dropped altogether. The departure from the normal usage arrests attention and heightens the effect. This may be observed in the following passages:

'Love was not in their looks...but guilt and shame and perturbation and despair and anger and obstinacy and hate and guile.'

'Fall, dark curtain, upon his pageant, his pride, his grief, his awful tragedy.'

The redundant use of conjunctions is called *Polysyndeton,* 'much-linked'; the omission of conjunctions is called *Asyndeton,* 'not linked.'

275. Omission of 'That.' The conjunction *that* is often omitted: 'He said (that) he was going,' 'I thought (that) I had done it.'

Notice the different parts of speech to which *that* belongs in the sentence 'I deny *that that that that* man said is true.' The first *that* is a conjunction; the second, a demonstrative pronoun; the third, a relative pronoun, equivalent to *which* ; the fourth, a demonstrative adjective.

276. Correlative Conjunctions. Conjunctions which occur in pairs are called Correlative. Such are *though...yet, either...or, whether...or, both...and.*

Similarly, the demonstrative adjectives *such* and *same* and the demonstrative adverb *so* have appropriate correlatives. In the sentences, 'This exercise has *such* mistakes *as* I never saw before,' 'This exercise is the *same as* you showed up yesterday,' *as* is a relative pronoun: in 'I am not *so* mean *as* to act thus,' *as* is a conjunctive adverb. *Such* and *so* are followed by the conjunction *that* when the result or purpose of an action is indicated: 'He made *such* mistakes *that* he failed to pass,' 'He took *such* pains *that* he might pass,' 'He worked *so* hard *that* he might pass.' In strictness *so* always requires a correlative to express the comparison which it implies; but in common speech *so* is used with the meaning of *very,* and the comparison is not expressed: 'She is *so* pretty, and he is *so* nice.'

The following sentence illustrates two common forms of error in connexion with the use of *neither*: 'You neither honour your father or your mother.'

Two points require correction here : (1) *neither...nor* are correlatives, not *neither...or*: (2) *neither* and *nor* must be placed before the words denoting the things or acts which we wish to exclude. Hence we must say (*a*) 'You honour neither your father nor your mother,' or (*b*) 'You do not honour either your father or your mother.' *Neither* placed before *honour* suggests some other verb to which *nor* should apply : 'You neither honour *nor obey* your father or your mother.' This misplacement of *neither* may often be found in the best writers, but this fact does not make it legitimate.

277. Idiomatic use of particular prepositions. Particular prepositions are appropriate after certain verbs, nouns, and adjectives: the use of a different preposition is a violation of idiom. Thus we say 'conform *to*,' but 'conformity *with*'; 'dependent *on*,' but 'independent *of*'; 'part *from* a person,' 'part *with* a thing'; 'disappointed *of* something' which we cannot get, 'disappointed *in* something' when we have got it. 'Differ' and 'different' are often used with the wrong preposition. When we disagree with a person we differ *from* him. Persons frequently say 'I beg to differ *with* you,' when they mean 'to differ *from* you.' If A and B agree in differing from C, we may say that A differs *with* B, but in no other sense is the use of *with* correct. Again, it is a common mistake to say 'different *to*'; 'different *from*' is prescribed by our idiom. We can speak however of 'a difference *with* a person' and of 'a difference *between* two things.' The student can test his familiarity with English usage by combining with suitable prepositions the words given in Question 5 at the end of this chapter.

Errors both of pleonasm and of ellipsis occur in the use of prepositions, especially in connexion with relative pronouns. Pleonasm, or redundancy, is seen in these sentences :

'It is to you to whom I am indebted for this favour.'

'It is to this last new feature of the game laws to which we intend to confine our notice.'

In the following, there is omission :

'My duelling pistols in rosewood case (same which I shot Captain Marker), £20.'

> 'Had I but served my God with half the zeal
> 'I served my king, he would not in mine age
> 'Have left me naked to mine enemies.'

' Participles express action with the time it happens.'

' And virgins smiled at what they blushed before.'

QUESTIONS.

1. Distinguish between an adverb and a conjunction. Parse the word *as* in both places in ' You are not *as* rich *as* he is.'

Classify adverbs according to their formation, giving examples.

Classify conjunctions. Write three short sentences in which the word *but* occurs as a conjunction, a preposition, and an adverb respectively.

2. What three parts of speech may *that* be? Construct three sentences to illustrate your answer.

3. What is a preposition? Distinguish between the uses of prepositions and conjunctions. Give two examples of *phrase-adverbs* and *phrase-prepositions*.

[*Phrase-adverbs* : ' of a truth,' ' nowadays,' ' by no means,' ' at times,' ' in front,' ' for ever and ever,' ' in a canter,' ' head over ears.'

Phrase-prepositions : ' by means of,' ' in accordance with,' ' in consequence of,' ' in reply to,' ' with a view to,' ' for the sake of.']

4. Correct :—' Should the frost continue as sharp as last week, which I do hope it may, the large pond will bear.'

[How can we compare a frost with a week ?]

' They know that as well as me.'

' She had a very fair complexion, and which was quite different to her sister's.'

' Many an emigrant have regretted the domestic pleasures from which they have been deprived, and which were impossible to be carried to their new country.'

' I hope to see you next week, and believe me, yours sincerely.'

5. What Prepositions are found in combination with the following words :—*absolve, abhorrence, acquit, adapted, agreeable, averse, call, change, confer, confide, correspond, discourage, eager, exception, expert, glad, made, need, prejudice, provide, taste, thirst, worthy ?*

Correct :—' It bears some remote analogy with what I have described.'

' You are in no danger of him.'

6. Certain words are used in English sometimes as prepositions, sometimes as conjunctions. Give examples and write sentences in which such words occur, specifying the part of speech in each example.

Write four sentences containing the word *after* and make it (1) an adjective, (2) an adverb, (3) a preposition, (4) a conjunction.

Form sentences to show the different uses of the words *for, since, but,* mentioning in each case the part of speech which the word is.

7.   The following sentences are faulty as regards the order of the words[1].   The meaning is not free from ambiguity, and rearrangement is necessary.

'I saw many dead soldiers riding across the battle-field.'

'I never remember to have seen such a storm.'

'His success is neither the result of system nor strategy.'

'Lost near the market-place a large Spanish blue gentleman's cloak.'

'He seldom took up the Bible, which he frequently did, without shedding tears.'

'The beaux of that day used the abominable art of painting their faces as well as the women.'

'Erected to the memory of John Phillips accidentally shot as a mark of affection by his brother.'

'Wanted a pianoforte for a gentleman with carved legs.'

'Rats and gentlemen catched and waited on by Solomon Gundy.'

'We regret to say that a mad dog yesterday bit the editor of the *Western News* and several other dogs.'

'Wanted a boy to open oysters with a reference.'

'The procession was very impressive and nearly a mile in length as was also the sermon of the minister.'

'A man was run over in Cheapside this morning by a cab while drunk.'

'Raw cows' milk is better for children than boiled.'

'A transitive verb is when its action passes to an object.'

[Change the position of the word 'transitive': a verb is a word, not a time.]

8.   Many sentences are faulty owing to incoherence of thought, although they may contain no violation of grammatical rules.   Point out any incoherence or confusion in the following sentences :

'The horse is a noble animal, but if you treat him unkindly he will not do so.'

'Prisoner at the bar, Providence has endowed you with great bodily strength, instead of which you go about the country stealing ducks.'

'Salt is what makes the potatoes taste nasty when you don't put any on.'

'If I am not mistaken, I met you yesterday.'

'Towards the close of his life he committed suicide.'

'I shan't do more than I can help.'

'The guilelessness of his own heart led him to expect none in others.

'This is the most wonderful preparation of modern times for the entire restoration of dimness or partial loss of sight.'

'I shall have much pleasure in accepting your kind invitation.'

[1] A large collection of examples is given in Hodgson's *Errors in the use of English* : also in Salmon's *School Composition.*

9. Distinguish the different meanings obtained by changing the position of the word *only* in the following:—' John attempted only three problems.'

Is any alteration necessary in the sentence—' I called, only I could not stop long ' ?

[*Only* is often used instead of *but*, as a conjunction to express opposition to what precedes : ' I called, but in one respect my call was limited, namely, that I could not stop long.']

Distinguish between—' Only he lost his child,' ' He only lost his child,' ' He lost only his child,' ' He lost his only child,' ' He lost his child only.'

10. What meaning do you attach to the following sentences ?—

' You punished me more severely than she.'

' You punished me more severely than her.'

Correct where necessary :—' Wilt boast boldlier than me ? '

[In Elizabethan literature examples often occur of the comparison of adverbs in *-ly* by adding *-er* and *-est* Tennyson and Carlyle have imitated the archaism with ' gentlier ' and ' proudlier.' Thus *boldlier* is not ungrammatical, though *more boldly* would be in closer conformity with our usage. *Me* should be *I*, the same case as *thou*, which is for rhetorical purposes suppressed after *wilt*.]

' It is easier said than done.'

' He did not get so many marks as me.'

' John never wrote a better letter, nor as good, as James.'

' You will soon find such peace which it is not in the power of the world to give.'

' He neither knows French nor German.'

' Neither John or Thomas considered that morning or evening are the best time for study.'

' He was neither learned in the languages or philosophy.'

Construct sentences containing the following phrases, rightly used :—
' Better than he,' ' Better than him,' ' Than whom,' ' And which,' ' As good as I,' ' As good as me,' ' Would that.'

11. Give one example of (*a*) Relative use of ' but '; (*b*) Adverbial use of ' no ' ; (*c*) Antecedent implied in Possessive ; (*d*) Infinitive Absolute ; (*e*) Object placed before Verb.

[For (*a*) see p. 129. 'There is no one *but* thinks you mad,' *i.e.* who does not think you mad, (*b*) ' He is *no* better.'

(*c*)   ' Poor is *our* sacrifice *whose* eyes
                              ' Are lighted from above.'

' *Our* sacrifice whose ' is for ' the sacrifice *of us* whose.'

(*d*) ' *To tell the truth* I dislike him.'   (*e*) See p. 239.]

12. How may conjunctions best be distinguished from adverbs? Sometimes conjunctions are used in pairs or are correlative : give examples of the use of *although* and *not only* with their correlatives.

13. Comment on—' I will try and go.'
[This colloquial use of *and* instead of *to* is common with such verbs as *try*, *come*, *go*, but it cannot be justified logically in the case of the verb *try*. For though the expressions 'Come and see,' 'Go and ask' admit of defence on the ground that two distinct actions are commanded,— to come and to see, to go and to ask,—only one action is commanded when we say 'Try and go': we mean 'Try in order that you may go.']

14. Show that in the following sentences there is Pleonasm, that is, redundancy or excess of expression.
' Traveller, from whence comest thou ? '
' Between you and me, I fancy there will be nobody else there but you and me.'
' The river of Kishon swept them away, that ancient river, the river Kishon.'
' After the most straitest sect of our religion I lived a Pharisee.'
' He behaved with great magnanimity of mind.'
' He stooped down to pick up a stone.'
' The transparency of his motive is clear to every one.'
' It is not nor it cannot come to good.'
' I do not like the house in which I live in.'
' Of the tree of the knowledge of good and evil thou shalt not eat of it.'
' And, perhaps, it may be worth revealing the fact that my distrust of our present social arrangements was deeply increased by a second visit to the United States.'
' I would be the veriest demagogue if I suggested that I had found a panacea for the immediate remedy of all those social evils.'
[What does *panacea* mean ?]

' He has eaten no bread nor drunk no wine these two days.'
[What is the construction of *these two days*? See § 243 (5), p. 238.]

' The king then entered on that career of misgovernment which. that he was able to pursue it, is a disgrace to our history.'

> ' And that no woman has ; nor never none
> Shall mistress be of it, save I alone.'

> ' What shall we say, since silent now is he
> Who, when he spoke, all things would silent be.'

' I have now the perfect use of all my limbs, except my left arm, which I can hardly tell what is the matter with it.'
' Money is the most universal incitement of human misery.'

15. Write sentences which exemplify the right use of the following combinations:—*correspond with* and *to*; *confide in* and *to*; *agree to* and *with*; *differ with* and *from*; *difference between* and *with*; *provide with*, *for* and *against*; *regard for* and *to*; *wait on*, *at* and *for*.

16. Append to the following words the appropriate prepositions:—*independent, different, angry, composed, dissent, conversant, conformable, disapprove, full, replete.*

How is the meaning of the verb *fall* affected when it is followed by the words *in, off, out, to, under, upon*, in combination with it?

17. Point out and explain any peculiarity in the following pair of sentences:—

(1) 'Excuse my answering your question.'
(2) 'Excuse my not answering your question.'

[In spite of the *not*, the two sentences have the same meaning. This is due to the fact that *excuse* in (1) signifies 'dispense with,' and in (2) 'pardon.']

18. Explain and illustrate by examples (*a*) absolute use of participle, (*b*) reflexive pronoun, (*c*) inflected subjunctive, (*d*) correlative conjunction.

19. Give examples of (*a*) compound gerunds, (*b*) words which are conjunctions and something besides, (*c*) verbs of incomplete predication, (*d*) the oldest inflexions still in use.

20. What do you understand by the following terms?—Aryan, runes, hybrid, prosody, solecism.

21. Correct the following sentences wherever the form of expression is ungrammatical or misleading:

'It is better for you and I as it is.'

'He having none but them, they having none but he.'

> 'A thousand weary miles now stretch
> Between my love and I.'

'We might have placed Smith in the first class with no more impropriety than we have placed Jones in the second.'

[To avoid this slip-shod construction, recast the sentence after the word *than*.]

'Neither he nor she are at hand.'

'The porch was the same width with the temple.'

'If he permits this, we shall speedily become as poor as them.'

'I don't believe you have got a better bicycle or even as good as me.'

'He can do it easy enough, if he don't get nervous.'

> 'And now I never dare to write
> As funny as I can.'

'From my shoulder to my fingers' ends are as if half dead.'

> 'A perfect judge will read each work of wit
> With the same spirit that its author writ.'

' Miss Smith will have much pleasure in accepting Mrs Brown's kind invitation.'

[Whatever pleasure Miss Smith finds in the acceptance of the invitation she *has* at the time when she writes to accept. The pleasure which she *will have* is the pleasure of going to the party.]

' Thersites' body is as good as Ajax', when neither are alive.'

' Luckily the monks had recently given away a couple of dogs, which were returned to them, or the breed would have been lost.'

' He was shot at by a secretary under notice to quit, with whom he was finding fault, very fortunately without effect.'

Old Friend to Artist: ' Look here, old man, I'll tell you what really brought me here to-day. The fact is, my wife wants her mother painted very badly,—and I naturally thought of you.'

' I saw a gentleman who had shot hundreds of buffaloes in London a month ago.'

' Gibbon was the eldest of five brothers who died in infancy, and of a sister who lived a little longer, and whom he knew well enough to regret her.'

' Adversity both teaches men to think and to feel.'

' These kind of books neither interest or gratify you and I.'

' The army, whom its chief had abandoned, pursued their miserable march.'

' Each of the horses reared and threw their riders.'

' This was in reality the easiest matter of the two.'

' Whom do you think I am ?'

' I am a man that have travelled far.'

            ' O Thou my voice inspire
       Who touched Isaiah's hallowed lips with fire.'

' Each of the girls went to their separate rooms to rest themselves.'

' He was angry at me quitting the house.'

      ' Art thou proud yet?'

                   'Ay, that I am not thee.'

' Whoever the king favours the cardinal will find employment for.'

' No one expressed their opinion so clearly as him.'

' Everybody has a right to look after their own interests.'

' He talks like Charles and not like you do.'

' His is a poem, one of the completest works that exists in any language.'

' Did he not confess his fault and begged to be forgiven ?'

' The town mentioned is the warmest of the two.'

' If the king gave us leave, you or I may as lawfully preach as them that do.'

' The largest circulation of any Liberal newspaper.'

' The largest circulation of any other Liberal newspaper.'

' A larger circulation than any Liberal newspaper.'

22. Give a few simple rules for Punctuation.

[It is customary to use—

(1) a Full-stop at the end of a sentence and after abbreviations:—*e.g.*, *viz.*, *ult.*, *i.e.*, M.P., B.A., K.G., Bart.

(2) a Colon or a Semicolon between sentences grammatically independent, but closely connected in sense and not very long. These stops are not used extensively by most writers at the present day. Rapid readers like to have their sentences chopped up short, so that the meaning may be taken in at a glance.

(3) a Comma to separate—
   (*a*) short co-ordinate sentences:
   (*b*) subordinate from principal clauses :
   (*c*) the noun in apposition :
   (*d*) and the nominative of address :
   (*e*) and quotations:
   (*f*) and a series of words having the same construction : *e.g.* 'Remote, unfriended, melancholy, slow.'

(4) a Dash, to separate parentheses and introduce quotations. Some writers have a fondness for the dash and employ it in places where the comma or semicolon would do equally well. Sterne in the last century and Mr Besant in our own make free use of the dash.

(5) Inverted Commas, to introduce and to end a quotation.

(6) a Note of Interrogation after direct questions.

(7) a Note of Exclamation after interjections and exclamations.

These rules are 'few and simple.' The student must bear in mind that in using stops at all our sole object is to make our meaning clear ; that the insertion of unnecessary stops is a hindrance rather than a help to the reader ; that punctuation admits of very few hard and fast laws ; that the usage of different writers varies; and that the author is frequently at the mercy of the printer in the matter of stops. Hence it seems a waste of time to burden the memory with elaborate principles of punctuation.]

23. Punctuate the following passage and insert capitals:

No one venerates the peerage more than I do but my lords I must say that the peerage solicited me not I the peerage nay more I can say and will say that as a peer of parliament as speaker of this right honourable house as keeper of the great seal as guardian of his majesty's conscience as lord high chancellor of england nay even in that character alone in which the noble duke would think it an affront to be considered as a man I am at this moment as respectable I beg leave to add I am at this moment as much respected as the proudest peer I now look down upon. *Thurlow.*

APPENDIX I.

DEFINITIONS OF SOME OF THE PRINCIPAL GRAMMATICAL TERMS.

Grammar is the science which treats of words and their correct use.

Orthoëpy deals with the correct pronunciation of words.

Orthography deals with the correct spelling or writing of words.

Etymology deals with the classification of words, their derivation and inflexion.

Syntax deals with the combination of words in sentences, their government, agreement, and order.

Parts of Speech are the classes into which the words of a language fall, when they are arranged according to their separate functions in a sentence.

Inflexion is a variation in the form of a word to mark a modification of its meaning.

The **Accidence** of a language consists of the sum-total of the inflexions which the words in a language undergo.

Analytic and **synthetic** are terms applied respectively to languages which have few or many inflexions.

A **Noun** is the name of anything.

A **Common Noun** is one which can be applied to an indefinite number of things in the same sense.

A **Singular Noun** is one which can be applied to only one thing in the same sense.

A **Proper Noun** is a singular name assigned to an individual as a mere distinguishing mark.

A **Collective Noun** is one which denotes a number of things regarded as forming a whole.

A **Concrete Noun** is the name of a thing regarded as possessing attributes.

An **Abstract Noun** is the name of an attribute or quality of a thing.

The sum-total of the inflexions marking number and case of a noun or pronoun is called its **Declension.**

Gender is the form of a noun or pronoun corresponding in English to the sex of the thing named.

Number is an inflexion which shows whether we are speaking of one thing or of more than one.

Case is the form of a noun or pronoun which shows its relation to other words in the sentence.

An **Adjective** is a word which is used with a noun to limit its application.

A **Pronoun** is a word used instead of a noun.

A **Relative Pronoun** is one which refers to some other noun or pronoun, called its antecedent, and has the force of a conjunction.

A **Verb** is a word with which we can make an assertion.

A **Transitive Verb** is one which indicates an action directed towards some object.

An **Intransitive Verb** is one which indicates a state, or an action which is not directed towards an object.

A **Reflexive Verb** is one in which the subject and the object are the same.

A **Verb of Incomplete Predication** is one which requires the addition of some other word to complete its meaning.

The word which is added to complete the meaning of a verb of Incomplete Predication is called the **Complement** of the Predicate.

An **Auxiliary Verb** is one which is used to supply the place of inflexions in the conjugation of another verb.

A **Notional Verb** is one which has a meaning of its own.

An **Impersonal Verb** is one in which the source of the action is not expressed.

The sum-total of the inflexions of a verb is called its **Conjugation.**

Voice is the form of a verb which shows whether the subject of the sentence stands for the doer or for the object of the action expressed by the verb.

The **Active Voice** is that form of the verb which shows that the subject of the sentence stands for the doer of the action expressed by the verb.

The **Passive Voice** is that form of the verb which shows that the subject of the sentence stands for the object of the action expressed by the verb.

Mood is the form of a verb which shows the mode or manner in which the action is represented.

The **Indicative Mood** contains the forms used (1) to make statements of fact, (2) to ask questions, and (3) to express suppositions in which the events are treated as if they were facts.

The **Imperative Mood** contains the form used to give commands.

The **Subjunctive Mood** contains the forms used to represent actions or states conceived as possible or contingent, but not asserted as facts.

The **Infinitive Mood** is the form which denotes actions or states without reference to person, number, or time.

A **Gerund** is a verbal noun in *-ing* which, when formed from a transitive verb, can take after it an object.

A **Participle** is a verbal adjective. The active participle of a transitive verb differs from an ordinary adjective in taking an object.

Tense is the form of a verb which shows the time at which the action is represented as occurring and the completeness or incompleteness of the action.

A **Simple Tense** is one which is expressed by a single word.

A **Compound Tense** is one which is expressed by the help of an auxiliary verb.

Perfect and **Imperfect** are terms applied respectively to tenses denoting actions which are completed or in progress.

A **Weak Verb** is one which forms its past tense by adding *-ed, -d,* or *-t,* to the present.

A **Strong Verb** is one which forms its past tense by change of vowel without the addition of any suffix.

Person is the form of a verb which shows whether the subject of the sentence stands for the speaker, for the person addressed, or for some other thing.

An **Adverb** is a word which modifies the meaning of a verb, adjective, or other adverb.

A **Conjunctive Adverb** is one which joins sentences.

A **Preposition** is a word which is used with a noun, or pronoun, to show its relation to some other word in the sentence.

A **Conjunction** is a word, other than a relative pronoun or conjunctive adverb, which joins words and sentences.

A **Co-ordinating Conjunction** is one which joins co-ordinate or independent clauses.

A **Subordinating Conjunction** is one which joins a dependent clause to the principal clause.

A **Sentence** is the complete expression of a thought in words.

A **Clause** is a part of a sentence containing a finite verb.

A **Phrase** is a collection of words without a finite verb.

A **Simple Sentence** contains only one subject and one finite verb.

A **Compound Sentence** contains two or more independent clauses joined by co-ordinating conjunctions.

A **Complex Sentence** contains two or more clauses, of which at least one is dependent.

It might also be defined as a sentence which contains a clause introduced by a subordinating conjunction.

The **Subject** of a sentence is the word which stands for the thing about which the assertion is made.

The **Predicate** is the word by means of which the assertion is made.

The **Object** of a verb is the word which stands for the thing towards which the action indicated by the verb is directed.

Concord is the agreement of two or more connected words as regards their gender, number, case, or person.

Government is the influence exercised upon the case of a noun, or pronoun, by another word.

Order is the arrangement of words in a sentence.

When one noun is used to explain another, it is put in the same case and is said to be in **Apposition**.

A noun, or pronoun, and a participle, which are independent in construction of the rest of the sentence, are said to be in the **Absolute** construction.

Ellipsis is the omission of a word or words necessary to complete the grammatical structure of the sentence.

Pleonasm is redundancy or excess of expression.

Solecism is an error in grammar or pronunciation.

Anomaly is the name given to any irregularity of accidence.

Anacoluthon is the confusion of two constructions.

The deviation of a word from its right construction, owing to the improper influence of some adjacent word, is said to be due to **Attraction**.

Asyndeton is the omission of conjunctions.

Polysyndeton is the redundant use of conjunctions.

Composition is the formation of a word by joining words together.

Derivation is the formation of a new word (1) by adding to a word a part not significant by itself, or (2) by modifying an existing sound.

A sound not significant by itself which is added to a word to form a derivative is called an **Affix**. Attached at the beginning of a word it is called a **Prefix**, attached at the end, a **Suffix**.

A **Hybrid** is a compound or derivative containing elements which come from different languages.

A **Syllable** consists of a single vowel sound with or without accompanying consonants.

Analysis is the resolution of a sentence into its essential parts.

Parsing is the statement of the part of speech to which a word belongs, its inflexion if it has any, and its syntactical relations with other words in the sentence.

An **Alphabet** is the complete collection of the letters used in writing a language.

A **Phonetic System** of spelling is one in which words are written according to their sound.

Orthographical expedients are devices by which the deficiencies of an alphabet are supplied.

Accent is the stress of the voice laid upon a syllable in a word.

Emphasis is the stress of the voice laid upon a word or words in a sentence.

Metathesis is a transposition of letters in a word.

Umlaut is the modification of a root-vowel owing to the influence of a suffix.

Changes in words arising from a desire to economise effort in speech are said to be due to **Euphony.**

A **Vowel** is a sound by the aid of which any consonantal sound can be audibly produced.

A **Consonant** is a sound which will not enable us to produce audibly sounds which are by themselves almost inaudible.

A **Diphthong** is a combination of two vowel sounds in the same syllable.

APPENDIX II.

PASSAGES FOR ANALYSIS.

1. Who is this?—Why are you so late?—Give me your hand.—To bliss domestic he his heart resigned.—There is said to have been a battle.—He will succeed or die.—Twilight's soft dews steal o'er the village green.—Let me stay at home.—His horse being killed, he was taken prisoner.—Your voiceless lips, O flowers, are living preachers.

2. Whatever the consequences may be, I shall go my way.—Uneasy lies the head that wears a crown.—No other allegorist has ever been able to make abstractions objects of terror, of pity, and of love.—None but the brave deserves the fair.—This is made of the same material as that.

3. Who will undertake it, if it be not also a service of honour?— Won is the glory, and the grief is past.—It is not true that he said that. —Plain living and high thinking are no more.—To the great virtues of that gentleman I shall always join with my country in paying a just tribute of applause.

4.   I am monarch of all I survey,
          My right there is none to dispute.

5.   Sweet was the sound, when oft, at evening's close,
        Up yonder hill the village murmur rose.

6.   Hope for a season bade the world farewell,
        And Freedom shrieked as Kosciusko fell.

7.   The stag at eve had drunk his fill,
        Where danced the moon on Monan's rill,
        And deep his midnight lair had made
        In lone Glenartney's hazel shade.

8.   He that has light within his own clear breast
        May sit i' the centre and enjoy bright day.

9.   To me the meanest flower that blows can give
        Thoughts that do often lie too deep for tears.

10.
       Stone walls do not a prison make,
        Nor iron bars a cage;
       A free and quiet mind can take
        These for a hermitage.

11.
          High on a throne of royal state
       Satan exalted sat, by merit raised
       To that bad eminence.

12.
       Last noon beheld them full of lusty light;
        Last eve, in beauty's circle proudly gay;
       The midnight brought the signal sound of strife,
        The morn, the marshalling of arms.

13.
       The World is too much with us: late and soon,
       Getting and spending, we lay waste our powers:
       Little we see in Nature that is ours;
       We have given our hearts away, a sordid boon!

14.
       This vesper-service closed, without delay,
       From that exalted station to the plain
       Descending, we pursued our homeward course,
       In mute composure, o'er the shadowy lake,
       Under a fated sky.

15.
       Full many a gem of purest ray serene,
        The dark unfathom'd caves of ocean bear;
       Full many a flower is born to blush unseen,
        And waste its sweetness on the desert air.

16.
       The innocent are gay; the lark is gay,
       That dries his feathers, saturate with dew,
       Beneath the rosy cloud, while yet the beams
       Of dayspring overshoot his humble nest.

17.
       In this poor gown my dear lord found me first,
       And loved me serving in my father's hall:
       And this poor gown I will not cast aside
       Until himself arise a living man
       And bid me cast it.

18.
       The heights, by great men reached and kept,
       Were not attained by sudden flight;
       But they, while their companions slept,
       Were toiling upward in the night.

19.
          Then burst his mighty heart;
       And, in his mantle muffling up his face,
       Even at the base of Pompey's statue,
       Which all the while ran blood, great Cæsar fell.

20.   How happy is he born and taught,
     That serveth not another's will;
     Whose armour is his honest thought,
     And simple truth his utmost skill!

21.   And statesmen at her council met
      Who knew the seasons when to take
      Occasion by the hand, and make
     The bounds of freedom wider yet.

22. When the men who were exploring the pit ascertained that the water had reached a certain level, they knew that the imprisoned colliers could not be rescued without great difficulty.

23.   Soon as the evening shades prevail,
     The moon takes up the wondrous tale,
     And nightly to the listening earth
     Repeats the story of her birth :
     Whilst all the stars that round her burn,
     And all the planets in their turn
     Confirm the tidings as they roll,
     And spread the truth from pole to pole.

24.   He many an evening to his distant home
     In solitude returning saw the hills
     Grow larger in the darkness; all alone
     Beheld the stars come out above his head,
     And travelled through the wood with no one near.

25.   Intermit no watch
     Against a wakeful foe, while I, abroad,
     Through all the coasts of dark destruction seek
     Deliverance for us all.

26.   The lively Grecian, in a land of hills,
     Rivers and fertile plains, and sounding shores,
     Under a cope of sky more variable,
     Could find commodious place for every god,
     Promptly received, as prodigally brought,
     From the surrounding countries, at the choice
     Of all adventurers.

27.   Thus with the year
     Seasons return : but not to me returns
     Day, or the sweet approach of even or noon,
     Or sight of vernal bloom or summer's rose,
     Or flocks, or herds, or human face divine;
     But clouds instead and ever during dark
     Surrounds me, from the cheerful ways of men
     Cut off.

28. Breathes there the man with soul so dead,
Who never to himself hath said,
This is my own, my native land!
Whose heart hath ne'er within him burned,
As home his footsteps he hath turned
From wandering on a foreign strand?

29. Now is the winter of our discontent
Made glorious summer by this sun of York,
And all the clouds that lour'd upon our house
In the deep bosom of the ocean buried.

30. That time of year thou mayst in me behold
When yellow leaves, or none, or few do hang
Upon those boughs which shake against the cold
Bare ruin'd choirs, where late the sweet birds sang.

31. And where two raging fires meet together,
They do consume the thing that feeds their fury:
Though little fire grows great with little wind,
Yet extreme gusts will blow out fire and all.

32. There at the foot of yonder nodding beech
That wreathes its old fantastic roots so high,
His listless length at noon-tide would he stretch,
And pore upon the brook that babbles by.

33. As travellers oft look back at eve
When eastward darkly going,
To gaze upon that light they leave
Still faint behind them glowing,—
So, when the close of pleasure's day
To gloom hath near consigned us,
We turn to catch one fading ray
Of joy that's left behind us.

34. But whilst, unconscious of the silent change
Thus stol'n around him, o'er the dying bard
Hung Wolfram, on the breeze there came a sound
Of mourning moving down the narrow glen;
And looking up, he suddenly was ware
Of four white maidens, moving in the van
Of four black monks who bore upon her bier
The flower-strewn corpse of young Elizabeth.

35. Once on a time, an emperor, a wise man,
No matter where, in China or Japan,
Decreed that whosoever should offend
Against the well-known duties of a friend,
Convicted once, should ever after wear
But half a coat, and show his bosom bare.

36. The swallow stopt as he hunted the bee,
    The snake slipt under a spray,
  The wild hawk stood with the down on his beak,
    And stared, with his foot on the prey,
  And the nightingale thought, 'I have sung many songs,
    'But never a one so gay,
  'For he sings of what the world will be
    'When the years have died away.'

37.   Daughter of Jove, relentless power,
      Thou tamer of the human breast,
    Whose iron scourge and torturing hour
      The bad affright, afflict the best!
    Bound in thy adamantine chain
    The proud are taught to taste of pain,
    And purple tyrants vainly groan
  With pangs unfelt before, unpitied and alone.

33.   Orpheus with his lute made trees
    And the mountain tops that freeze
      Bow themselves, when he did sing;
    To his music plants and flowers
    Ever sprung, as sun and showers
      There had made a lasting spring.

39.   We leave the well-beloved place
      Where first we gazed upon the sky;
      The roofs, that heard our earliest cry,
    Will shelter one of stranger race.

    We go, but ere we go from home,
      As down the garden walks I move,
      Two spirits of a diverse love
    Contend for loving masterdom.

40.   If this great world of joy and pain
      Revolve in one sure track;
    If freedom set will rise again,
      And virtue flown come back;
    Woe to the purblind crew who fill
      The heart with each day's care;
    Nor gain, from past or future, skill
      To bear and to forbear.

41.   In such a place as this, at such an hour,
    If ancestry in aught can be believed,
    Descending spirits have conversed with man,
    And told the secrets of the world unknown.

42. Those who reason in this manner do not observe that they are setting up a general rule, of all the least to be endured; namely, that secrecy, whenever secrecy is practicable, will justify any action.

43.
> To thine own self be true,
> And it must follow, as the night the day,
> Thou canst not then be false to any man.

44. Being angry with one who controverts an opinion which you value, is a necessary consequence of the uneasiness which you feel.

45.
> This is the state of man; to-day he puts forth
> The tender leaves of hope; to-morrow blossoms,
> And bears his blushing honours thick upon him:
> The third day comes a frost, a killing frost,
> And when he thinks, good easy man, full surely
> His greatness is a-ripening, nips his root,
> And then he falls, as I do.

46.
> Wide through the landscape of his dream
> The lordly Niger flowed;
> Beneath the palm-trees on the plain
> Once more a king he strode,
> And heard the tinkling caravans
> Descend the mountain road.

47.
> What stronger breast-plate than a heart untainted?
> Thrice is he armed, that hath his quarrel just;
> And he but naked, though locked up in steel,
> Whose conscience with injustice is corrupted.

48.
> Deaf to King Robert's threats and cries and prayers,
> They thrust him from the hall and down the stairs;
> A group of tittering pages ran before,
> And, as they opened wide the folding-door,
> His heart failed, for he heard, with strange alarms,
> The boisterous laughter of the men-at-arms,
> And all the vaulted chamber roar and ring,
> With the mock plaudits of 'Long live the king.'

49.
> But when the sun was sinking in the sea
> He seized his harp, which he at times could string
> And strike, albeit with untaught melody,
> When deem'd he no strange ear was listening:
> And now his fingers o'er it he did fling,
> And tuned his farewell in the dim twilight.

50.
> They heard, and were abashed, and up they sprung,
> Upon the wing, as when men wont to watch
> On duty, sleeping found by whom they dread,
> Rouse and bestir themselves ere well awake.

51. So cheered he his fair spouse, and she was cheer'd;
But silently a gentle tear let fall
From either eye, and wip'd them with her hair;
Two other precious drops that ready stood,
Each in their crystal sluice, he ere they fell
Kiss'd, as the gracious signs of sweet remorse
And pious awe, that feared to have offended.

52. Hadst thou but shook thy head, or made a pause,
When I spake darkly what I purposed;
Or turn'd an eye of doubt upon my face,
As bid me tell my tale in express words;
Deep shame had struck me dumb, made me break off,
And those thy fears might have wrought fears in me.

53.   Long time in even scale
The battle hung; till Satan, who that day
Prodigious power had shown, and met in arms
No equal, ranging through the dire attack
Of fighting seraphim confused, at length
Saw where the sword of Michael smote, and felled
Squadrons at once.

54. Long time they thus together traveiled,
Till, weary of their way, they came at last,
Where grew two goodly trees, that faire did spred
Their armes abroad, with gray mosse overcast;
And their greene leaves trembling with every blast,
Made a calme shadow far in compasse round.

55.   While some on earnest business bent
        Their murmuring labours ply
      Gainst graver hours, that bring constraint
        To sweeten liberty,
      Some bold adventurers disdain
      The limits of their little reign
      And unknown regions dare descry:
      Still as they run they look behind,
      They hear a voice in every wind
        And snatch a fearful joy.

56. Though a scholar must have faith in his master, yet a man well instructed must judge for himself; for learners owe to their masters only a temporary belief, and a suspension of their own judgment till they are fully instructed, and not an absolute resignation or perpetual captivity.

57.   Fame is the spur that the clear spirit doth raise,
      That last infirmity of noble mind,
   To scorn delights and live laborious days,
      But the fair guerdon when we hope to find
   And think to burst out into sudden blaze
      Comes the blind Fury with th' abhorred shears
      And slits the thin-spun life.

58.   Since words are only names for things, it would be more convenient for all men to carry about them such things as are necessary to express the particular business they are to discourse on.

59.   Bless'd are those
   Whose blood and judgment are so well commingled,
   That they are not a pipe for fortune's finger
   To sound what stop she please. Give me that man
   That is not passion's slave, and I will wear him
   In my heart's core, ay, in my heart of heart,
   As I do thee.

60.   Dangerous it were for the feeble brain of man to wade far into the doings of the Most High; whom although to know be life, and joy to make mention of His name, yet our soundest knowledge is to know that we know Him not as indeed He is, neither can know Him.

ON

ESSAY-WRITING.

CONTENTS.

ON ESSAY-WRITING.

1. Elements of an Essay. The following pages contain precepts for the guidance of pupils who are studying how to write well, not a scientific exposition of the principles on which good writing depends.

Composition is an Art. Every essay is a product of Art, and like other products of Art it possesses Matter and Form. Its matter consists of thoughts, expressed in words. In a good essay good matter is presented in a good form. The matter is undoubtedly of greater importance than the form, yet a learned essayist may remain unread, because he lacks the ability to display his valuable materials in an attractive dress, while an unlearned essayist may meet the public taste, because of the appetising way in which his worthless materials are served up. The matter for your essays will increase in quantity and improve in quality with each addition to your knowledge. As your knowledge extends, you will get more ideas and a larger vocabulary with which to express them.

Now to knowledge there are no short cuts. In order to 'get understanding' three things are necessary. You must (1) read widely, (2) observe closely, (3) think over what you read and observe; and the last is the hardest of the three. So long as your reading is confined to reports of cricket and football matches, or to twaddling stories in magazines, you will make but a poor hand at any essay which requires much intelligence in its writer. If for a change you read now and then an essay by Goldsmith, or Macaulay, or

Thackeray, or Bagehot, or Froude, or Matthew Arnold, three results may be looked for: (1) you will add to your stock of ideas: (2) you will enlarge your vocabulary: (3) you will get a better notion of excellence of style than books about style will ever impart.

2. Vocabulary. To express your thoughts you need words, and to use words correctly you must understand their meanings. The vocabulary which serves for conversation is quite insufficient for literary purposes. In one of Lord Beaconsfield's novels a foreigner remarks that English is an expressive language, but not difficult to master, as it consists of four words,—'nice,' 'jolly,' 'charming,' and 'bore,' to which some grammarians add 'fond.' Good reading is therefore indispensable, if you are ever to get the vocabulary wanted for good writing. Making lists of synonyms is also a useful exercise. Take, for example, the word *useful* in the last sentence and put down all the adjectives of like meaning that occur to you, *e.g. beneficial, serviceable, profitable, advantageous.* Note also that the synonymous words cannot invariably be interchanged. Thus, we can say that the horse is a useful animal, but not that it is a beneficial or an advantageous animal.

Make sure that you understand the meaning of your words. Dogberry and Mrs Malaprop exemplify the dangers which attend the use of long words by the illiterate. The authoress who wrote of 'lapses from ebriety' doubtless thought that as *inebriety* means intoxication *ebriety* must mean the opposite.

A writer may easily avoid gross errors of this sort and yet use words in a sense not strictly their own. Thus *aggravate* is commonly used for 'exasperate,' though rightly it means 'intensify.' You aggravate an offence if you add insult to injury, but you cannot properly be said to aggravate the person offended. A man's calling or business in life is his *vocation* : what takes him away from his business is his *avocation.* For boys and girls at school, study is the vocation, games are the avocation. Unfortunately the words are now commonly used as if synonymous. The literal sense of *eliminate* is 'to turn out of doors,' 'to expel.' Yet people talk of 'eliminating the truth' when they mean, not getting rid of the truth, but eliciting it or drawing it forth. The words *decimate, individual, mutual, verbal,* are used more often than not with like inaccuracy[1].

3. **Choice of a subject.** If you are allowed a choice between several subjects for an essay, choose the subject of which you know most and on which you are therefore likely to write best. A Descriptive essay on Dogs must be within the reach of everybody., A Narrative essay on Nelson is within the reach of those who know the principal facts of Nelson's life. A Reflective essay on the aphorism, 'Knowledge is Power,' or on the question, 'Can Persecution be defended?' is within the reach only of those who can think for themselves.

4. **Advantages of an Outline.** Having chosen your subject, spend a portion of the allotted time (say one-sixth) in making an outline of your essay, so as to secure (1) Orderly arrangement of the materials, and (2) Suitable proportion between the parts. The signs by which you mark, in this preliminary sketch, the divisions of the subject, such as I. 1. (*a*) etc., are for your own guidance and not for reproduction in the essay, to which they would give the appearance of a scientific treatise. The outline will also be (3) a Safeguard against Digression, for which in a short essay there is properly no room. Keep to the point. If your subject is Railways, a passing reference to

---

[1] See Hodgson's *Errors in the Use of English,* a storehouse of information about the uses and abuses of words.

Stage-coaches and Motor-cars, for the purpose of contrast, is appropriate, but if your pen runs away with you and three-fourths of your pages are filled with a picturesque description of travelling by stage-coach or by motor-car, your essay misses its mark.

5. Qualities of Style.   Aim at expressing your thoughts in language which is

>   (1) Correct grammatically,
>   (2) Clear,
>   (3) Condensed,
>   (4) Forcible,
>   (5) Pleasing.

If your composition possesses the qualities of Correctness, Clearness, Brevity, Force, and Charm, you may not indeed be a master of style, but you will certainly be a good writer.

There is something to be said about each of these five requisites.

6. I. Grammatical Correctness. Illustrations of the principal errors of syntax are given in the paragraphs mentioned below   Refresh your memory from time to time by a reference to them.

§ 234.   Erroneous application of the Participial adjunct.   See other examples in § 246.   This is one of the commonest pitfalls in Periodic sentences.

§ 250.   Constructions in connexion with the Distributive Pronouns and nouns of similar import, *they, their,* &c., being used with reference to *every, each, anyone, nobody,* &c.   Instances often occur in practice which are not so easily dealt with as are the examples of the text. Consider the following sentences :

'The duke and the duchess quarrelled, and each thought *himself or herself* (themselves) in the right.'

'Although the room was full of men and women, nobody troubled *himself or herself* (themselves) to utter a protest.'

'No man, woman, or child should be deprived of *his, her, or its* (their) rights.'

The italicised forms are intolerable : the alternatives in brackets are unfortunately not grammatical. If we had an Academy, these ungrammatical but convenient forms might receive the sanction of authority. In the absence of this authority the safest course is to avoid such constructions altogether. It is interesting to notice that the form of expression sometimes varies according to the sex of the writer. A man writes, Every one knows that *his* life is uncertain,' understanding that *his* includes *her*, as it might do in an Act of Parliament. A woman writes, ' Every one knows that *their* life is uncertain.'

§ 251. Erroneous uses of Comparative and Superlative.

§ 253. Ambiguity in the use of the Article.

§ 254. Misuse of *like* as a conjunction : a most offensive error, to which people in the Midlands especially are addicted.

§ 260. Problems connected with the Concord of the Verb and errors of Concord arising from Attraction.

§ 273. Errors due to Ellipsis.

§ 277. Violation of idiom in the use of Prepositions.

P. 266, Q. 29. The 'split' Infinitive.

Among the Questions which follow Chapters XXIII—XXVI, you will find upwards of 200 sentences for correction, illustrating errors into which even great writers have fallen. If you employ a form of expression which is condemned as ungrammatical at the present day, it is no valid defence to urge that Pope, or Swift, or Addison used the same. For, in the first place, usage (which really decides what is and what is not grammatical) may have changed during the last two centuries, and, in the second place, a great writer occasionally makes a slip. A senior wrangler may add up a column in his cash-book wrong, but his doing so does not invalidate the rules of arithmetic.

7. II. Clearness : accuracy of expression needed. It is better that you should give yourself a good deal of trouble to express your meaning clearly than that you should give the reader a good deal of trouble to discover what your meaning is.

Be careful in using pronouns that the reference is free from ambiguity. Obscurity often lurks in paragraphs where *he, it, they, who, which* abound. You need not be afraid of repeating the noun. Johnson always repeated the noun instead of writing *the former* and *the latter*. To what is said upon this point in §§ 257–9, a caution must be added respecting the ambiguous reference of *who* and *which*, 'the sin of *which*craft,' as it has been called. To avoid ambiguity it is sometimes wise to alter the construction of the sentence. Thus, in the following sentence, 'He might have increased his popularity by yielding to their request, *which* would have gained for him also the gratitude of the government,' the antecedent in the writer's mind was *yielding*, not *request*. The ambiguity is removed if for *which* we substitute 'Such a course,' or 'His so doing.' Again, in the sentence, 'This is one of the books *which* deserve a place in a library, to *which* recourse is often necessary,' does the second 'which' refer to 'books' or to 'library'? If to 'books,' instead of *to which* write 'for to them.'

The misplacement of *only* should be guarded against : see § 268.

8. Preciosity. One may write with grammatical accuracy, use the pronouns without ambiguity, even put *only* in the right place, and yet produce obscurity owing to the adoption of a radically vicious style. From the desire for originality or effect, some writers take great pains to express their thoughts in a manner as far removed as possible from the manner of ordinary men. Hence they cultivate fastidiousness of expression and twist words from their usual signification with an elaborate ingenuity worthy of a better aim.

Preciosity is the name given to this unwholesome quality of style[1]. Like measles it is a malady for the most part incidental to youth. In one of the *Bab Ballads* there is a couplet which pokes fun at Martin Tupper, a poet now forgotten :

' " A fool is bent upon a twig, but wise men dread a bandit,"
Which I knew was very clever, but I didn't understand it.'

On much of the writing infected with Preciosity a plain man will pass a similar judgment,—'It seemed extremely clever, but I didn't understand it,'—not without a suspicion

[1] Molière's *Les Precieuses Ridicules* (1659) was directed against the charmed circle which met at the Hôtel de Rambouillet.

sometimes that the style has been deliberately obscured in order to hide the poverty of the thoughts.

As an example of Preciosity take the following criticism on an eminent novelist of a past generation :

'Hers was an apocalyptic gift of psychological fiction, free from the fetters of convention, deaf to the resonant rotundity of rule, ignoring the clamant importunity of whatever is banal, and depicting with curious felicity all that is *bizarre* and *recherché* in human personality '

Precious words indeed ! Yet so far as they mean anything at all they mean merely this, that she possessed insight into character, handled her materials in a way of her own, and had a happy knack of describing odd people.

9. Parenthetic Style. Another vicious style is the Parenthetic. Some writers repeatedly interrupt the progress of their sentences by inserting parentheses and parenthetic qualifying words, fancying that they are thereby giving to their writing the ease of conversation. The only kind of conversation which their sentences suggest is conversation with a confirmed stammerer. Simplifying an expression by removing the brackets is an operation that should be confined to algebra and not made necessary in literature.

Let us illustrate the peculiarity.

Johnson concludes his *Life of Swift* as follows :

'It was said, in a Preface to one of the Irish editions, that Swift had never been known to take a single thought from any writer, ancient or modern. This is not literally true ; but perhaps no other writer can easily be found that has borrowed so little, or that in all his excellences and all his defects has so well maintained his claim to be considered as original.'

We will now rewrite the passage in the Parenthetical style :

'That Swift had never been known to take a single thought from any other writer, ancient or modern [the assertion is made (to the best of our recollection) in a Preface to one of the editions published (we believe) in Ireland], is not true (or at any rate not literally true), but perhaps another writer will not be found {or [if found at all (and we will not assert that this is impossible)] will be found certainly not without considerable difficulty} who has borrowed so little, or who in all his excellences (which must be admitted to be great) and all his defects (probably not fewer and possibly even more numerous than his excellences) has on the whole so well (if we take all the circumstances into consideration) maintained his claim to be regarded in large measure as original.'

A single paragraph written in this hiccoughing style is fatiguing : a whole essay would be unreadable.

10. Allusiveness. Excessive Allusiveness is the bane of some writers.

Take the following statement :

'Macaulay and Carlyle formed different estimates of Boswell's character.'

Adopting the allusive style, we may transcribe the sentence thus :

'The author of the *Lays of Ancient Rome* and the Sage of Chelsea formed different estimates of the character of the man to whom we owe the best biography in the English language.'

Now a writer's object is to be read, and this object he is not likely to gain, if he irritates, annoys, or disgusts those who might possibly be his readers. On the sentence thus transcribed a plain man's criticism would probably be to this effect : 'It is no business of yours to require me to guess conundrums, or to answer questions in a General Knowledge Paper. If you mean Macaulay, Carlyle, and Boswell, why not say so?'

It is only allusiveness in excess however that is to be condemned. Occasional allusiveness, if appropriate, is a pleasant and useful feature of style. If, for example, you are maintaining that Macaulay is a true poet, and you say, 'The author of the *Lays of Ancient Rome* is a true poet,' your circumlocution suggests an argument. The reader understands you to imply, 'That Macaulay is a true poet is proved by his *Lays of Ancient Rome*.' Again, if you say,

'The man who wrote the best biography in the English language was no simpleton,' the reader understands you to mean, 'Boswell was no simpleton: had he been one he could never have written the best biography in the English language.' Once more, if you say, 'The Sage of Chelsea should have changed his quarters, since the noises of the neighbourhood disturbed his peace,' you remind the reader that Carlyle, as a philosopher, would need quiet for meditation, and that as a resident in London he would be surrounded by noises. Thus in each of these three sentences the use of the circumlocution is justified. With regard to the last, however, note that the phrase 'Sage of Chelsea' has passed into the vocabulary of third-rate journalists and should therefore be dropped.

11. Simplicity. Keep your compositions free from mannerisms and tricks of style. Be simple and natural, both in the choice of your words and in the construction of your sentences. Avoid whatever is far-fetched and suggestive of pedantry. Some people like to show off by writing *meticulous, phenomenal, oblivious* and *eventuate.* It is much better to write *timid, extraordinary, forgetful* and *happen.* Simplicity is a protection against Obscurity. If your language is simple, your meaning stands a good chance of being clear.

But simplicity of style can be carried so far that it degenerates into mere childishness. A child will tell you a story in this fashion :

'A fox saw some grapes in a vineyard one day. And they were very nice grapes. So he tried to reach them. But he couldn't, because he wasn't tall enough. So at last he gave up trying, and said, "Never mind, I daresay the grapes are sour." '

Prattle of this kind is pleasing in the nursery, but unsuitable for an essay.

12. III. Brevity. When Brevity is recommended,

you are not to suppose that you are advised to make your essay short. The length of your essay should depend on the amount of matter which you have to put into it. In any case of course it is Quality and not Quantity that affects its excellence. But if the subject is a large one, the shortness of an essay may be due to the writer's ignorance, or to his want of reflexion. The brevity to be aimed at is brevity due to condensation. Avoid wordiness and long-windedness. Polonius asks Hamlet, 'What do you read, my lord?' 'Words, words, words,' says Hamlet. 'Words, words, words,' grumbles the reader, as he turns the pages of an author, fluent and diffuse.

Try to put your points tersely. Drive them home by the clearness and directness of your sentences. Any force which they might otherwise have will only be frittered away by verbosity and prolixity. In public speaking a certain amount of repetition is necessary, for if some of the audience miss a point, unless it is repeated they lose it altogether. But the reader who misses a point always has it in his power to look back a page or two and refresh his memory.

13. Length of Sentences. Is Brevity to be aimed at also in the construction of sentences? Are short sentences better than long sentences?

We reply that both are good and that, to prevent monotony of style, a good writer will use both. The style of an author who writes nothing but short sentences may be described, by an expressive colloquialism, as 'snippety.' The style of an author who writes nothing but long sentences becomes ponderous and wearisome. A judicious writer will occasionally insert a short sentence between two long ones, or with a weighty long sentence conclude a series of short ones. But while your essay-writing is at an early stage, you will do well to aim at making your sentences short. Your short sentences will probably be grammatical : in your long ones, the end of the sentence may sometimes forget the beginning and the result will be a muddle. Tradesmen's circulars and letters in provincial newspapers show, from the tangled construction of their contents, that half-educated people find it easier to write a long sentence ungrammatically than to write a short sentence in good English.

Break up your composition into paragraphs. Whether the paragraphs should be long or short must depend upon the amount of matter properly belonging to each. When you have dealt with one branch of the subject and pass to another, begin a new paragraph, so as to show the reader that the topic is about to be changed.

14. IV. Force. If your composition is correct, clear, and condensed, it possesses three excellent qualities, and nobody is entitled to say that you are a bad writer. Yet you may be dull and heavy, and if you are dull and heavy you may be quite sure that, in the present busy age, nobody will stop to read you. Try therefore to express your meaning, not only correctly, clearly and briefly, but also forcibly, or, as we sometimes say, with point. Are there any expedients, you may ask, for arresting the reader's attention?

The endeavours of a writer dull by nature to acquire vivacity of style by adopting various literary devices remind one of the German gentleman who was discovered jumping over the drawing-room chairs *pour devenir vif.* Sometimes, however, a composition is dull, not because it reflects the temperament of the writer, but because the writer was inexperienced in using just those literary devices to impart energy, strength and vivacity to his style.

15. Periodic Sentences. The occasional use of Periodic Sentences is one device for adding force to a composition. In a Periodic sentence the reader's attention is kept on the alert, because the sense is not completed until the end of the sentence is reached (*i.e.* until we come to the 'Period,' or full-stop).

Suppose that a master says to a boy, 'If you bring me fifty lines before dinner, you may go to cricket this afternoon.' The boy, not knowing how the sentence is going to end, waits with interest for its close. Now suppose that the master says, 'You may go to cricket this afternoon, *if* you bring me fifty lines before dinner,' reversing the order of the clauses. The boy is relieved of anxiety when the sentence is only half finished : about a possible remainder he feels indifferent. The first form is Periodic : the second is not.

Take two other short examples :

'While the magistrates were deliberating about the punishment which they should inflict, the prisoner escaped.'

'Though they offered me five pounds, I would not tell them the name of my informant.'

These are Periodic sentences and the reader's attention is kept on the stretch to the end. Make them non-periodic, by transposing the clauses, and the reader's attention becomes less keen, when he is half way through.

Here is a longer example :

'Roughly handled by the head master | who suspected him of dishonourable conduct | of which he had never been guilty, ‖ frowned upon in the family circle | where his depressed manner was attributed to ill-temper, ‖ treated with cold politeness by those who had once been his chums, ‖ insulted by the baser crew among his schoolfellows, ‖ and deliberately cut by the rest, ‖ the boy led an unhappy life.'

This Periodic sentence keeps the reader in suspense to its close. Now place the words, 'The boy led an unhappy life,' at the beginning, thus converting the form of the sentence to non-periodic. Mark the result. Although the sentence goes dribbling on with a long series of participial adjuncts, it might very well come to an end at any of the places where we have inserted a bar.

One danger to which in a long Periodic sentence you

are exposed has already been mentioned. Absorbed in the accumulation of participial adjuncts, you may easily forget the noun to which they properly refer. Thus, in the last example, you might conclude with the words, 'the boy's life was an unhappy one.' But it was the *boy*, not the boy's *life*, that was roughly handled, frowned upon, treated with cold politeness, insulted and cut. This mistake could hardly occur, if the sentence began with the words for which, in the Periodic form, we have to wait till we reach the end.

Periodic sentences introduced in moderation give variety and add force to a composition. When many of them are crowded together, they suggest artificiality, or, what is worse, pomposity.

16. Impressive Opening and Conclusion. Try at any rate to begin and to finish your essay with an effective sentence. How impressively Bacon sometimes opens an essay, with a sentence which comes down like the blow of a hammer! Thus, writing on Truth, he starts with the words, 'What is Truth? said jesting Pilate': on Death, 'Men fear death as children fear to go in the dark': on Marriage, 'He that hath wife and children hath given hostages to fortune': on Gardens, 'God Almighty first planted a garden.'

Avoid the conventional opening, dear to the young essayist: 'Few subjects are more interesting and important than'...whatever the subject in hand may be,—perhaps Punctuality, or Crocodiles, or Lawn Tennis, or The British Museum. The first sentence of an essay is often the most difficult to write. You may sometimes make a good start with a quotation. Thus, if your subject is Procrastination, you may begin, ' "Delays are dangerous," says the proverb,' or,

> 'There is a tide in the affairs of men,
> Which, taken at the flood, leads on to fortune.'

17. Adjectives in excess. For adding force to his sentences, a good writer employs many expedients. These are for the most part so subtle that they cannot be taught by simple rules. Your best way of acquiring them is to take note of an impressive sentence, when you meet with one, and to consider why it impresses you. A caution may be useful, however, against the employment of certain devices which are often unwisely employed to produce effect.

Many writers think that they add force to their sentences by increasing the number of their adjectives, until every noun marches with its adjective at its heels. So far from the force being increased by this expedient, the force is diminished. As a great critic remarked long ago, 'The adjective is the enemy of the noun.'

Let us illustrate the point.

Junius writes:

'They are still base enough to encourage the follies of your age, as they once did the vices of your youth.'

This is effective. But many a modern journalist, having read the sentence, would exclaim, 'What, no adjectives!' and would bring Junius up to present-day standards in this fashion:

'They are still base enough to encourage the *consummate* follies of your *unhonoured* age, as they once did the *egregious* vices of your *callow* youth.'

By these adjectival embellishments the force of the original passage has been entirely destroyed.

18. Bombast. Avoid Bombast. It is not always easy to say exactly where a writer takes the false step which leads from sublime rhetoric to ridiculous bombast. What is magnificent in a suitable context may become absurd in humbler surroundings. The elevated diction of poetry seems grotesque when employed in the service of ordinary prose.

The following passage is open to hardly any objection on the score of the words. It contains but little Fine Writing, in the sense in which that term of reproach is commonly used. Yet we feel that it is inflated, pompous, what in the United States people call 'highfalutin.' Hence it is not likely to please readers of taste.

'The long-deferred message of hope brings gladness to the heart, just as the sun, shining forth, after a protracted season of unsettled weather, in all his gorgeous brilliance, dispels with golden rays the clouds and mists from the sky, causing the birds to break forth in song, the trees of the forest to rejoice, and the fields to clothe themselves in floral splendour.'

19. Italics. To underline those words which you consider important is a poor device. Try to construct your sentences so as to lay the stress where the stress is required. The use of italics is no compliment either to yourself or to your reader. It implies that you think one of two things : either that you are so devoid of literary skill that you cannot produce an impression on the reader without employing a mechanical device, or that the reader is so devoid of intelligence that, in order to produce an impression on his mind, a mechanical device is required.

20. V. Charm. We come now to the last of the five qualities by which a good style is characterised. You were told to aim at expressing your thoughts in language which shall be pleasing to the reader. If in this endeavour you attain a high degree of success, your composition will be said to possess Beauty, or Grace, or Charm.

Now it is evident that, if it was a difficult matter to give a pupil rules for investing his style with Force, still more difficult must it be to give him rules for investing his style with a quality so elusive and hard to analyse as Beauty or

Charm. To write so as to give pleasure to people of refined taste, the writer must himself be a person of refined taste, and refined taste requires a good many years for its development. You cannot be taught how to make your essays charming any more than you can be taught how to make them witty. But although it is impossible to lay down positive precepts for the attainment of this end, saying, 'Do this and you will make your style charming,' it is quite possible to lay down negative precepts, saying, 'Do not do this, for, if you do, you will offend against the canons of good taste and banish all charm, grace, beauty and capacity for giving pleasure from your style.' Let us consider some of the things which, in a composition, are offences against good taste.

21. Arrogance. Purge your character of Arrogance. When arrogance infests a man's nature it also infects his style Jerrold went up one day to a consequential-looking gentleman and said, 'Pray, sir, are you anybody in particular?' There are a good many contemporary writers to whom one would like to put Jerrold's question.

Exceptional arrogance is displayed in the following remarks on Thackeray:

'That he possesses humour of a sort we should be the last to deny, but the vein is soon exhausted. Lack of imaginative range and prolixity of common-place reflexion are his essential characteristics. With regret we are obliged to refuse him a place among great writers, but truth is our paramount consideration, and such must be our verdict.'

On one occasion when Johnson's critical taste had been outraged, he relieved his feelings by ejaculating, 'Puppy!'

Think modestly and express yourself modestly, especially when you are writing about great men. Check any tendency to flippancy, pertness, or smartness of expression. Think reverently and express yourself reverently, when you are writing on subjects connected with morality or religion.

22. Pomposity. Avoid Pomposity. This sometimes
arises, not from arrogance, but from shyness, or from
awkwardness, or from the want of a sense of humour.
Keep your essay free from such expressions as, 'I have yet
to learn,' or 'All history teaches.' When he comes across
language of this sort, the judicious reader smiles and thinks
that you have probably a good many things yet to learn
and that, whatever all history teaches, you have not yet
been taught all history.

23. Jokes. Refrain from introducing jokes into your
essay. Perhaps you think yourself rather a wag and ask
why you should not make yourself amusing. But jokes so
seldom are amusing, and nothing is drearier than a joke
which fails to go off. If you indulge in a little mild irony,
give the reader credit for intelligence enough to detect it
without the assistance of the symbols (!) or (?) or italics.
Thus, if in your facetious description of a thunderstorm
you say, 'It is extremely pleasant (?) for the pedestrian to
feel the rain coming through the garment which he bought
last week as a waterproof (!) and to realise that, if the down-
pour goes on much longer, he will get home *swimmingly*,'
remove the typographical aids to the discovery of your
jests. The reader will be much better pleased if he finds
out your fun for himself, and even if he misses it his loss
will not be great.

24. Vulgarity: Slang. Avoid Vulgarity in all its
forms. In an essay Slang is vulgar, though not necessarily
vulgar in conversation. To say of a man that he is a prig,
or a smug, or a bounder, or a bore, is to describe him in
one word more effectively than could be done in a circumlocution requiring twenty, and no one but a precisian of
painful propriety would object to the use of these terms in
the freedom of everyday speech. But all persons of taste

will agree in banishing them from a serious composition. With even greater rigour must you exclude from an essay words of which the ordinary meaning has been perverted to a slang sense, such as *awful*, for 'very,' *ripping*, for 'agreeable,' *row*, for 'quarrel,' and phrases such as 'keep one's hair on,' 'get in a wax,' 'put on side,' etc.

There is, of course, much slang which is vulgar and silly, not only in an essay, but in all places and at all times.

25. Fine Writing. Fine Writing is a form of Vulgarity, though it probably arose from a mistaken notion on the part of half-educated people that vulgarity lay rather in using the common words of everyday life. Specimens of Fine Writing abound in country newspapers, among the items of local intelligence and the letters to the editor For convenience one may call this style Journalese, but the term does grave injustice to journalists as a class. On the staff of many of our leading papers there are journalists who deserve to take rank with the best writers of the day.

The Penny-a-liner will contribute to the provincial paper a column of paragraphs in this style :

'After assisting at the function in the Town Hall, the Duke partook of refreshments with the civic dignitaries in the Council Chamber.'

'The erection of Mr Smith's new emporium, in proximity to the Parish Church, is rapidly approaching completion.'

'We regret to announce a disastrous fatality which transpired yesterday afternoon. The Mayor was proceeding to his residence on his bicycle, when he was precipitated from his machine and sustained a fractured leg.'

Translating these statements from Journalese we should write :

'The Duke was present at the meeting in the Town Hall and afterwards lunched with the Mayor and Corporation in the Council Chamber.'

'Mr Smith's new shop near the Parish Church is almost finished.'

'We are sorry to say that the Mayor met with a bad accident yesterday afternoon. As he was riding home, he fell from his bicycle and broke his leg.'

26. Patchwork. Another irritating form of Vulgarity is the frequent use of hackneyed quotations and allusions, or of well-worn Latin and French phrases. Such expressions as the following are entitled to a century of repose : after that interval they may come out fresh :—'the cup that cheers,' 'last but not least,' 'few and far between,' 'the light fantastic toe,' 'born to blush unseen,' 'thereby hangs a tale,' 'coign of vantage.'

Allusions to Oliver Twist's request 'for more,' to Mr Micawber's expectation that something would 'turn up,' and to Mr Dick's difficulty in keeping King Charles's head out of the memorial, should be strictly prohibited. Perhaps Bruce's spider, Mrs Partington's mop, and Macaulay's New Zealander on London Bridge may as well go along with them.

Some writers are so fond of exhibiting their scraps of Latin and French that their composition becomes a piece of polyglot. The following importations from abroad should be avoided, some because they are hackneyed, others because they are unnecessary, convenient equivalents of English origin being available : *tempora mutantur, mens sana in corpore sano, experientia docet, nil desperandum, otium cum dignitate, dolce far niente, nous avons changé tout cela, comme il faut, nous verrons, entre nous, bêtise, canaille, de nouveau,* etc.

If, however, the foreign phrase or word expresses succinctly what we should have to express in English by a long circumlocution, or might even be unable to express at all, its use is justified. Thus, to the following, objection would be pedantic : *ad hominem, ad captandum, ex parte, lucus a non lucendo, sine die, ne plus ultra, sic vos non vobis, éclat, esprit, coup d'état, canard, bizarre, chic, arrière pensée, prestige, naïveté,* etc.

If you introduce a word from another language, be careful to spell it correctly. Write *sobriquet, à outrance, coûte. que coûte*, not *soubriquet*, *à l'outrance*, *coute qui coute*. The plural of *scandalum magnatum* is not *scandala magnata*, as some writers have supposed. If you wish to mention more than one *animalculum*, write *animalcules* in English, or *animalcula* in Latin, but not *animalculæ*, which is neither Latin nor English.

27. · Quotations. It is only from stale Quotations that you are recommended to abstain. Quotations which are fairly fresh and apposite are always welcome. In reading a contemporary author, it is sometimes a pleasure if a quotation carries one's thoughts away to Pope, or Shakespeare, or Horace. It is an unusual pleasure moreover to find that a young writer knows any good literature from which to quote, and in the present utilitarian age it is a further pleasure to find that he can quote Latin. Quote therefore without fear, taking care only that your quotations are to the point and that they are correct. Write with Pope,

'A little learning is a dangerous thing,'

not

'A little knowledge is a dangerous thing,'

which indeed is not true and which Pope never wrote.

Note that Hamlet speaks of

'The undiscovered country from whose bourn
No traveller returns.'

In popular misquotation this becomes 'the bourn from which no traveller returns.'

Prior's words are,

'Fine by degrees and beautifully less,'

not 'small by degrees,' as people commonly represent.

Write,

'Sunt bona, sunt quædam mediocria, sunt mala plura,'

following Martial, not *sunt plura mala*, an arrangement

which is open to the twofold objection that the line fails to scan and that, if it scanned, *plura mala* would mean 'many apples,' a meaning which was not in the author's mind.

Quotations should bubble up spontaneously from a well-stored memory. If on the one hand they must not be too hackneyed, on the other hand they must not be too recondite. With Horace and Virgil we are supposed to have a nodding acquaintance, but if you quote Lucretius or Persius, we fancy that you have been digging up passages and storing them for the purpose of quotation, and we smell Pedantry.

28. Pedantry. A pedant is a man who lays great stress on the knowledge of small points and likes to parade his learning. By his pedantry an author sometimes robs his style of grace and charm. Pedantry drives men in one direction to choose big words of classical origin in place of simple words of native origin, and the result is Journalese. Pedantry drives men in the opposite direction to use a vocabulary exclusively English, and accordingly they revive words which have long been obsolete in ordinary speech. They begin their books with a *Foreword*, which other people call a Preface, and they sprinkle their pages with *whilom, eftsoons, fordo, methinks, nathless, sheen, ween, yclept,* and the like. Pedantry drives men in yet another direction to adopt Gallicisms, imposing on English words French idioms or French meanings. Thus they write, 'The window *gives* upon the street'; 'The Mayor *assisted* at the dinner'; 'This *goes without saying*'; 'His motives are very much *in evidence*'; 'He *exploited* their patriotic feelings for his own advertisement.'

All these forms of pedantry are affectation. Avoid affectation.

29. Imitation of other writers. Some authorities on Composition tell you that you must on no account try to imitate the style of other writers, for to do so would be insincere : you must 'be yourself.' The soundness of this advice seems open to question. The handwriting of nine people out of ten possesses more character than their style, but we do not therefore tell boys and girls to 'be themselves' and to scribble as they please. On the contrary, when they are at school we give them copy-books. In spite of their early instruction, when they are grown up, there is something distinctive about the handwriting of each. All may write good hands and yet all the hands are different.

Now you compose essays in the hope of improving your mode of expression, and if you can improve your mode of expression by copying the style of somebody else, the only point of importance is to make sure that you choose a good model. If you copy the mannerisms of a style which has marked mannerisms, you will make yourself ridiculous.

Fifty years ago there were literary giants in the land. Carlyle, Dickens, Macaulay, Thackeray, were prose writers of genius, but the mannerisms of Carlyle and Dickens made their style quite unfit for imitation. Yet literary pygmies, long since forgotten, tried hard to imitate these two giants, writing epileptic sentences which were conceived to be in the manner of Carlyle, and reproducing in an exaggerated form the faults of Dickens. Those who followed Macaulay as their model fared better. Much good writing at the present day is due to the influence of Macaulay. Yet in the hands of many of his imitators his style degenerated into what Matthew Arnold called 'middle-class Macaulayese,' the defects of which are painfully obvious.

Imitate therefore no writer whose style, though it may strike you as clever or brilliant, is eccentric or deficient in good taste. Carlyle, Dickens, American Humourists, their English disciples, authors of the Precious or of the Parenthetic school, Impressionists, noisy writers, writers of Bombast,—admire them, enjoy them, if you like, but never try to copy them. If on the other hand your fancy is taken by a writer whose style is clear and pleasant and free from tricks, you will do well if you not only admire and enjoy but also imitate. For you are more likely to acquire the art of writing clearly and pleasantly by copying from a good model than by continuing to 'be yourself.'

SUBJECTS FOR ESSAYS.

1.	Dogs.	36.	Camping out.
2.	English wild birds.	37.	Cycling.
3.	A rookery.	38.	The first day at school.
4.	Wasps.	39.	School friendships.
5.	Bees.	40.	School punishments.
6.	Butterflies.	41.	Holiday tasks.
7.	Wild flowers.	42.	The Bully.
8.	A garden.	43.	The choice of a profession.
9.	Ferns.	44.	Bores.
10.	Trees.	45.	Stupid people.
11.	A country walk.	46.	Gipsies.
12.	Clouds.	47.	Money.
13.	Sunrise.	48.	'Time is money.'
14.	Twilight.	49.	Responsibilities of wealth.
15.	A backward Spring.	50.	Luxuries.
16.	April.	51.	Fashion.
17.	May Day.	52.	The Post-office.
18.	A summer night.	53.	The morning newspaper.
19.	A shower in summer.	54.	A railway-bookstall.
20.	Harvest.	55.	Railways.
21.	Winter.	56.	Strikes.
22.	A frosty morning.	57.	The rivalry of nations.
23.	How to pass a wet day.	58.	European disarmament.
24.	Moorland scenery.	59.	Patriotism.
25.	A storm at sea.	60.	Conscription.
26.	A sailor's life.	61.	School cadet corps.
27.	A Bank Holiday.	62.	Chivalry.
28.	An alarm of fire.	63.	Slavery.
29.	Shops.	64.	Puritanism.
30.	Games.	65.	What is civilisation?
31.	A cricket match.	66.	John Bull.
32.	A regatta.	67.	The British Constitution.
33.	Lawn-tennis.	68.	Trial by jury.
34.	Compulsory football.	69.	Freedom of the press.
35.	A day's fishing.	70.	Party government.

71. A general election.
72. Old-age pensions.
73. The future of England.
74. 'Trade follows the flag.'
75. Technical education.
76. Free Libraries.
77. 'Knowledge is power.'
78. International Exhibitions.
79. Emigration.
80. Intelligence of animals.
81. Instinct and Reason.
82. Memory.
83. Sleep.
84. Solitude.
85. Discontent.
86. Cheerfulness.
87. Sympathy.
88. Heroism.
89. Fortitude under reverses.
90. Self-help.
91. Observation.
92. 'Look before you leap.'
93. 'More haste less speed.'
94. Punctuality.
95. Affectation.
96. Common sense.
97. Competition.
98. The force of example.
99. Home influences.
100. Good and bad habits.
101. Early rising.
102. Conversation.
103. Wit and humour.
104. Simple pleasures.
105. Hobbies.
106. Collecting postage-stamps.
107. Gardening.
108. Castles in the air.
109. The Christmas pantomime.
110. Private theatricals.

111. Music.
112. Gambling.
113. Vivisection.
114. Popular superstitions.
115. Ghosts.
116. Astrology.
117. Fairy tales.
118. Parodies.
119. The influence of fiction.
120. Novels.
121. A favourite book.
122. The pleasures of reading.
123. 'The fairy tales of science.'
124. Aerial navigation.
125. Telescopes.
126. Photography.
127. The invention of printing.
128. African explorers.
129. Arctic exploration.
130. Ulysses.
131. Alfred the Great.
132. Joan of Arc.
133. Sir Thomas More.
134. Nelson.
135. Sir John Franklin.
136. Tennyson.
137. Ruskin.
138. The Siege of Troy.
139. The Spanish Armada.
140. The Great Plague.
141. The French Revolution.
142. The English Lakes.
143. The Thames.
144. Stonehenge.
145. Westminster Abbey.
146. Egypt.
147. The Nile.
148. The Suez Canal.
149. Vesuvius.
150. Johannesburg.

151. Recent advances in the applications of electricity.
152. The coal supply of the world.
153. The qualities that make a great man.
154. Which do you consider the greatest of the Queens of England?
155. The inspiring influences of noble associations, corporate or local.
156. The causes of England's preeminence as a colonising nation.
157. Life in an English colony.
158. Warfare in ancient and modern times.
159. Is war an unmixed evil?
160. To be prepared for war is one of the most effectual means of preserving peace.
161. Are people better off now than they were a century ago?
162. Travelling—now and in the olden days.
163. The best way of spending a million pounds to benefit the poor of a large town.
164. The value of a classical education.
165. The gains and losses of spending holidays abroad.
166. The disadvantages of mid-term holidays.
167. The use and abuse of athletics.
168. Your ideal of a happy life.
169. Can persecution be defended?
170. John Bunyan and his books.
171. Sir Walter Scott as a novelist.
172. A poem by Browning.
173. 'Some books are to be tasted, others to be swallowed, and some few to be chewed and digested.'
174. 'Travel is a part of education.'
175. 'Every man is the architect of his own fortune.'
176. 'Necessity is the mother of invention.'
177. 'Prevention is better than cure.'
178. 'As the twig's bent the tree's inclined.'
179. 'A little learning is a dangerous thing.'
180. 'Sweet are the uses of adversity.'
181. 'God made the country, and man made the town.'
182. 'All that glisters is not gold.'
183. 'A bird in the hand is worth two in the bush.'
184. 'An ounce of sweete is worth a pound of sowre.'
185. 'Conscience does make cowards of us all.'

186. 'The evil that men do lives after them.'
187. 'Teach thy tongue to say, I do not know.'
188. 'We live in deeds, not years.'
189. 'The old order changeth, yielding place to new.'
190. 'A lie which is half a truth is ever the blackest of lies.'
191. 'The world knows nothing of its greatest men.'
192. Duty, 'stern Daughter of the Voice of God.'

193. 'He prayeth well, who loveth well
     Both man and bird and beast.'

194. 'A man's reach should exceed his grasp,
     Or what's a heaven for?'

195. 'He is the freeman whom the Truth makes free,
     And all are slaves beside.'

196.   'Peace hath her victories
     Not less renowned than war.'

197. 'Full many a gem of purest ray serene
         The dark unfathom'd caves of ocean bear:
     Full many a flower is born to blush unseen,
         And waste its sweetness on the desert air.'

198. 'Evil is wrought by want of thought
     As well as want of heart.'

199. 'He that is truly wise and great
     Lives both too early and too late.'

200. 'The heights, by great men reached and kept,
     Were not attained by sudden flight.'

INDEX.

For EU product safety concerns, contact us at Calle de José Abascal, 56–1°,
28003 Madrid, Spain or eugpsr@cambridge.org.

 www.ingramcontent.com/pod-product-compliance
Ingram Content Group UK Ltd.
Pitfield, Milton Keynes, MK11 3LW, UK
UKHW012329130625
459647UK00009B/154